Legacies of Struggle

Legacies of Struggle

Conflict and Cooperation
in Korean American Politics

Angie Y. Chung

Stanford University Press
Stanford, California
2007

Stanford University Press

Stanford, California

©2007 by the Board of Trustees of the Leland Stanford Junior University. All rights reserved.

Printed in the United States of America on acid-free, archival-quality paper

Library of Congress Cataloging-in-Publication Data

Chung, Angie Y., 1973–
  Legacies of struggle : conflict and cooperation in Korean American politics / Angie Y. Chung.
       p. cm.
  Includes bibliographical references and index.
  ISBN 978-0-8047-5657-0 (cloth : alk. paper)—ISBN 978-0-8047-5658-7 (pbk. : alk. paper)
  1. Korean Americans—Politics and government. 2. Korean Americans—Ethnic identity. 3. Korean Americans—Societies, etc.—Case studies. 4. Children of immigrants—United States—Political activity. 5. Children of immigrants—United States—Societies, etc.—Case studies. 6. Intergenerational relations—United States. 7. Elite (Social sciences)—United States. 8. Power (Social sciences)—United States. 9. Community life—United States. 10. United States—Ethnic relations. I. Title.

E184.K6C53 2007
305.895'7073009045—dc22   2007000343

Typeset by Thompson Type in 10/14 Minion

To my parents, Connie and Ye Hyun,
whose love and lives have inspired me
to cross the generational divide

Contents

Tables and Maps

Tables

Maps

Preface

THE TASK OF LEARNING AND WRITING about Korean American politics is not an easy one to say the least. Among other things, it requires an honest discussion of the internal problems that beset different generations of leaders and organizations in trying to service and empower the Koreatown community without undermining the contributions they make in areas where American society has failed them. What my time in the field has taught me is that we must learn to explore internal divisions in order to find our way to unity. I have tried to emphasize the importance of looking at all facets of identity and interest, including race, ethnicity, nativity, class, gender, and sexual orientation, in order to provide a more complex picture of ethnic political solidarity in the post-1965 era. Although acknowledging the multiple problems that leaders face today, I dispute the general perception of ethnic organizations within the Korean American community as overridden by conflict and corruption and instead view the community as struggling to define itself and produce diverse forms of political leadership to meet the needs of different constituencies amid mainstream indifference, internal inequality, and intergenerational conflicts. This is certainly an admirable feat in an era in which community-based organizations must increasingly compete for limited resources and juggle conflicting loyalties and interests, all of which do not always accommodate easily to one another.

I would like to emphasize the fact that my investigation of hierarchies within ethnic politics is certainly not an attempt to claim that certain groups within the Korean American community have been fully empowered by their class or gender privilege. Instead, my use of the term "ethnic elite" is meant to imply that this privilege is only relative to others within the community yet still marginal in respect to White elite powerholders in the United States. I suggest that in some ways the unequal distribution of power and resources within the ethnic community may be partly attributed to larger mainstream hierarchies and cultural perceptions. As such, this book is an effort to broaden current understandings of empowerment based on the differential access of indigenous groups to valued networks, resources, and institutions within both the ethnic community and mainstream society.

No matter what type of organization they work in, how many benefits they derive from this line of work, or how they are situated within this political hierarchy, individuals who have participated in such organizations have played a role in contributing to the betterment of the broader community in some way. My in-depth observations of board, staff, and volunteers within two such organizations have demonstrated to me the extraordinary level of commitment, humanitarianism, and effort that goes into nonprofit work, even at the expense of emotional, physical, and financial well-being. Nor is this type of dedication regularly rewarded. Interviewees have related to me the struggles they've encountered from a media culture that sensationalizes the troubles of the community, other leaders who question their personal motives and political loyalties, and even family and community members who pressure them about pursuing more higher-paying, prestigious occupations.

Having said this, I cannot even begin to express my gratitude to organizational clients, members, and leaders I have interviewed for assisting me with my research despite time limitations and personal conflicts. I am especially indebted to the staff of the Korean Immigrant Workers Advocates (KIWA) and the Korean Youth and Community Center (KYCC) for not only allowing me access into their personal lives and experiences but also for teaching me the importance of giving back to the community. Although I cannot refer to them by name, I owe a special debt of gratitude to those interviewees who were willing to open up old wounds or relate to me private stories in order to contribute to this research and the community at large. I can only hope that I have done some justice to the sacrifices they've made and have made my own contribution to the Korean American community.

Taking this into consideration, I've tried my best to publicize the political concerns, personal hardships, and unheard voices of internally marginalized groups within the Korean American community while protecting the confidentiality of my interviewees and recognizing the great work that both first and 1.5/second generation organizations have achieved. I also want to avoid the danger of characterizing these incidents as individual- or organi-zation-specific weaknesses, but clarify the relevance of such issues to other community-based organizations both within and outside the Korean Ameri-can community. For this reason, readers may note that parts of chapters may refer to specific incidents and controversies in a somewhat broad and ambigu-ous manner. I use pseudonyms for all my interviewees, but as I've warned them, certain figures may be easily recognizable to those even remotely fa-miliar with the Korean American community. I did make two exceptions by including the names of select academics to give them appropriate credit for their insights and KIWA's and KYCC's former and current executive direc-tors (with their permission), because it seemed that their prominent status made both their views and actions well known to the general public. To get some organizational feedback, I also consulted with a few interviewees and the past and present executive directors of KIWA and KYCC, who were gra-cious enough to read draft chapters.

I refrain from describing this book as a completely balanced and compre-hensive overview of Korean American politics in the United States but instead as an effort to look beyond the generational divide. As a second generation Korean American striving to think like a 1.5 generation one, I have had to overcome a number of obstacles in order to understand the needs and per-spectives of both generations, including language, cultural, budget, and time limitations. For one, the bulk of interview data was collected during my grad-uate school years. My position as a relatively young, second generation female graduate student proved to be an impediment in trying to solicit interviews from some immigrant leaders, some of whom were used to communicating on the basis of social status. Like most second generation community workers, I tried my best to balance my respect for and understanding of Korean immi-grant culture with the need to assert my worthiness to those with whom I in-teracted. Of course, I must also recognize those other first generation leaders who were more than eager and willing to help me as a fellow Korean Ameri-can. With my intermediate-level Korean, I made an extra effort to conduct interviews whenever I could and relied on student translators when I could not. However, these limitations prevented me from getting a comprehensive perspective on the views of immigrant leaders on certain issues.

Lastly, I'd like to point out how much I've learned by reengaging in volun-teer work and conducting research in Los Angeles from both a personal and political standpoint. As one friend reminded me, both students and professors alike have a tendency to lose sight of their own role within the communities they study and fall into the dangerous habit of exploiting such communities for their own academic needs. Long after the project is over, scholars should use this kind of opportunity to reconsider their own position within the communities they study and reengage themselves within the communities they live. I'm the last one to say that I've resolved all the internal conflicts and contradictions that this study has raised for me, but it is exactly this that I would like to convey through this research—the constant "personal-slash-political" process through which we confront our own privilege and how we can use that to change the world around us. It is the recognition that no one has found the one answer to social liberation, but it is this experience of challenging ourselves, as well as working toward the greater good (however that may be defined) that can be valuable in itself. Neither the quest for solidarity nor the valor of dissent should be devalued since both contribute to our individual and collective empowerment. If anything, I think that is one of the lessons that we have learned since the devastations of *sa-i-gu* (or 4-29) when the rioting first erupted and changed the course of Korean American politics.

I should note at this juncture that I use "Los Angeles civil unrest" and "Los Angeles riots" interchangeably throughout the book in order to recognize the two conflicting meanings that sa-i-gu has held for its victims and participants. On the one hand, there are those who claim that poor minorities took to the streets as a form of political protest against the conditions of poverty and discrimination that ravaged their communities—in other words, downplaying the chaos, irrationality, and lawlessness that the term *riot* implies. But then, there are others who adamantly maintain there could be no other word to express the tragedy and destruction the looters and arsonists spread by preying on powerless Korean immigrant merchants, who had little control over crime and poverty in urban areas and were being scapegoated for society's ills. I believe both sides represent some of the contradictions that emerge from social inequality in American cities today and are in that sense both legitimate despite their opposing claims.[1]

It is said that the topic we choose to study oftentimes reflects something that is near and dear to our personal histories, and this book has been no different in that respect. This study represents the culmination of all the years I have spent trying to understand my own ethnic identity and experiences, as well as those of family members and close friends. As such, I see those who have been gracious enough to allow me insight into their lives, to offer ideas and critiques on my manuscript, or to help alleviate some of the emotional anguishes of writing a dissertation as having shared not only in the research processes but a part of me as well.

My study was most formatively shaped by the intellectual and spiritual guidance of my dissertation advisors and lifetime mentors, Min Zhou and Walter Allen, who have enriched my personal and academic development with their unending support, intellectual insights, and perceptive analysis of life experiences. Min's unbounded knowledge, caring guardianship of her students, and individual success as an Asian American female professor have given me much to emulate in my academic career. Although all have benefited from his endless wisdom and kindness, I have come to believe that Walter is the ideal mentor for students of color who have lost their way in the maze of graduate life, and I can only wish that everyone has the fortune to find someone as spiritually supportive and intellectually inspiring as he has been to me.

I would also like to express gratitude to my other two committee members, John Horton and Edward Park, for having put so much faith in my work and adding their own wisdom to the dissertation. As one of the top specialists and activists in Korean American politics, Edward Park graciously shared his knowledge, insights, and resources on the organizations discussed in this book and also commented on draft chapters from this study. A long-time mentor and a dear friend from my undergraduate years, Edward T. Chang, has also read and commented on parts of my dissertation and has indirectly helped me through the academic process with much-needed advice and support. Both were as much a part of these communities I studied as they were brilliant scholars, so they also teach by example.

I owe a special thanks to my esteemed colleague, Richard Lachmann, who commented on many draft versions of the manuscript and also helped me to navigate the book-publishing process. I am also fortunate to have been part of a warm and accomplished community of scholars in the Sociology Department at the University at Albany, including Richard Alba, John Logan, Glenna Spitze, Glenn Deane, Zai Liang, and Nancy Denton. Special thanks to Minjeong Kim for her impeccable editorial/research assistance and also to Karen Tejada, Jin-Wook Lee, Wenquan Zhang, the staff at the CSDA and Lewis Mumford Centers, and various undergraduate assistants including Young-Gi Kim for their help with translating or transcribing different aspects of the research. Im Cho, Terry Cho, and Bob Lee also helped me to recruit interviewees in the early stages of the project.

I would like to extend a special thanks to the acquisitions editor Kate Wahl and the staff at Stanford University Press for their editorial commentary and enthusiastic support for this book. Although I cannot mention them all individually, I would also like to recognize all the professors who have helped me throughout the different stages of my undergraduate (Yale) and graduate studies (UCLA). Abel Valenzuela, Paul Johnston, Dina Okamoto, Valerie Hunt, Gina Masequesmay, Vincent Fu, Susan Suh, Andy Yan, Irene Bloemraad, Glenn Omatsu, and Bill Ong Hing also influenced the way I approached the study with their intellectual insights, technical support, and community experiences. I've also had the benefit of receiving chapter comments from well-respected scholars through various workshops and conferences, including Kyeyoung Park and Rafael Alarcon (SSRC Minority Dissertation Workshop), Roger Waldinger (UCLA-SSRC Summer Institute), and Yen Le Espiritu (CCIS presentation).

This book would never have come about without the support of various foundations and departments that have taken a chance in providing me funding throughout the research, presentation, and writing processes. Funding sources included the Edward Bouchet Fellowship (Yale University), Project 88 (UCLA), the Research Mentorship Fellowship and the Institute of American Cultures Research Grant (UCLA Asian American Studies), the Dr. Nuala McGann Drescher Affirmative Action/Diversity Leave Program (United University Professions), the Young Scholars Program (the Jacobs Foundation in Switzerland), and the Social Science Research Council (SSRC) Minority Dissertation Workshop and Post-Doctoral Fellowship (International Migration Program). The Department of Sociology and College of Arts and Sciences at the University at Albany also offered me some seed grants and support for the Drescher leave. I would also like to commend the International Migration Program at SSRC for providing unending support to its scholars in the form of fellowships, workshops, publication opportunities, and networking events. Thanks to the Center for Comparative Immigration Studies (CCIS) for giving me office space and support during my post-doctoral year at UC-San Diego, and Rob Teranishi and the NYU Steinhardt Institute for Higher Education Policy for providing me temporary office space to work on revisions. Dr. Jae Ho Yeom, Dr. Gil-Sung Park, and the staff at the Institute of International Studies at Korea University also offered me unique teaching opportunities that not only helped me to fund the book-writing process, but also to gain insight into modern Korean culture.

Of course, these acknowledgments would not be complete without recognizing the most important people in my life—my family and friends—who have been my richest source of inspiration and spiritual guidance. Every work that I have produced has sprung from my deep-seated desire to understand and appreciate the immigration experiences of my parents, Connie and Ye Hyun, whose love, support, and past struggles have allowed me to enjoy the privileges of higher education. I also owe much to my *dong-seng* Mike for his no-nonsense advice and his deep compassion for family that has held us all together. My heartfelt appreciation to Eddie Poteat, Cheng Chen, Monica Rhee, Yumi Shin, Eric C. Liu, Melissa Moskof, Allison Yoh, and my other close friends for dealing with my occasional fits of insanity and for offering the emotional support I need for my professional development.

Legacies of Struggle

1 Introduction

THE SCENE THAT PLAYED OUT on the television screens of Americans across the nation in April 1992 could have been taken straight out of a film noir on postapocalyptic Los Angeles. With law enforcement officials nowhere to be found, poor minority rioters were shown ravaging the unprotected stores of impoverished neighborhoods, pelting passing White motorists with stones and debris, and torching select establishments in angry reaction to the injustices of ghetto poverty and the American justice system. On the other end, gun-toting Korean immigrant merchants, in a desperate attempt to protect their lifetime investments, stood defiantly on the rooftops of buildings and dared looters to rob them of their American Dream. Unaffected outside observers mostly remember the riots as the event when African Americans took to the streets to protest the unjust exoneration of four White police officers caught on videotape beating up an unarmed Black motorist. For those who read a little deeper, the riots may also conjure up images of a Korean immigrant storeowner, Soon Ja Du, who shot a black teenage girl in a dispute over a bottle of orange juice. This was one version of the story that the news media would continue to replay in decontextualized soundbites of conflict, lawlessness, and chaos and one that would be contested in years to come. Yet as most pundits will assert, the reality, both past and present, is much more complex.

Whereas most Americans may vividly recall the days leading up to the 1992 civil unrest, Korean immigrants have had to overcome not only the shock of a past in ruins, but the heavy burden of a future to rebuild. Caught between the Black and Latino ghettoes of South Central Los Angeles and the la-la dreamland of Hollywood, the storefronts and mini-malls of Koreatown suffered the worst of the rioters' wrath, with Korean business owners losing several hundred million dollars worth of property. However, numbers alone cannot convey the long history of struggle and sacrifice that had gone into building these businesses and the dreams that evaporated with their destruction. As renowned Korean American scholar, Elaine Kim (1993), tragically describes it, the 1992 upheavals became the day when Korean Americans relived their *han*, which is best translated as the "sorrow and anger that grows from the accumulated experiences of oppression." She laments:

> Seeing those buildings in flames and those anguished Korean faces, I had the terrible thought that there would be no belonging and that we were, just as I had always suspected, a people destined to carry our han around with us, wherever we went in the world. The destiny that had spelled centuries of extreme suffering from invasion, colonization, war, and national division had smuggled itself into the U.S. with our baggage. (215)

To survey the ever-expanding domain of Koreatown now, one can hardly imagine that the three days of rioting that hit the enclave community could have so completely overturned the lives of countless Korean store owners and their employees and caused many immigrants to overhaul their faith in the American Dream. The charred remains of looted stores, the furious explosion of century-old grievances and poverty unaddressed, the reverberating silence of law enforcement and government officials, and the soulful wails of dreams forsaken seem to be long forgotten as residents and business owners tend to the economic exigencies of day-to-day survival. From the dark pit of loss and despair grow the seeds of a new institutional empire—a dizzying array of restaurants, pool halls, hot spas, and golf ranges—that extend way beyond the boundaries that once contained them. Unlike its predecessor, the new Koreatown boasts strong roots in an ethnic community dispersed, at the same time it draws strength from the multiracial neighborhood around it. In the end, the resilient spirit of Korean immigrants built on centuries of oppression and domination in their ancestral land and the subsequent resurrection of new businesses and organizations in post-1992 Koreatown may appear to have wiped away most physical traces of the 1992 civil unrest, or "pok-dong" (riots) as more embittered Korean Americans call it.

But underneath the hustle and bustle of everyday life, the wounds run deep and the lessons are not so easily forgotten for Korean Americans, both young and old. Among other things, the events of 1992 preceded a broader transformation in the political consciousness and internal power structures of the

Korean American community. Having been left to defend themselves at the height of the crisis, Korean immigrants learned the painful lesson that blind dependency on the Seoul government in Korea, marked indifference to the society around them, and unconditional donations to local politicians would not earn them the respect and stature they needed to demand outside protection and prevent future calamities within the community. The series of politically tumultuous events thus mobilized the community into action and forced the leadership to reconsider its tenuous relationship with the outside world. In the aftermath, the immigrant and American-born Korean leadership have taken various steps to forge stronger relations with local government and Los Angeles Police Department (LAPD) officials and gain better representation within the media. Responding to the heated confrontations with African Americans before and during the riots, Korean Americans have also begun to reacquaint themselves with the neighborhoods around them and acquire the skills to communicate and collaborate with their Black and Latino neighbors.

The conflicts between Korean merchants and Black patrons and the victimization of Korean immigrants during the riots made many Americans first aware of the presence of Korean Americans in their midst and, in the process, paved the way for new leaders and organizations to establish their presence in the American political scene. Korean American leaders have been able to command the full attention of their American counterparts and tap into strong networks of support that have enabled them to run for elected office or get appointed on local, state, and national levels. Between 1987 and 1992, a notable fifteen Korean Americans were included on electoral ballots from the city council to the House and the Senate, seven of whom were elected to office (Cha 1994). The most distinguished government positions to be offered to Korean Americans include the 1992 election of Jay Kim to Congress and President Bill Clinton's 1997 appointment of Angela Oh to the Advisory Board on the President's Initiative on Race.

Over time, Korean Americans have increasingly learned to carve their own ethnic niche within the arena of mainstream politics. Community-based organizations that could once barely afford to manage a full-time staff have been taking in millions of dollars of postriot funds to implement ambitious programs on youth leadership, economic development, and interracial cooperation. Where there was once silence, the mainstream media has now taken an avid interest in everything from the residential patterns of the Korean community to the proliferation of Koreatown enterprises to protest campaigns within the enclave. Meanwhile, immigrant and American-born Koreans have joined ranks to launch massive voter registration drives and advocate for new redistricting plans that will consolidate the electoral power of a divided Koreatown. When all else fails, some of the more militant Korean Americans have found both the courage and the backing to mount aggressive but peaceful protest demonstrations against city hall, the media, the LAPD, and even fellow Korean Americans.

More recent events in international politics since September 11, 2001, have added fuel to collective activism among Korean Americans, young and old. In response to the September 11 terrorist attacks on the World Trade Center and the Pentagon, President George W. Bush in his State of the Union address declared an unofficial campaign against the "three axes of evil," including Iran, Iraq, and North Korea. The address represented the culmination of three decades of fluctuating tensions in U.S.-North Korea relations, ever since Korea had been divided in half after World War II. Although activism in homeland politics began long before these events, mounting tensions in U.S.-North Korea relations, increasing resentment of U.S. military occupation in South Korea, and the persistence of prodemocratic and labor rights movements in the ancestral land have raised Korean American consciousness of political activities abroad.

Political visibility and awareness has been accompanied by the rise of new political leadership better able to mediate the racially diversifying population of Koreatown and assert its position within mainstream society without losing sight of their coethnic[1] constituency. Aside from transforming the worldview of existing ethnic leadership, the internal disruptions have introduced organizational actors among the younger, English-speaking generation of Korean Americans who have been able to foster new relationships with mainstream institutions of power and create solid alliances with other racial and ethnic communities. Ethnic-based organizations like these that can bridge multiple communities of interest are becoming almost a necessity, especially for ethnic enclaves in multicultural cities that have been changing in a way that their early immigrant predecessors could never have imagined. In so doing, these newly emerging ethnic organizations have raised new possibilities for organizing the diversifying population of Koreatown and have completely transformed the fragmenting political landscapes of the broader ethnic community.

Nevertheless, calls for political action have posed as many challenges as they have opened up windows of opportunity. Rather than underlining the community's collective solidarity amid crisis, organizational responses to these different issues have highlighted the complex nature of intergenerational tensions in ethnic power structures like this. This book is a study on the way these bridging ethnic organizations are able to cultivate ethnic political solidarity despite increasing residential dispersal, class polarization, and generational clashes within the ethnic community. As they integrate into American society, how do these Korean American organizations justify and maintain strong relations with the immigrant-dominated ethnic population? Who represents this steadily diversifying Korean American community and, conversely, whose interests do these organizations represent? Who are their friends and who are their enemies? What compelling interests or ideologies will bring the next generation of middle-class Korean Americans back to the ethnic community? What kind of relationships should they nurture with their African American and Latino neighbors? Should this be a story of growth and power or a story about social justice?

Straddling the Generational Divide

Indeed, the fate of ethnic communities in general may depend on bridging organizations like these that help to facilitate the transition from immigrant to ethnic-based mainstream politics. Numerous studies have shown that the long-term integration of immigrants is contingent upon the capacity of neighborhoods, workplaces, and institutional structures to create extensive networks with mainstream groups and institutions (Fernandez-Kelly 1995). Along with occupation and education, political action is one of the channels through which immigrants and their children enter into the organized structures of mainstream society. Organizations must reach out to noncoethnic organizations in order to gain access to new sources of information, resources, and other opportunities unavailable within the ethnic community, thus broadening their potential to enact social change. Such organizations also create bridges by providing the knowledge, resources, and networks necessary for socioeconomic mobility through culturally appropriate channels and instilling in their membership the cultural norms and values of "American society." And more importantly, outside institutional linkages also help ethnic organizations to establish their political presence within mainstream society.

The increasing embeddedness of ethnic community-based organizations into the institutional structures of American society raises new questions about the salience of ethnicity among future generations of Asian Americans.

Although theorists have recognized the continuing significance of racial political solidarity for Black and Latino communities, there have been few studies that have analyzed how post-1965 Asian immigrant communities are able
to sustain ethnic political solidarity amid increasing generational cleavages,
class polarization, and residential dispersal. The possibility of maintaining
ethnic solidarity without residential concentration has become a particularly
poignant one, considering the rapid pace at which Korean, Chinese, Japanese,
and other Asian American groups have achieved socioeconomic mobility and
spread out into diverse residential settings. There is growing literature on the
role of mainstream politics in shaping the development and political integration of immigrant organizations into the host society,[2] but there are relatively
few works that have looked at political organizations, relationships, and inequality *within* ethnic opportunity structures. In this light, ethnic community-
based organizations may better help us to understand what happens with generational transitions in political leadership.

The main interest of this book lies in ethnic organizations primarily led
and operated by the 1.5/second generations. These generations, respectively,
refer to those children of immigrants who were either born in Korea and
educated in the United States or were born and raised as Americans. Such
organizations are to be differentiated from traditional ethnic organizations
run by first generation immigrants, such as the Korean-American Federation,
which dominated ethnic politics in the early years of Korean American history. Whereas the old ethnic organizations are almost exclusively comprised
of Korean-speaking immigrants and have stronger ties with the homeland,
new ethnic organizations are comprised primarily of English-speaking and
bilingual 1.5/second generation members, who have adopted different strategies and ways of approaching issues in the Koreatown community. Furthermore, these types of organizations have taken on more significant roles in
Asian America in recent years, as a result of demographic and structural shifts
in post-1965 ethnic communities in the United States.[3] Because of their ties to
both the ethnic community and mainstream society, these newly emerging
organizations have played a crucial bridging function within ethnic organizational structures.

While immigrant organizations may take on some of these responsibilities, 1.5/second generation-led organizations are the more ideal conduits for
such bridging social networks because of their greater English-speaking ability, cultural and political knowledge of mainstream bureaucratic systems, and

institutional ties to outside groups and organizations. Although bicultural in nature, not all 1.5/second generation organizations are necessarily "bridging organizations" since some groups may maintain themselves through funds and support networks garnered within the ethnic community, focus almost exclusively on coethnic staff and clientele, and function with little support from mainstream institutions. Alternatively, there are 1.5/second generation organizations that draw heavily on outside support networks and serve a racially mixed clientele, especially in diverse cities like Los Angeles. In contrast, all bridging organizations rely on both ethnic and mainstream institutions for some degree of support.

In particular, there are two ideal types of bridging organizations among the 1.5/second generation that unify communities whose residential, entrepreneurial, institutional, and social structures are not bounded by space. *Translocal ethnic organizations* are what we typically refer to as "national ethnic organizations" that have one corporate headquarters along with various membership and affiliate branches scattered in different cities throughout the nation. Although the different branches may solicit support from mainstream organizations, these types of organizations tend to depend less on local non-coethnic residents for their core membership and clientele and focus more of their efforts on bringing together coethnic members across local, regional, and national boundaries based on a conventional framework of ethnic political solidarity. Among other things, national organizations will share resources and sponsorship and hold conferences that bring together its multiple branches. Examples of translocal organizations within the Koreatown community include the Korean American Coalition (KAC); the National Korean American Service and Education Consortium (NAKASEC); and Korean Health, Education, Information and Research Center (KHEIR), all of which have Korean American membership branches in different locations.

In contrast, *geoethnic organizations* tend to construct more dynamic and flexible frameworks of ethnic solidarity that accommodate to the diversifying context of the geographically bounded enclave upon which they depend. These organizations do not usually have national branches or centralized corporate headquarters from which they can draw resources and support. As such, geoethnic organizations firmly maintain their core leadership and political culture within the ethnic community but may strategically expand their membership and clientele base to include other racial/ethnic populations in the local neighborhood. Although they do straddle both ideal types, the two organizations in this research, the Korean Youth and Community Center (KYCC) and Korean Immigrant Workers Advocates (KIWA), have come to be considered geoethnic bridging organizations. For the purposes of convenience, I loosely use the term *bridging organizations* to refer to geoethnic organizations throughout the book.

Both KYCC and KIWA are relatively liberal 1.5/second generation Korean American organizations that took center stage in the politics of the ethnic community through ties with mainstream institutions after the 1992 civil unrest. This is where most of their similarities end. Aside from their prominent status within post-1992 Koreatown politics, the case studies were selected to represent two distinct organizational structures that have established strategically distinct relations with the immigrant elite and have thus relied on different bases of organizational support both within and outside the Korean American community. These organizations were not intended to be comparative case studies but to represent different ways in which 1.5/second generation bridging organizations have been politically integrated into ethnic power structures. Most of the liberal 1.5/second generation organizations in Koreatown generally fall in a continuum between these two organizations in terms of their relations with the immigrant leadership. This book will show how these new organizational frameworks of ethnic political solidarity offer important venues for organizing diverse segments of the Korean American and Koreatown community in a manner that most effectively enables them to achieve their political agenda.

The first case study, the KYCC, is a nonprofit social service agency that was originally established in 1975 to service economically disadvantaged youths and their families but has expanded its programs to encompass a variety of other health, advocacy, community, business, housing, and employment-related services. The organization is led by a strong executive board primarily (but not exclusively) comprised of Korean Americans and a long line of 1.5/second generation Korean American executive directors. The staff members are dominated by 1.5/second generation Korean Americans but with a growing body of non–Korean Americans, including non–Korean Asian Americans, African Americans, and Latinos. The clientele includes both Korean and Latinos from the Koreatown neighborhood, depending on the program. Located in the upper tiers of ethnic organizational structures, KYCC has made a name for itself among established organizations and the ethnic elite of Koreatown, as well as politicians and corporations in mainstream society. Despite occasional intergenerational conflicts on community-related issues, KYCC has struggled to maintain relatively stable relations with immigrant community leaders and business owners through its governing board.

Founded in March 1992, the second organization, KIWA, has worked to organize, empower, and advocate for workers in the Koreatown community through legal assistance, protest demonstrations, educational seminars, and other political activities. The organization has maintained a semidemocratic governing structure of staff members, only partly dominated by 1.5/second generation Korean Americans along with a mix of non–Korean Asian Americans and Latinos, depending on the time period in question. So far, the executive directorship has been occupied by two 1.5 generation Korean American male leaders with a history of activism in leftist politics. Reflecting the demographics of Koreatown workers, the organization's clientele has a good balance of Korean immigrants and Latino immigrants. Although actively working with Korean immigrant workers in the community, the organization has been known to butt heads with immigrant powerholders because of its leftist stance on various social issues and publicized struggles against Korean business owners. As a result of tensions with the ethnic elite, KIWA has found alternative sources of support with progressive Korean American organizations, American labor unions, progressive racial and ethnic groups, and activist organizations in Korea and Mexico.

Residential Propinquity and Ethnic Solidarity

The processes of migration require that immigrants uproot themselves from the security of jobs, homes, families, and friends in their homelands and move to foreign societies that are oftentimes hostile to immigrants. Such social and economic shifts can have a dislocating effect on the emotional and material lives of new immigrants. Generally, most scholars agree that ethnic-based organizations are instrumental to the early stages of immigrant adaptation by re-creating a sociocultural environment that is friendly to incoming migrants; by establishing an institutionalized setting within which members can share information, resources, and other forms of assistance; and by offering a self-enclosed sanctuary away from the exclusionary practices of native groups. The institutional infrastructure of the enclave lays the foundations upon which immigrants and their children create and maintain strong ties with other members of the surrounding ethnic community. Hence, ethnic political solidarity itself is in many ways predicated on the common values and interests that arise from residential proximity and intersecting life chances.

Immigration scholars have long attested to the significance of institutional development in tempering the disruptive effects of immigration and hence consolidating the fates of ethnic groups in deteriorating urban neighborhoods. Drawing on the experiences of early-twentieth-century European immigrants, Robert E. Park and his colleagues from the Chicago School of Race and Ethnicity depicted urban spaces as emerging from a natural competition among different social groups that would ultimately assemble people with common social characteristics into distinct but interdependent ecological niches within the city. The scholars (Burgess 1925) viewed the city as "a mosaic of little worlds which touch but do not interpenetrate (40)," segregated partly by the desire of groups to maintain their own "moral order" through independent social and political organizations. Like the segregated ghettoes of native-born African Americans, immigrant enclaves were generally situated in dilapidated sections of the city, nestled in between the central business district and more racially integrated, middle-class neighborhoods on the fringes.

Ethnic enclaves were conceptualized as socially and spatially bound areas occupied by immigrants whose low-income status, residential segregation, and lack of effective modes of transportation rendered them highly dependent on the institutional structures of the local neighborhood in the early stages of migration. Unlike their African American counterparts, European immigrants were able to resurrect homeland social structures and shape their neighborhood surroundings in a way that sustained strong networks of support, preserved the cultural traditions of their homeland, and facilitated the adaptation and mobility of second generation youth. The immigrant colony was built like a "transplanted village," containing all the ethnic institutions that are integral to living in a society, including businesses, churches, media, and mutual aid organizations (Park 1950). Ethnic-based organizations offered immigrants a variety of social services and cultural resources, a space for building social relationships, and resources for finding jobs and housing within the spatial confines of the enclave.

These ethnic institutions are considered to be important vehicles for adaptation into the host society because of their capacity to provide ethnic support networks and culturally sensitive services that aid immigrants in adjusting to their new environment. Common values and interests emerging from shared economic situations, cultural isolation, and day-to-day interactions reaffirm a general sense of ethnic cohesion within the transplanted community. Immigrants and their children rely on this type of familiar support structure to find psychological fulfillment, social support, and overall security living in a physically declining urban neighborhood while gradually acculturating into a new society. For this reason, those populations that are part of ethnic communities with highly developed social and economic infrastructures are shown to be better adapted to their surrounding environment than those that lack any ties to an institutionally developed enclave.

However, assimilation scholars generally do not make a broader connection between the institutional development of an ethnic enclave and the persistence of ethnic solidarity among the children of immigrants. Because ethnic distinctions are based on the constraints imposed by economic marginality and social isolation, theorists have argued that residential mobility, acculturation, and racial intermixing will inevitably dissolve mutual interests and those relationships created within the ethnic enclave. Over time, the children of immigrants broaden their primary relationships with other racial/ethnic groups and become increasingly incorporated into the social cliques, clubs, and institutions of mainstream society (Gordon 1964). Those who achieve higher status are predicted to move out into better neighborhoods and relinquish their old ties for the promises of individual success (Massey 1985; Ward 1989).[4] Although ethnic groups may become part of the mainstream in their own way and at their own pace, ethnic differences along with their associated social ties and cultural traditions do eventually lose their relevance in the day-to-day lives of immigrants and their children, who choose to improve their individual situations within mainstream opportunity structures (Alba and Nee 2003). Once these groups move into outlying middle-class neighborhoods and begin to intermix equally with other racial groups, ethnic-specific problems faced by immigrants and their children will dissipate as the advantages of assimilation increase and future generations find more effective avenues of empowerment through mainstream American institutions.

Nevertheless, the heterogeneity of today's immigrant population has caused some scholars to give pause on earlier assumptions about the incorporation of ethnic groups into American society, primarily because they do not all start out on equal footing. Some immigrants migrate with substantial resources and skills, build vibrant enclave economies, and are well received by the host society, while less privileged others flee war-torn countries, lack sufficient capital, and are met with hostility because of their distinguishing physical features. Unlike early European immigrants, the children of Asian and Latino immigrants today are also socialized into diverse neighborhood contexts—from middle-class White neighborhoods to ethnic enclaves to poor minority ghettos—and are thus exposed to different opportunity structures, ethnic support systems, and peer influences. Depending on the context of their migration and their incorporation into the host society, immigrants and their children may consequently find that ethnicity may be a personal option, a means to achieve upward mobility, or a source of social stigma (Portes and Rumbaut 1996). In other words, ethnic solidarity does not necessarily hinder the socioeconomic progress of second generation children; instead, preexisting ethnic networks and communities may be integral in off-setting some of the negative effects of acculturating into diverse neighborhood contexts.

To address these weaknesses, some scholars have begun to place greater emphasis on the ability of more resource-rich immigrant groups to respond to the structural conditions of the receiving society by creating alternative ladders of social mobility through the enclave economy. From this perspective, ethnic organizations have the capacity to facilitate the socioeconomic mobility of ethnic groups, compensate for structural deficiencies in the local neighborhood environment (for example, schools), and contribute to the long-term integration of future generations into mainstream society. Research suggests that the information, resources, and assistance derived from ethnic media, banks, churches, after-school programs, mutual aid associations, and businesses may actually help ethnic groups to overcome some of the disadvantages associated with marginal social status and residential isolation in low-income urban communities and eventually achieve middle-class status. In other words, institutions create new ethnic-based opportunity structures and hence alternative opportunities for mobility for both immigrants and their children.

These scholars contend that the ethnic enclave economy can offer a different mode of socioeconomic incorporation for immigrants, who experience cultural and structural disadvantages in mainstream labor markets (Light and Bonacich 1988; Portes and Stepick 1993; Zhou 1992). More specifically, new immigrants can seek greater financial returns for their skills, education, and knowledge in the long term by taking on jobs or owning small businesses in the ethnic enclave than through low-paying, dead-end jobs in the secondary labor market. The ethnic enclave economy also creates a crucial stepping stone for low-skilled workers by endowing them with invaluable training and coethnic support in exchange for their labor in ethnic-owned firms. From this vantage point, the institutional vitality of the enclave contributes to the economic goals of its residents and is thus seen as a vehicle for socioeconomic mobility, above all else.

In turn, a community's level of social organization, or what Breton (1964) calls its "institutional completeness," facilitates the individual's interpersonal integration into the host society. The more equipped an ethnic community is able to provide for the fundamental needs of their members, the less likely those immigrants and their children will need to depend on social relationships outside their respective communities. By offering structural support for ethnic cohesion, immigrants within such institutionally developed communities are more likely to cultivate ethnic attachments and remain culturally distinct from outside groups, even as their secondary integration within the workplace, school, and political settings gradually encourages them to participate in the broader society.

Needless to say, the ability of immigrant populations to cultivate a strong institutional structure depends heavily on the resource base of the ethnic community. Ethnic enclave economies are semiautonomous, highly specialized, and capital-rich economies that provide valuable jobs, capital, and resources to members of the ethnic community. Because of the immense socioeconomic heterogeneity of post-1965 immigration, however, ethnic communities vary greatly in terms of their ability to sustain such economically active communities. Enclaves created by immigrants who came with substantial physical, financial, and human capital, such as the Cubans in Miami, the Koreans in Los Angeles, and the Chinese in New York, have dramatically converted declining urban neighborhoods into thriving ethnic economies. Other enclaves among low-income Mexican, Haitian, and Vietnamese populations that lack entrepreneurial and institutional development have not been as successful in comparison.

The state of the ethnic enclave economy determines the quantity, quality, and heterogeneity of institutions that arise in the neighborhood and, along with it, the ability of ethnic groups to advance their political interests. In turn, community-based organizations are integral components in the production and reproduction of cultural solidarity and ethnic-based networks that drive the ethnic economy. Strong social networks embedded in both the formal and informal institutions of the enclave aid immigrants in their struggle to find jobs, accumulate capital, and promote the economic goals of parents and the educational aspirations of immigrant children. These networks of organizations and informal relationships enable immigrant groups to live out their day-to-day lives within the confines of ethnic boundaries. Organizations may even help to institutionalize expanding networks that socially link sending communities in the homeland to migrant areas in the receiving society—thus encouraging the flow of not only people but also capital in the form of remittances overseas (Massey et al. 1987). Thus, the more developed the institutional structure of the ethnic enclave, the greater the potential for uplifting the members of the ethnic community.

To be sure, residential clustering and institutional completeness may provide the structural context for organizing and mobilizing around common political interests, but there are several problems with simply applying conventional theories on institutional assimilation to ethnic political solidarity among Koreatown organizations. For one, most studies on immigrant adaptation presume that the common ethnic and class-based (or "eth-class") interests of immigrants are best articulated and sustained within the residential context of the ethnic enclave neighborhood. Ethnic solidarity entails the presence of a spatially concentrated ethnic community from which members can draw resources, build institutions, and act on shared political interests. Without this, there is little reason to preserve ethnic organizations or ethnic political solidarity in general. In the early stages of adaptation, immigrant organizations may take shape around residential and eth-class-based interests, yet these models do not clearly explain why the children of immigrants might continue to stay politically involved in a community that is divided by class, ideological, and generational differences.

Related to this, most theories also assume that resource mobilization is the sole basis for building ethnic institutions—a focus that neglects the non-instrumental appeal of such collective expressions of solidarity. Although interests may certainly play a part in giving rise to such organizations, the purpose of the book is to explore the complexities of ethnic identity formation and the diverse experiences that may draw 1.5/second generations to ethnic community work. Clearly, the strategic ways bridging organizations approach ethnic political solidarity becomes more critical in the case of spatially dispersed populations that would otherwise have little inspiration to "return to the community." Organizations provide the institutional setting within which to shape and regulate the shared ideologies and cultures of affiliates around politicized frameworks of ethnicity, which in turn help to attract, retain, and mobilize the 1.5/second generation members.

Conversely, these theories have yet to address adequately how spatial mobility and increasing ideological tensions between the immigrant and native-born generations may further transform the dynamics of ethnicity, other than making it disappear. Most studies on institutional assimilation have a tendency to advance a homogeneous notion of ethnic political solidarity that downplays the effects of both uneven and complementary empowerment in shaping the political loyalties of various institutions *within* the community. Using residential proximity as their starting point, these studies focus on how the spatial isolation of ethnic enclaves facilitates the emergence of self-governing political entities that can act in the best interests of the "ethnic community" because of compelling interests associated with coinciding cultural values and shared life chances. Yet the foundation for political solidarity is expected to dissipate with the emergence of a new generation of political leadership, whose more Americanized perspectives create conflict with the old guard and thus undermine any basis for intraethnic cooperation.

More contemporary works on Asian American enclaves (Kwong 1993; Lin 1998; Zhou and Kim 2001) reveal how the reality of ethnic power structures is much more complex. Detachment from mainstream society contributes to the formation of a male-dominated entrepreneurial elite that is able to manipulate the political agenda and resources of the self-governing ethnic community, often at the expense of workers and women within. Yet there is less discussion on how these internal hierarchies pass their legacy onto the next generation of ethnic leadership. Indeed, the contradictions of merging common ethnic-based interests with divergent political agendas may lead to atypical alliances and strange political bedfellows among the second generation. Thus, the idea that singular conceptions of ethnic solidarity will prompt the emergence of homogeneous institutions neglects the political complexities introduced by stratified ethnic opportunity structures and the paths more Americanized ethnic organizations must take to mediate the various paradoxes of ethnic solidarity.

Institutions as Bridging Community

Shared socioeconomic status and residential propinquity may provide the most stable structural foundations for ethnic solidarity, but new research studies on contemporary Asian immigrant communities suggest that they may not constitute the *only* basis for ethnic solidarity. This is particularly true for newer Asian immigrant groups, many of whom have bypassed the ethnic enclave and dispersed into diverse middle-class neighborhoods while other poor and newly arriving immigrants maintain their livelihoods near the traditional enclave centers. With this in mind, a number of studies have begun to explore the rise of "communities without propinquity," or communities that arise not from traditional spatially clustered residential neighborhoods but ethnic-based interactions and activities maintained through social networks, cultural events, and various institutions (Agocs 1981; Ling 2004; Pfeifer 1999; Zelinsky 2001).

Ethnic communities without residential propinquity have emerged within the context of changing American laws and societal attitudes that have accelerated the spatial integration of select immigrant groups into middle-class American neighborhoods. Immigration laws instituted after the 1960s helped to diversify the socioeconomic profiles of contemporary immigrants, which set the conditions for divergent trajectories of adaptation into American society. Aided by the elimination of residential segregation statutes and new social attitudes toward minorities in the postcivil rights era, more affluent immigrants have used their premigration skills and resources to migrate out of or even leapfrog the central enclave to middle-class neighborhoods away from the urban core. New technological advances in travel and communication have also made out-migration more viable and accessible even to less privileged ethnic groups. Regardless of socioeconomic background, immigrants are less likely to cluster near the central business district in the tradition of early-twentieth-century immigrants because of increasing congestion and unfavorable housing market conditions in inner-city areas.

From this perspective, socioeconomic and residential mobility does not necessarily entail the disintegration of "ethnic community" in all its sociocultural, economic, and political manifestations. Studies have shown that even in the absence of spatial propinquity, some groups are able to forge ethnic bonds, carry on cultural values and traditions, retain a strong sense of ethnic identity, collectively organize, and share ethnic-based resources and knowledge through various networks of affiliation. These networks can be as informal as bonds with family and extended kin to more fully developed ties embedded in institutions like churches, athletic leagues, social clubs, cultural centers, and political organizations. Some networks are localized within entrepreneurially developed communities, while others transcend national boundaries as discussed in the growing literature on transnationalism. Some relationships require regular visits, face-to-face interaction, and direct physical contact, while others are sustained through the virtual medium of telecommunications, media, and internet technology.

As a result, recent scholarly interest in deterritorialized post-1965 ethnic communities has given rise to new categories of community that no longer assume a direct linkage between residential proximity and ethnic solidarity. Although enclaves may continue to serve as a starting point for the eventual assimilation of immigrant groups, various scholars have raised the possibility that immigrants and their descendents may opt to settle in ethnically segregated suburban neighborhoods even when integration into racially mixed neighborhoods is feasible (Alba et al. 1999; Li 1998). Immigrant groups like the Chinese and Taiwanese in Los Angeles and New York have reconstructed new ethnic communities in satellite suburban or middle-class neighborhoods near the original enclave center (Horton 1995; Hum 2002; Lin 1998). Other groups like the Chinese in St. Louis; the Vietnamese in Toronto; and the Indians, Filipinos, and Japanese in various metropolitan areas have relied less on residential concentration and more on interpersonal networks to sustain vibrant ethnic communities (Ling 2004; Pfeifer 1999). And still other populations like the Korean Americans in Washington and the Germans in metropolitan Detroit (Agocs 1981; Zelinsky and Lee 1998) choose to live in residentially dispersed neighborhoods but commute to institutions within traditional enclaves to satisfy their ethnic tastes and needs.

Based on these new residential patterns, Table 1 presents four ideal-types of ethnic communities that may promote different configurations of ethnic solidarity. *Residential clustering* refers to ethnic populations that have mainly concentrated themselves in one or two traditional ethnic enclaves within the metropolitan area, while *residential dispersal* refers to those groups that have reclustered in various satellite communities or spread themselves thin in diverse neighborhood contexts. *Ethnic enclave economy* indicates whether the ethnic group has access to an institutionally developed, entrepreneurial ethnic economy within the metropolitan region, irrespective of their place of residence.

Because of their roots in ethnic-based residential neighborhoods, traditional ethnic enclaves and ghettos/barrios were seen as the only settings within which immigrants and their descendants would be expected to maintain a strong sense of ethnic solidarity. The main point of distinction between the two place-based communities was whether or not they were equipped with the kind of developed institutional structure that would allow future genera-

Table 1.1 Ideal-type classification of post-1965 ethnic communities

	Residential clustering	*Residential dispersal*
Access to developed ethnic enclave economy	Traditional ethnic enclave	Institutionally-centered communities
Lacks developed ethnic enclave economy	Ghettoes/ barrios	Cultural communities

SOURCE: Courtesy of author

tions to assimilate into American society or remain trapped forever in low-income minority ghettos and barrios. However, the literature on communities without propinquity has also considered two alternative scenarios for more spatially dispersed communities, including those that cultivate ethnic bonds through businesses and institutions in the central enclave and those that rely more on informal social networks and activities.

It is this third type of community, the institutionally centered community, that has laid the foundations for ethnic political solidarity among Korean Americans in Los Angeles. The case of Koreatown shows how the traditional image of early-twentieth-century ethnic enclaves as homogeneous, self-contained, and socially isolated stopping points on the pathway to American assimilation is becoming difficult to sustain in metropolitan regions that are themselves becoming increasingly global. Located at the nexus of developing Pacific Rim economies, ethnic enclaves like Koreatown serve as critical gateways for new streams of labor and capital that support social processes closely linked to the broader global economy. Replicating the class-polarized structure of global cities, the local economies of these neighborhoods are rebuilding their infrastructures around the upper circuits of transnational finance and corporate investment, as well as the lower circuits of small, labor-intensive businesses like restaurants and garment sweatshops (Lin 1998; Sassen 1988). In the process, the characteristics of such areas have shifted from internally oriented, isolated venues for ethnic succession and assimilation to globally integrated, capital-rich, and hierarchically structured institutional bases for new ethnic communities (Hum 2002; Vo and Bonus 2002). This economic transformation has prompted new notions of citizenship, cultural appropriation, and political resistance centered on both the concentrated power of ethnic enclaves and the broader global processes of inequality that sustain them (Lin 1998; Smith 2001; Vo 2004).

The resulting surge of entrepreneurial activity has enabled enclaves to expand in leaps and bounds, even as upwardly mobile residents continue to scatter across the urban metropolis. Indeed, it is the economic effects of globalization that has strengthened the institutional foundations of those developed enclave economies best equipped to meet the demands of the new capitalist order. In the postindustrial context, middle-class Asian immigrants and their children who relocate to suburban areas are able to take advantage of ethnic-based networks and institutions clustered within the primary enclave, because of the stability of entrepreneurial structures that support such institutionally complete communities. Ethnic-owned businesses in urban enclaves have a distinct competitive advantage over those choosing to locate in outer neighborhoods, because of their greater access to concentrated social networks, lower overhead costs, proximity to cheap labor, and interconnectedness with the Pacific Rim economy. As a result, immigrant-owned businesses are slower to leave the central enclave than are the residents who own and patronize these businesses. Even as Korean Americans disperse into distant suburban neighborhoods throughout Los Angeles and Orange Counties, entrepreneurial growth stimulates the expansion of social, cultural, political and economic institutions within the central enclave—a trend that has profoundly impacted Korean American politics today.

The Dynamics of Ethnic Political Solidarity

So what does this all mean for the political development of institutionally centered communities like Koreatown Los Angeles? One thing to note is that the pace at which ethnic groups socioeconomically assimilate does not necessarily parallel the pace at which they achieve political and social recognition from their White American peers and discard ethnic ties and identities. In the case of Korean Americans, the extent to which many Korean immigrants and their children have assimilated into mainstream economic structures may have lessened some of the socioeconomic hardships of the upwardly mobile but have not necessarily fulfilled all of their social and political needs. Events like the 1992 Los Angeles riots impressed upon the community the need to build their base of political empowerment, even as their ability to mobilize votes has become increasingly diluted by residential out-migration.

In this light, institutional concentration can provide a strong political foundation for communities whose voting power is significantly diminished by small population size and residential diffusion. Spatial clustering enables such organizations to coordinate their services, combine resources, and instantly band together in response to urgent events. Of course, internal ethnic solidarity does not fully compensate for the disadvantaged status of Korean Americans in mainstream politics, but maintaining the integrity of such institutions gives them the political cohesiveness necessary to advocate for greater representation, to create alliances with other racial and ethnic communities, and to establish their presence in mainstream politics during the formative years of the community's development.

Within this context, the book explores another possible function of ethnic institutions—that of bridging community. Although weakened by stratified eth-class interests, institutional infrastructures in more developed ethnic economies can play an important role in promoting ethnic political solidarity when residential ties disappear. In such communities, the key to understanding the rootedness of ethnic organizational politics is the continuing value of enclave resources, which are largely controlled by members of the "ethnic elite." In the Korean American community, the ethnic elite primarily consists of immigrant business owners, church leaders, and Seoul-linked immigrant organizations, who control access to critical community resources and wield significant political influence over the immigrant-dominated population.

In the early stages of immigration, overriding commonalities in interest and the hegemonic influence of the ethnic elite minimize the likelihood of intraethnic conflicts. However, exigent political upheavals, the processes of Americanization, and the introduction of outside support networks give voice to younger generations of ethnic leaders, who bring with them diverse and innovative ideas about political empowerment, along with invaluable ties to mainstream institutions. This new leadership is important in helping community members to initiate and manage contacts and resources with institutions outside the evolving ethnic enclave community. Drawing on ethnic and mainstream networks, bridging organizations provide the kind of institutional support necessary to promote ethnic political solidarity among the next generation as the population becomes increasingly divided by spatial assimilation and acculturation.

Yet contrary to assimilationist predictions about the growing autonomy of younger organizations from their immigrant predecessors, 1.5/second generation organizations must negotiate their political agendas within the traditional hierarchies of the immigrant community because of their partial dependency on the enclave-based influence and resources of the ethnic elite. Simply put, the first generation leadership relies on the second generation for specific resources they lack and vice versa because of their respective embeddedness within different networks of support—the former with stronger networks within the immigrant-dominated enclave population and the latter with stronger outside institutional support. Although more advantaged than the first generation organizations in terms of political expertise, English proficiency, citizenship rights, and access to mainstream resources, 1.5/second generation Korean American organizations are still constrained by the hierarchical structures of the immigrant community and their relations with first generation powerholders who are better equipped to mobilize financial capital, ethnic-based networks of support, and other resources within the immigrant-dominated enclave. Thus, despite intense intergenerational conflict and competition, access to different networks of support ironically creates the condition for intergenerational dependency and engagement between those who dominate the institutions of the traditional ethnic community and those who have the tools to create new bridges into mainstream society.

While there may be good reason for intergenerational cooperation, the question then is *how* such bridging organizations construct a sense of ethnic political solidarity in a community fragmented by so many competing interests. For one, the political agendas of bridging organizations do not necessarily accommodate easily to immigrant power structures, as my two case studies will show. These organizations bring with them Americanized ideas about the ethnic community and its place within mainstream society that clash with the traditional ideologies and value systems of the immigrant elite to varying degrees. Second, not all ethnic organizations will have equal access to ethnic community resources depending on the extent to which they can adjust their political ideals to those of the traditional leadership. Indeed, this study emphasizes the importance of internal inequities in structuring political agendas and interorganizational relationships within the Koreatown community.

The key is in understanding the diverse and specialized ways that organizations may attract 1.5/second generation Korean Americans to community work based on distinct notions of "ethnic political solidarity." Because of the expansion of ethnic organizational structures with the influx of mainstream resources in the postriot era, organizations have created a multitude of political spaces within which young generations of Korean Americans can understand and articulate their diverse ethnic-based experiences beyond traditional notions of ethnicity. These organizational frameworks focus on the salience of ethnicity as a central feature of the American experience, yet how they conceptualize the ethnic community and where this fits within the broader schemata of ethnic politics varies depending on the way they navigate immigrant power structures. In the process, organizations create diverse and multifaceted notions of citizenship and ethnicity that appeal to specific segments of the Korean American population.

Networks with groups outside the ethnic community are particularly instrumental in allowing organizations to achieve their political agenda. Conflict with the immigrant leadership and the availability of mainstream resources motivate particular 1.5/second generation ethnic organizations to look outward for assistance in dealing with the traditional leaders of the community. This book reveals that as opposed to fragmenting political leadership along generational lines, non-coethnic networks have allowed the new wave of Korean American organizations to renegotiate their status within Koreatown's political structures. In other words, these organizations have used their alternative resources to engage with, not detach from, the broader ethnic community. Hence, support from outside constituencies has not diminished the salience of ethnicity in these community-based organizations so much as given them the tools to promote new frameworks of "Korean Americanness" within the collective discourse. In the process, bridging organizations have completely rearticulated the sociopolitical meanings of "ethnic solidarity" no longer based on spatially bound, monolithic conceptualizations of community, but rather on political agendas that arise from navigating the rapidly diversifying context of Koreatown and the Korean American community.

Overview of the Book

Using interviews, participant observation, and other methodological techniques,[5] the book aims to understand the different ways 1.5/second generation bridging organizations in Koreatown, Los Angeles, cultivate and maintain ethnic solidarity among their membership despite the internal fragmentation of the ethnic community. The research is mainly based on five years of exploring Koreatown, roughly two years of volunteer work at KIWA and KYCC, and seventy in-depth interviews with community leaders, including organizational members/volunteers, business owners, workers, religious leaders, academics, and youth.

The book consists of two parts: Based on interviews with community leaders and secondary sources, Part 1 of the book describes the new demographic and political context within which 1.5/second generation Korean American organizations must build a sense of ethnic political solidarity in order to attain political empowerment. In particular, it traces the evolution of Koreatown politics from the more traditional, homogeneous notions of ethnic political solidarity fostered by the immigrant elite in Koreatown to the more diverse, specialized organizational subcultures of the 1.5/second generation leadership. Unlike past European immigrant communities, these newly emerging organizations in Koreatown have found ways to adapt to the potentially divisive effects of residential dispersal, the racial diversification of ethnic enclaves, and intergenerational fragmentation by strategically using both ethnic and mainstream resources to maintain the "institutional completeness" of Koreatown and fostering ethnic political solidarity among specific segments of the Korean American community.

Chapter 2 explains how entrepreneurial growth and global economic processes have prompted Koreatown's transition from a traditional immigrant enclave to the institutional home base of a class-polarized and spatially fragmented ethnic community. In this sense, the internally and externally imposed image of Koreatown as a center of entrepreneurship, conservatism, ethnic solidarity, and hard-working model minorities fails to capture the internal complexities of the population. Drawing on field observations and data from the 2000 U.S. Census, the chapter reveals how the population has been increasingly characterized by class polarization, residential dispersal, and intergenerational fragmentation yet grounded by the steady proliferation of ethnic-based businesses and institutions—all of which have led to the rise of Koreatown as an institutional community without propinquity.

Chapter 3 describes the relatively homogeneous, isolated, and hegemonic nature of ethnic political solidarity in the early stages of Koreatown politics, beginning with the emergence of the "ethnic elite"—namely, church leaders, entrepreneurs, and leaders of select Seoul-linked immigrant organizations. Political formations during this stage are more reminiscent of traditional geographically bounded enclave structures. Political isolation and common interests rooted in the shared migration experiences, residential spaces, and day-to-day struggles of Korean immigrants laid the basis for ethnic political solidarity and the uncontested dominance of the ethnic elite. Because of limited resources and marginal status within the host society, ethnic organizations became an important medium for providing mutual aid to incoming immigrants and raising the status of individual leaders within the community.

Chapter 4 focuses on a series of political crises from the Kwangju Rebellions in Korea to the Korean-Black conflicts to the 1992 Los Angeles riots that set the context for Koreatown's transformation from a traditional, secluded community to an externally oriented one and provided an entryway for 1.5/ second generation Korean American leaders and organizations. Although the process of generational transition was hastened by these three events, the study does generally show that access to mainstream resources and networks of support changes the political dynamics of ethnic power structures by intro- ducing a new generation of American-raised leadership whose interests and ideologies are more diverse than their immigrant predecessors. These events weakened the stronghold of the ethnic elite, politicized the 1.5/second genera- tion, and enhanced the influence of this newly emerging leadership through the introduction of mainstream resources and outside political opportunities. However, organizational responses in the aftermath of the 1992 Los Angeles riots also demonstrate how ethnic politics is characterized by both intergen- erational conflict and accommodation as different actors struggled to engage themselves within the political structures of Koreatown.

Chapter 5 explores how this process eventually changed power relations among the current organizational leadership, with specific attention to the diversification and specialization of Korean American organizational struc- tures centered on the community-based resources of the immigrant elite. The chapter begins by describing the internal tensions and conflicts that divide the traditional elite from the new 1.5/second generation leadership, as well as the complementary resources that bring them together. The chapter seeks to move beyond the generational divide by examining the internal stratification of contemporary ethnic organizational structures, not so much around gen- erational differences but more around unequal relations with the immigrant elite.

Based on interviews and field observations, Part 2 takes a closer look at two different 1.5/second generation ethnic organizations and the ways in which they have cultivated and maintained ethnic political solidarity among their membership within the constraints of ethnic and mainstream power structures. In particular, the chapters show how these bridging organizations have been able to reconcile some of the inherent contradictions of ethnicity in this type of context by constructing distinct, specialized frameworks of eth- nic political solidarity based on different relationships with the ethnic elite. Although they may not be able to address the general concerns of the entire Korean American population as the immigrant elite was able to do in the early years, they are able to construct specialized organizational subcultures that strongly appeal to the diverse "ethnic-centered" experiences of 1.5/second generation Korean Americans and therefore enhance attachments to and feelings of ethnic community among an otherwise divided population.

Chapter 6 covers the historical emergence of two 1.5/second generation Korean American organizations (KYCC and KIWA), from their humble roots in grassroots community work to their divergent paths into contemporary power structures. The chapter describes how each organization has strategically negotiated their political agendas within traditional immigrant hierarchies, drawing on different support networks and how this has provided them with unique political resources.

Chapter 7 then takes a look at the way these bridging organizations have had to politicize the new second generation and negotiate their emergent political agendas within the constraints of both ethnic and mainstream support networks, with particular attention to federal restrictions on political activities among nonprofits. It is shown how this strategic approach to politics shapes the internal political cultures of these two organizations in terms of their response to community-related issues, the way they cultivate youth leadership, and their incorporation of Latino members and clientele.

The case of KYCC and KIWA are testaments to how social service agencies and advocacy organizations have come to fill a political void in marginalized ethnic communities like Koreatown. Through an analysis of these two organizations, Chapter 8 asks why 1.5/second generation Korean Americans who work in these organizations feel compelled to return to the ethnic enclave community. Namely, bridging organizations create a sense of "place" for 1.5/second generation Korean Americans and a political framework for understanding ethnic-centered struggles and experiences that emerge from living in diverse neighborhood settings outside the traditional enclave of Koreatown. The chapter explores the differential appeal of organizations like KIWA and KYCC that have cultivated distinct frameworks of ethnic political solidarity based on their individual networks of support—one based on an eth-class model of solidarity and the other on a flexible notion of Korean Americanness and social justice

Chapter 9 examines how women have played a particularly unique role in bridging the various microchasms that may emerge between the organization and the communities they serve by promoting a more subjective, inclusive, and humanistic approach to community work. Because of the hegemonic nature of ethnic political structures, women have had few organizational spaces for contesting gender inequality within the community and have thus focused their efforts on "engendering" community work based on gendered roles and responsibilities in existing ethnic organizations. Within this context, the chapter explains how KYCC and KIWA have incorporated women into their organizations in a way that sustains their organizational cultures and re-affirms their respective frameworks of ethnic political solidarity.

Finally, Chapter 10 considers the broader theoretical implications of the study on the development of ethnic politics among post-1965 Asian American communities. Here, the chapter discusses the need to come up with new ways of conceptualizing "community" for Asian Americans in the post-1965 era, the continuing significance of ethnic political solidarity based on a more nuanced approach to internal and external inequality, and the future evolution of Asian American politics within the context of race relations and globalization.

Part One
Burning Bridges

2 The Making of Koreatown, L.A.

THE NAME "KOREATOWN" COMES FROM the visible and influential proliferation of Korean-owned businesses throughout the community, the "success" of which has caught the interest of numerous academic studies and the
popular media in recent decades (Abelmann and Lie 1995; Light and Bonacich 1988; Min 1996). Situated west of downtown Los Angeles and north
of South Central, the enclave has undergone many transformations since its
inception at the fringes of a declining inner-city neighborhood. In the early
years of its development, Koreatown served as the major destination point
for incoming Korean immigrants in the United States, because it offered
abundant economic opportunities for entrepreneurs and laborers as well as
social networks and cultural resources for the "unassimilated." Unlike their
European predecessors, immigrants from Asia and other third world countries also had to deal with a host of discriminatory laws, including anti-
immigration policies, restrictive covenants on housing, and antimiscegenation
statutes that spatially and socially confined them to declining neighborhoods
within the city. Both cultural solidarity and discrimination pushed Korean
residents to cluster in physical proximity to their coethnic-oriented businesses.

Over time, immigrants have used their class resources and entrepreneurial skills to renovate declining inner-city neighborhoods into vibrant enclave
communities. However, since the 1960s, upwardly mobile Korean Americans
have taken advantage of fair-housing policies to scatter into suburban neighborhoods throughout Los Angeles and Orange Counties, leaving behind only
elderly and working-class immigrants who cannot afford to leave the ethnic
neighborhood. Despite this wave of out-migration, the booming ethnic econ-

omy continues to attract a steady stream of tourists and investment capital from other countries—a trend that has made Koreatown one of several transnational headquarters for the Pacific Rim economy of Los Angeles. Today, numerous colorful signs written in Korean lettering mark the presence of countless Korean business establishments, churches, nonprofit organizations, and strip malls lined along the main business corridors of the enclave. The economic prosperity of this growing entrepreneurial community has been sustained by both the hard labor of low-skilled Korean and Latino workers and the patronage of its less privileged, multiethnic residents. In this respect, Koreatown represents a significant departure from traditional European enclaves of the early twentieth century.

This chapter discusses Koreatown's historical transition from a small, isolated immigrant enclave to its institutional expansion at the nexus of the current global economy. Several developments in the global era, including the passage of the 1965 Immigration and Nationality Act, played a key role in determining the heterogeneous and entrepreneurial character of Korean migration that would shape the dynamics of social inequality in Koreatown's ethnic power structures. The concentrated influence of Korean immigrant entrepreneurship, the growth of ethnic-based support networks, and the influx of transnational capital have all helped to establish Koreatown as the institutional home base of a rapidly dispersing Korean American population. The unchecked growth of ethnic businesses and institutions has had far-reaching effects on both Korean and non–Korean American residents who live and work within the vicinity of the enclave economy.

Immigration and Entrepreneurship After 1965

Historical and Demographic Patterns

Less than twenty years ago, few pundits would have considered Korean Americans formative players either in the dynamic spaces of Asian American grassroots activism or the electoral stages of mainstream American politics. In part, the roots of the community's political obscurity can be traced back to the demographic and historical context of Korean migration. Korean migration, like that of most other Asian ethnic groups, had been largely curtailed by restrictive quotas implemented in the early twentieth century as a result of widespread working-class discontent and nativist movements across the nation. Migration from Korea was severely curtailed when Japan took control of

Korea as a protectorate in 1905 and then formally annexed the country in 1910; this takeover made the nation subject to the immigration restrictions negotiated between the United States and Japan under the Gentleman's Agreement. The subsequent enactment of the 1924 National Origins Act, which instituted quotas on the immigration flows of individual sending nations, virtually signaled the end of immigration from Asia for almost half of the century. Aside from a small flow of students, G. I. wives, and adoptee children during the Korean War (1950–53), Korean migration to both Hawaii and the U.S. mainland was virtually nonexistent until the passage of the 1965 Immigration and Nationality Act.

Major upheavals in the social and economic structures of American society would ease the nation's reductionist approach toward immigration and push Congress to implement new and less stringent requirements for entry into the country. Since the 1970s and 1980s, economic restructuring has transformed the world economy from an internationally linked world system in which goods and services are traded across national boundaries to a globally interdependent economy governed by the oligopolistic economic activities of multinational corporations. Within the context of heightened global competition and rising energy prices, the United States and other developed nations experienced a major transition from a manufacturing industrial economy to a technological and service-oriented economy during this time period.

Immigrants played a critical role in the emergence of the new global economy by allowing capitalists to cut the costs of labor through the employment of low-wage workers from the third world, while simultaneously fulfilling the need for technological innovation and development through the incorporation of highly skilled and well-educated managers and professionals. As the main recipients of these transnational flows of labor and capital, ethnic enclaves have become the primary sites for the growth of unregulated and highly exploitative economic activities that provide light manufacturing services (for example, garment manufacturing) and specialized ethnic-based markets (for example, ethnic restaurants) through the employment of cheap immigrant labor. Around the same time period, American society was also experiencing a gradual change in its attitudes toward racial and ethnic minority groups as a result of the civil rights movement, which pushed for a more open-door policy to foreigners from other nations.

Partly in response to these different social and economic shifts, the U.S. Congress replaced the earlier quota system with a new preference system that stimulated massive immigration from Asia, Latin America, and the Caribbean. The 1965 Immigration and Nationality Act established a system of preferences for the admission of specific immigrant groups. The most important categories would be immigrants with highly skilled, managerial, and professional backgrounds and those with family and kinship ties to either citizens or permanent residents of the United States. As we shall see, the stipulations of this immigration act have had a profound impact on the internal demographic and institutional structure of ethnic enclaves in the United States by dramatically expanding, diversifying, and transforming their immigrant populations.

About 23 million immigrants came to the United States between 1971 and 2002. Most immigrants initially situated themselves in major metropolitan areas across the country, including Los Angeles, which is now considered the "New Ellis Island" (Waldinger and Bozorgmehr 1996). Political turmoil in Asia and Latin America and undocumented migration primarily from Mexico and other Central American countries added more fuel to migration flows to Los Angeles, which became home to the second largest foreign-born population next to Miami (Waldinger and Bozorgmehr 1996). More importantly, contemporary immigration represents a significant departure from early waves of European immigration in terms of its vast ethnic and class heterogeneity, which has laid the foundations for the emergence of diverse ethnic communities in both urban and suburban regions throughout the United States.

The passage of the 1965 Immigration and Nationality Act was also a major turning point in Korean American history, because it allowed for the rapid expansion and immigration of a diverse Korean American population that had barely existed before the 1960s. According to the Bureau of Citizenship and Immigration Services (formerly known as the Immigration and Naturalization Service), Koreans constituted the fourth largest ethnic group to enter the United States between 1971 and 1981 and the seventh largest group between 1981 and 1996, behind larger countries such as Mexico, Philippines, Vietnam, and China. The latest figures from the 2000 U.S. Census indicate that Korean Americans continue to be among the top five Asian Pacific American groups in the United States in terms of the overall size of their residential population. The statistics indicate that there are currently over a million Koreans living in the United States. Within the County of Los Angeles, the Korean American population grew from 9,000 in 1970 to 145,000 in 1990. Today, roughly 258,000 Korean Americans live in the combined metropolitan areas of Los Angeles, Riverside, and Orange Counties.

Of course, immigration policies alone do not account for the major flow of Koreans that entered the United States. The nation had established strong international linkages with South Korea through its long-standing military and political presence and economic ties that spurred the movement of cheap labor and Asian goods into the United States. At the height of Korean migration during the 1980s, wages in the United States were much more competitive than South Korean wages, which became the main impetus for Korean movement to America. (Light and Bonacich 1988). In turn, the United States was more than happy to receive this relatively cheap but highly educated workforce in order to fill shortages in skilled labor and keep pace with the global economy. South Korean dependency on the export economy also worked to undermine workers' rights, as a result of efforts by U.S.-backed Korean administrations to keep workers' wages competitive in overseas contracts (Kim 1981). The rapid development and modernization of the South Korean economy within the global order produced a growing class of middle- and upper-class elites, whose newly emerging aspirations for upward mobility compelled them to venture abroad and send their children to schools in America. Population pressures and hyperurbanization in South Korea further encouraged the creation of emigration policies and recruitment companies that facilitated the movement of Koreans abroad. The globalization of American culture into Asia helped to advertise the American dream to potential immigrants.

As with many other post-1965 Asian immigrant groups, the socioeconomic and demographic profile of immigration waves from Korea gradually began to change over the past few decades in response to the stipulations of the 1965 Immigration and Nationality Act and changing economic conditions in the United States and abroad. The first wave of Korean immigrants was admitted under the occupational preferences category of the immigration act. Until the mid-1970s, about 30 percent of those eligible under the occupational preferences category were admitted each year (Yoon 1997). This group primarily consisted of those with four-year college degrees and from professional, technical, or managerial backgrounds, including doctors, nurses, scientists, and engineers. In addition, post-1965 Korean immigrants came primarily from major urban areas in South Korea, especially the capital of Seoul, easing their transition into U.S. urban areas. The selective nature of immigration may partly help to explain why we have seen higher rates of socioeconomic mobility, including the dramatic rise of small-business ownership among Koreans with middle-class backgrounds and resources.

Another defining characteristic of post-1965 Asian immigration has been the high proportion of women entering the United States. Historically, women did not constitute a large proportion of overall migration flows to the United States, especially if they were part of racially marginalized groups whose populations were often regulated by the fears and interests of capitalists and nativist White movements. However, family reunification policies, the high number of war brides, and the rising need for cheap immigrant labor in service industries and traditionally female occupations (for example, the garment industry) have bolstered the number of female immigrants to the United States. In the case of Korean immigrants, the migration of Korean nurses, war brides, and adoptees since the 1950s was enough to create an extreme gender imbalance in favor of women and children over men (Kim 1981). In contrast, current immigration from Korea has been characterized by the permanent settlement of stable, intact families, many of whom come to the United States to support their families, find better educational options for their children, or to reunite with their family members. In this sense, Korean women have been particularly important contributors to the processes of migration and settlement. In addition to taking care of domestic and childcare responsibilities on the home front, Korean immigrant women contribute to family welfare by working long hours in either family businesses or in the various service industries that sustain the Koreatown economy.

For all this talk about the wealth and success of the new model minority, an important development in recent decades has been the steady decline in the occupational and socioeconomic status of incoming Korean immigrants. Improving economic conditions in Korea throughout the early 1990s and limited opportunities in the United States have dampened some of the desires of middle-class Koreans to migrate. Furthermore, once the first wave of immigrants settled down in the United States and started to concentrate in higher numbers, they were able to bring in families and relatives through the second part of the 1965 Immigration and Nationality Act. The original 1965 Immigration and Nationality Act ranked family ties highest among all preference categories, yet Koreans could not take advantage of family preferences because of the small size of the community prior to 1965. Facing economic recession during the 1970s, however, Congress passed a series of legislation that made it more difficult for immigrants to enter through occupational preferences and placed more emphasis on those falling under the family reunification category.

As a result, data on immigration since the 1980s indicates a steady increase in the proportion of Koreans coming from lower- or working-class backgrounds. While immigration among those with higher skills and occupations still continues, a greater proportion of lower-class immigrants from Korea, including manual laborers, service workers, and farmers, have used their kinship ties with American citizens to enter the United States, as more Korean Americans begin to qualify for citizenship status over time. As a result, the median family income has declined while the proportion of Korean Americans living below poverty has steadily increased (Yoon 1997). In the end, the shifting character of Korean migration has molded the demographic and economic terrains of this globally driven enclave economy.

Entrepreneurship and the Enclave Economy   Not all ethnic populations are equipped to cultivate the type of resource-rich networks necessary for socioeconomic growth and mobility. Rather, it is the economic base that emerges from such densely clustered networks of support that differentiate declining *ethnic neighborhoods* from institutionally developed *ethnic enclave economies*. Ethnic neighborhoods are characterized by low levels of entrepreneurial activity, high concentrations of poor immigrants, and higher dependency on noncoethnic suppliers and consumer outlets. In contrast, ethnic enclave economies boast not only large numbers of businesses and institutions but also a wide range of economic activities, greater vertical integration[1] within the ethnic economy, and a highly differentiated labor force led by a strong class of entrepreneurial elites (Wilson and Martin 1982; Wilson and Portes 1980). Over time, entrepreneurial growth nurtures the kind of capital and organizing capacity necessary for the maturation of neighborhood infrastructures.

It is mainly the predominating influence of immigrant entrepreneurship that accounts for both the internal formation of political hierarchies and the rapid expansion of ethnic-based institutions within the Koreatown community. While some Korean immigrants are absorbed into the white-collar sectors of the market economy, Koreans have been most well known for their considerable success in entrepreneurship. According to more recent statistics, Koreans continue to have the highest rates of self-employment among all racial/ethnic groups. The 2000 census reports that in the United States, 25.9 percent of Korean men of working age are self-employed, as compared with 14 percent of White men and 5.5 percent of Black men. Within the L.A.-Long Beach metropolitan area, 25.8 percent of Korean men are reported to be self-employed, as compared with 16.2 percent of White men and 5.1 percent of Black men (Valdez forthcoming). Many of these immigrants have been able to use their middle- and upper-middle class urban backgrounds and a combination of family, ethnic, and class resources[2] to open small businesses in Koreatown and inner-city ghettos throughout cities across the nation. Korean immigrants have established strong niches in small firms within the retail trade, manufacturing, and service sectors, such as grocery and liquor stores, dry cleaning establishments, retail stores for Asian goods, and garment subcontracting.

Some Korean-owned businesses have filled economic gaps left by the withdrawal of large corporations from low-income minority neighborhoods in the past few decades. Establishing businesses in underserved areas of inner-city ghettos have been particularly appealing to Korean immigrants because of low overhead costs, little need for English proficiency, easy access to cheap labor, and/or less competition from established businesses. Although starting up a business in ethnic enclaves is relatively more competitive and expensive than in areas of South Central, some of the bolder or more capital-endowed immigrants prefer to establish themselves in places like Koreatown because of its slightly lower crime rates, strong ethnic support system, and common language and culture with coethnic patrons.

In addition, Korean immigrant business owners have been able to take advantage of economic opportunities made available by U.S.-South Korean ties and inequities in the new postindustrial economy. The South Korean export trade has provided important openings for Korean entrepreneurs in various industries catering to both coethnic and noncoethnic clientele. The many Korean supermarkets, travel agencies, and TV and newspaper media networks that populate Koreatown are some examples of businesses that rely on U.S.-Korea trade relations. Other entrepreneurs have capitalized on this extensive trade network to set up retail and wholesale businesses selling garments, wigs, and handbags produced by South Korean companies.

Entrepreneurship offers a viable alternative for immigrants who are reluctant to enter the secondary labor market, which is characterized by low-wage, menial jobs with little opportunities for upward mobility. Because of language barriers and nontransferable educational degrees or professional training, many Korean immigrants initially experience downward occupational mobility into lower job tiers within their profession or move to other occupations altogether. This situation results in what scholars term "status inconsistencies" between their education and income, between their education and occupation after migration, and between their occupational status before and after migration (Hurh and Kim 1984). In other words, Korean immigrants do

not do as well upon migration as their education or occupational background before migration would normally afford them. Within this context, business ownership is seen as the most ideal way to make money. Furthermore, Koreans prefer the sense of autonomy they feel in owning a business over working in a foreign American workplace environment where they do not relate to their co-workers and are more likely to encounter racial discrimination by superiors (Min 1990).

Establishing a small business does not require substantial capital but does require hard labor. Although the potential benefits can be high, studies have shown that operating a small business can entail considerable costs and risks including long hours, difficult working conditions, high rates of business failure, reliance on unpaid family labor, and tense relations with minority patrons in the case of inner-city businesses. What business owners save in terms of setup costs, they must pay for in terms of labor. Because of the marginal profits that businesses will make in any given day, merchants must spend longer hours in the store, raise the price of products to the ire of low-income customers, and utilize both cheap immigrant labor and unpaid family labor to make sufficient returns (Min 1996). Nevertheless, with a combination of luck, strenuous work, and various resources, owning a small business has greater potential to offer significant returns in terms of income.

Exemplified by the high rate of entrepreneurship among Korean immigrants in the United States, the myth of the so-called "model minority" has portrayed Asian Americans as the epitome of meritocracy and success in American society. However, such stereotypical generalizations have failed to recognize deep class bifurcations among Asian immigrants, ethnic and gender differences within the broader racial community, and racial differences with non-Hispanic Whites in terms of more immeasurable costs and sacrifices. More importantly, the prosperity of robust enclave economies like Koreatown depends on the maintenance of rigid racial and class hierarchies that enable a small class of elites to benefit through the exploitation of a poor minority. Because of the extreme competitiveness, low profitability, and general instability of the ethnic enclave economy, small ethnic firms must often rely on two forms of cheap and exploitable labor: low-wage workers and unpaid family members, especially women and children.

In this sense, we cannot understand the evolution of Koreatown power structures in the current global era until we explore the dark side of "entrepreneurial success." Labor-intensive enterprises in the enclave economy depend heavily on lowering workers' wages—a practice that enables ethnic-owned businesses to manufacture and sell corporate products at low costs and stay competitive with other firms within the global economy. Successful businesses are hence built on the backs of less fortunate Asian workers employed in the ethnic enclave economy. Like the secondary market, jobs in the ethnic enclave market are characterized by low wages, substandard working conditions, and high turnover rates. Poor working conditions are oftentimes exacerbated by the government's lax enforcement of labor laws in immigrant communities. Among the 100 Korean and Latino restaurant workers surveyed by the Korean Immigrant Workers Advocates (KIWA), 41.1 percent continued to earn below the minimum wage, 26.5 percent worked over sixty hours per week, and 40.6 percent suffered workplace injuries and lacked health insurance or workers compensation (KIWA 2000). One report finds that among the 145,431 Koreans in Los Angeles County, 16 percent lived under the poverty line in 1990, as compared to 13 percent of Asian Pacific Americans overall and 7 percent of Whites (Ong and Hee 1994). Some scholars argue that coethnic workers are willing to work under such inferior working conditions because they receive trade-offs in the form of high employment rates, cultural familiarity with the working environment, and greater potential for vertical mobility in the enclave economy (Wilson and Portes 1980; Zhou 1992).

As compared with Korean firms in other areas like South Central, unpaid family members and coethnic workers continue to form the main source of labor for businesses and industries in Koreatown, simply because they are easy to find. However, Latinos are beginning to make their presence in the lower-level workforce of many Koreatown industries, because of their greater willingness to accept low wages and political vulnerability arising from their undocumented status. In addition to being underpaid and overworked, Latinos are not likely to receive pay raises or promotions, endure continuous discrimination and verbal abuse from their supervisors, and live under the constant fear of being fired or, in the case of undocumented workers, deported.

Korean immigrant women also predominate in traditionally female-dominated occupations in Koreatown industries, such as the restaurant, bar/nightclub, and garment industries. Notwithstanding the large numbers of women who are employed in family businesses or immigrate as nurses, studies suggest that Korean immigrant women in Los Angeles and the United States as a whole are overrepresented in the personal services and unskilled labor sectors as compared with their American counterparts (Bonacich, Hossain, and

Park 1987). Because their wages are considered supplementary to the household income, women are also underpaid relative to their male counterparts. Although they have more opportunities to assume managerial positions than their Latino counterparts, women in these industries are vulnerable to verbal and physical abuse by their employers and sexual harassment from both clientele and employers. Many of these women also juggle with the dual burdens of low-wage work and domestic and familial responsibilities at home.

From an Ethnic Enclave to a Global Nexus

So then, how have the social and entrepreneurial characteristics of Korean migration shaped the urban terrains of Koreatown, Los Angeles, over the course of its history? Like most enclave communities of the time, Koreatown began as a small cluster of segregated homes and ethnic-owned businesses catering to the specialized tastes and needs of the local Korean population. In the early twentieth century, Korean residents were largely restricted to racially mixed, low-income districts as a result of racial covenant laws, particularly around the areas of Macy and Alameda Streets and Bunker Hill (Lewis 1974). During this period, racial discrimination also prevented Korean immigrants from entering most professions in the mainstream labor markets so that many chose to open up a limited variety of small businesses catering to coethnic patrons rather than assume menial jobs. Among other things, Korean immigrants established grocery stores, laundry establishments, restaurants, and wholesale companies throughout their neighborhoods. Various churches and community organizations such as the Korean Presbyterian Church (circa 1938) and the Korea National Association (circa 1910) continued to mark the presence of Koreans throughout the early part of the century (Lewis 1974; Yu, Phillips, and Yang 1982).

In the 1920s and 1930s, the Korean community shifted into the vicinity enclosed by Vermont Avenue, Western Avenue, Adams Boulevard, and Slauson Avenue and then moved northward into present-day Koreatown with the elimination of residential segregation statutes in 1948 (Lee 1995). The general area we now call Koreatown has undergone dramatic demographic changes throughout the twentieth century. Prior to the elimination of residential segregation statutes in 1948, this area began as an overwhelmingly White community in the 1940s (over 90 percent White), which gradually disappeared as more African Americans moved into the neighborhood from the growing communities of South Central to the south. The possible transition toward an inner-city ghetto however would be halted by new developments in immigration after the 1960s.

Initially drawn by the reasonable land value and the extensive job opportunities, Korean immigrants arrived in masses with the passage of the 1965 Immigration and Nationality Act, increasing the property value of the area and transforming the deteriorating district located on the peripheries of South Central into a center of thriving entrepreneurial activity. Once Korean-owned businesses started to gain momentum, the unofficial boundaries of Koreatown started to distend and shift in several directions until the community became a distinctive entity by the mid-1970s. With the assistance of the Korean Town Development Association, the City of Los Angeles officially designated the area as "Koreatown" in 1980, which signified the political visibility of Koreans in the city government and spurred further immigration (Light and Bonacich 1988).

Throughout the 1970s and 1980s, the number of Korean firms and their profits continued to soar. A new line of office complexes, grand hotels, storefronts, apartment buildings, and shopping centers lined the streets alongside the older homes of the original inhabitants. Over time, the businesses began to expand the range of services they provided to coethnic clientele, including professional services such as accounting, law, medicine, and real estate. The expansion of import and wholesale businesses has further strengthened the vertical integration of Korean retail store owners with coethnic suppliers within the ethnic economy. Although the spatial concentration of these businesses tended to focus on the vicinity within and around Koreatown, this period simultaneously witnessed a steady process of decentralization, as Korean immigrants began to venture into other underserved markets such as low-income minority ghettos (Lee 1995). By this time, Korean entrepreneurs had firmly established their presence within the power structures of Koreatown politics.

So what does the Korean American community look like today? When Pyong Gap Min (1996) wrote about the Los Angeles Korean American community in the mid-1990s, Koreatown was said to encompass a sixteen-square mile region bounded by Melrose Avenue on the north, Pico Boulevard on the south, Hoover Boulevard on the east, and Crenshaw Boulevard on the west. If one were to focus solely on Korean business concentration and the historical origins of the Korean American community within this particular region, the heart of Koreatown is generally located around Olympic Boulevard bounded by Vermont and Crenshaw to the east and the west, respectively. However, fueled by continuing immigration, business expansion, as well as corporate capital from abroad, Koreatown has since grown in leaps and bounds within the past decade alone, both in terms of its residential population and its entrepreneurial infrastructures.

As is true with most immigrants, the less fortunate arrivals continue to settle down in the central enclave, where resources are sparse and living standards low. The section of the community that remains is primarily the elderly who are too ingrained in the comforts of a "Korean" Koreatown life or poor Korean residents and business owners who cannot afford to move either their residence or business location. Map 2.1 depicts the socioeconomic composition of Koreatown based on median household income. As shown, Koreatown falls within some of the more impoverished areas of Los Angeles. The average median household income for Koreatown's core census tracts is $25,157 (not including the census tract outlier that partly falls into the more affluent areas

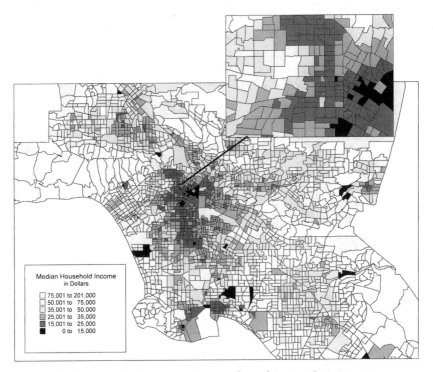

Map 2.1: Median household income in Los Angeles and Orange Counties, 2000
SOURCE: Data from 2000 U.S. Census

of Hancock Park), and almost a third of the households in Koreatown have incomes under the poverty level. A recent study classifies Koreatown as one of the nation's main Asian American neighborhoods in economic distress, with a quarter of its population below poverty level and stuck in low-wage jobs (Ong et al. 2002). Thus, regardless of the individual resources of Korean Americans in this area, the socioeconomic status of the neighborhood has serious implications on the ability of its occupants to demand certain political and economic services, as painfully captured during the 1992 Los Angeles civil unrest.

For this segment of the population, the institutional structure of Koreatown provides a familiar sociospatial context that enables them to adapt gradually to their new surroundings. Referring to the community as the "Korea away from Korea," many scholars have noted the striking similarities between the lifestyle and social structure of the community and that of Seoul, the rapidly modernizing capital of Korea. Unlike many other cities and districts in Los Angeles, the parochial quality of Koreatown is reaffirmed by the widespread availability of ethnic-based resources and networks that allow unacculturated Korean immigrants to fulfill their daily needs without knowing how to speak English. The reproduction of this social provincialism is intricately intertwined with the immigrants' firm nationalist ties to homeland politics, which manifests itself most clearly in the various ethnic newspapers and television networks that service the Los Angeles Korean community.

Yet despite its name, Koreatown is also a multiethnic residential neighborhood, dominated by Latino immigrants. Table 2.1 presents the racial/ethnic breakdown of residents in Koreatown based on data from the 1990 and 2000 U.S. Census. In 1990, we see that no single racial or ethnic group completely stands out in this diverse community, but Latinos now constitute almost half the population (49.5 percent) of Koreatown with the percentage steadily growing by 2000 (52.9 percent). Mexicans (20.8 percent), Salvadorans (7.5 percent), and Guatemalans (4.8 percent) are the largest Hispanic groups in the area relative to the residential population. Asian Pacific Americans comprise about a third of the residential population for both years. Although undoubtedly the largest among all Asian Pacific American groups and slowly growing, Koreans are only 21.5 percent of the Koreatown residential population. In contrast, the figures for non-Hispanic Whites and African Americans have been steadily declining in the past few decades.

Global restructuring has had a significant impact on the historical development of the Koreatown community by strengthening transnational linkages

Table 2.1 Racial and ethnic distribution of residents in Koreatown , 1990–2000

	1990 (172,094)	2000 (186,048)
NH Whites	15.4%	10.1%
NH Blacks	6.4	4.9
Asian Pacific Islanders	28.2	30.1
Koreans	18.4	21.5
Filipinos	6.3	4.9
Chinese	1.4	0.8
Japanese	1.5	0.9
Asian Indian	0.5	0.8
Persons of Spanish/Hispanic Origin[2]	49.5	52.9
Mexicans	17.6	20.8
Salvadorans	N/A	7.5
Guatemalan	N/A	4.8
Other Hispanic	31.9	19.7
American Indian, Eskimo, Aleut	0.2	0.2
Other	0.4	0.3

SOURCE: 1990 and 2000 U.S. Census

between immigrant communities in the United States and homeland economies. As the center of the developing Pacific Rim economy, Los Angeles has occupied a special position within the new global order mainly as a result of immigration. The rise of entrepreneurship in areas such as Koreatown has not only boosted the local economy but also facilitated international trade links with Asia. Moreover, the emergence of immigrant communities has attracted capitalists from abroad seeking investment opportunities in these areas. The resulting increase in speculative capital from South Korean corporations has contributed to the internal development and expansion of Koreatown. As a result, unlike most local economies, the Korean enclave economy is said to be less affected by the state of the broader American economy as it is by conditions abroad (Chang and Diaz-Veizades 1999).

An observational survey of Koreatown shows how territorial growth, various redevelopment projects, and the establishment of new businesses continue to transform the face of Koreatown with the advent of globalization. The spatial landscapes of Koreatown reflect the multifaceted entrepreneurial empire that makes up Los Angeles, including the small mom-and-pop shops that grow next door to U.S. and Korean corporate branch supermarkets and the multiracial base of consumers, workers, and merchants upon which these global economies are built. In any section of the Koreatown enclave, it is not odd to see a Korean acupuncturist office housed in a historical bungalow located not far from a McDonald's restaurant where Latinos and elderly Korean men lounge. Meanwhile, low wages coupled with the skyrocketing price of housing in Koreatown have intensified the paradoxes of spatial inequity, according to a recent report by KIWA. The lack of affordable housing has reached alarming proportions in Koreatown where two or three immigrant families may be forced to share a one-bedroom apartment not far down the block from a luxury apartment with high-tech security features.

At least five new Korean mall complexes and strip malls were being constructed along Wilshire Boulevard, Western Avenue, and Olympic Boulevard at the time of the study, along with several luxury apartment buildings advertising to wealthier incoming immigrants. In addition to the traditional signs and structures that permeate the landscape, major Korean corporations such as Korean Air have injected a modern, corporate element to traditional Korean culture from the capital of Seoul to the city of Los Angeles. In the past few years, these companies have erected grand glass-encased shopping malls and large-screen video monitors advertising various Seoul corporate products like Cosmos, Amore cosmetics, and KIA automobiles along the busiest intersections of the entrepreneurial district. The infusion of capital and cultural influences from South Korea have also given rise to a strong consumption culture among Korean Americans built on Louis Vuitton bags and fixed-up cars.

Ethnic consumers alone do not seem to be the only driving force behind the burgeoning Koreatown economy. Beyond the usual Korean immigrants that frequent the area, a diverse mix of Korean suburbanites, Latino locals, and outside spectators can be seen shopping at the many ethnic-owned businesses and institutions that sustain this flourishing enclave. As a recent headline in the *Los Angeles Times* (Chua 1994) proclaims, "Opening Up for Business Koreatown Looks to Other Ethnicities for Post-Riot Patrons." In contrast to smaller restaurants that specialize in specific Korean dishes, larger barbecue-style Korean restaurants that are more likely to cater to both Korean and non-Korean clientele have started to proliferate along the main corridors of the enclave. The increasing visibility of White women at Korean immigrant hangouts, such as women's saunas, have caused more than one Korean patron I spoke with to complain about the intrusion of outsiders. I also conversed with the female owner of one such recreational club in Koreatown, which has begun to draw in more non-Korean clientele in recent years. The club features a large women's spa and a golf driving range. With the help of her son's corporate connections, she has renovated one of the spaces into an elite dance club that attracts a racially mixed crowd interested in male revues and post–Grammy Awards parties.

Ironically, the very forces that prompted the internal development of the enclave economy also spurred the outward migration of its middle-class ethnic population. The uncontrolled growth of the enclave economy has contributed to air pollution, urban noise, traffic congestion, and the influx of poor minority groups. Ong (1994) finds that despite considerable economic growth, Koreatown still suffers from high poverty levels, low-quality schools, and increasing crime rates. Fear of crime, especially in the aftermath of the Los Angeles riots, has pushed more immigrant community leaders to nurture more positive relations with the local LAPD through financial donations, policeman dinners, public safety coalitions, and individual meetings. One fifty-three-year-old immigrant real estate executive argues that because of rising crime, "We lose the business, we lose the customers, and [when] some Caucasian people from my office go out to Koreatown, they don't even want to get out from the car. Why? Because they have a fear it's dangerous and it really is dangerous sometimes in certain locations, though *we [Koreans] feel it deep in our skin*" [Italics translated from Korean]. The excesses of entrepreneurial growth have caused more affluent and upwardly mobile Korean Americans to move to greener pastures in Los Angeles and Orange Counties.

With the disintegration of racial segregation statutes in the 1960s, affluent and socially mobile groups within the Koreatown community moved into secluded suburban neighborhoods far away from the urban core of Los Angeles. The high percentage of foreign-born Koreans in parts of Orange County also suggests that many immigrant groups have bypassed Koreatown altogether and moved directly to well-kept suburban neighborhoods. Some have even moved out to other cities throughout California or other states such as Washington, Utah, Arizona, and Kansas according to the *Los Angeles Times* (Carvajal 1994). Map 2.2 gives us a general idea of how the Korean American population has spread within this area from 1990 to 2000, although the residential growth is perhaps less dramatic as the development of its entrepreneurial infrastructure. Even if we look at residential distribution alone, it is apparent that Korean Americans have begun extending into neighboring areas, including the more upper-income neighborhoods of Hancock Park to the west and parts of Pico-Union to the East.

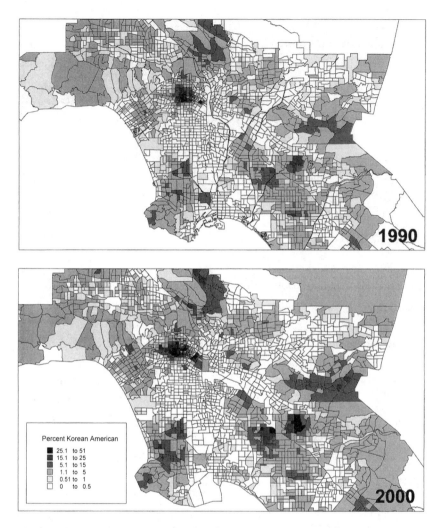

Map 2.2: Percent Korean American population in Los Angeles and Orange Counties, 1990 and 2000

SOURCE: Data from 1990 and 2000 U.S. Census

According to 2000 census data published by California State University Los Angeles (CSULA), Orange County is ranked as having the third largest Korean American population (55,573) in the United States, falling behind only Los Angeles County (186,350) and Queens County, New York (62,130). In addition, four of the top ten U.S. cities with the highest residential concentrations of Korean Americans are situated in outlying suburban and middle-class areas of Los Angeles (Glendale, Torrance, Fullerton, and Cerritos).

Demographic shifts have been followed by sudden growths in Korean organizational membership as well as business and real estate sales in areas of Orange County in the post-civil unrest period as reported in the *Los Angeles Times* (Carvajal 1994; Tran 1999).

Some move to traditionally white-dominated middle- and upper-class neighborhoods, but many Korean Americans are also opting to create their own "ethnic suburban" niches on the diverse outskirts of Los Angeles. Although Korean Americans are visible throughout different parts of Los Angeles, Orange County appears to be the prime real estate space for this rapidly suburbanizing population. Korean Americans have established a growing commercial center adjacent to the Vietnamese community near Westminster along Garden Grove Street that runs from Beach Boulevard to Brookhurst Street (roughly eight avenue-length blocks).

The commercial district of Garden Grove is lined with strip malls upon strip malls overtaken by the same range of specialized and diversified businesses as their downtown Koreatown counterpart, including tutoring schools, real estate agencies, restaurants, bank branches, warehouses, and medical offices. However, the commercial space is much smaller and less developed than Koreatown and, as one resident business owner tells it, caters to more Latinos and White American residents than does the original enclave. The spatial layout and physical appearance of the area itself also shows some remarkable contrasts to the urban enclave: like most of Orange County, the area is much more spacious and suffers from less traffic congestion, pollution, and street noise. There are fewer elderly Koreans waiting at bus stops or people walking along the sidewalks, making it more difficult for bystanders to see the mark that Koreans have made in these suburban communities, if it were not for the Korean business signs.

Furthermore, unlike their Vietnamese American neighbors who live and work in the same area, Korean Americans do not inhabit the same neighborhoods in which they work, opting instead to build homes in places like Cerritos, Anaheim, Fullerton, and Irvine with their upscale neighborhoods and higher-quality school systems (Vo and Danico 2005). While this may be a sign of greater socioeconomic success on their part, the researchers state that it also means that Korean Americans wield less political clout as an ethnic constituency because of their spatial dispersal. Thus, not surprisingly, Korean Americans have been less successful in electing coethnic politicians into local offices as compared with Vietnamese residents in neighboring communities.

Along with Korean residents, the location of businesses owned by Koreans has also dispersed to a lesser degree, although the typical pattern has been one where Koreans live in the suburbs while continuing to work in Koreatown or other urban minority areas. Due to the limited demand for mom-and-pop stores in suburban neighborhoods, many Korean businesses are generally less mobile than Korean households and thus continue to be concentrated in the central enclave community (Lee 1995). Real estate agents claim that immigrant business owners with more capital tend to find Koreatown to be a safer investment. As a result, one finds lower levels of self-employment among residents in Koreatown, while more than half of Korean merchants live in suburbs and commute to work (Min 1989–1990). In addition, Korean American banks have not followed their coethnic patrons into the outlying suburbs to the same degree as Chinese American banks (Li et al. forthcoming). Regardless of their place of residence, Korean immigrants continue to patronize Koreatown restaurants because they offer the best food for the lowest prices as a result of strong business competition within Koreatown (Min 1989–1990). Thus, while Korean immigrants regard the area as a place of temporary residence because of its high crime rates and inferior schools, the businesses and institutions of the central enclave continue to attract visitors and coethnic suburbanites from afar.

The Institutional Completeness of "K-town"

Despite residential out-migration in recent decades, Koreatown has maintained its identity as the institutional hub of the Korean American community. Indeed, Koreatown derives its name not so much from the diminishing number of Korean residents who occupy this enclave, but rather the businesses and institutions that continue to attract Koreans and non-Koreans from all over Los Angeles County. In addition to its entrepreneurial base, we may note three types of institutions that have proliferated and shaped the social milieu of Koreatown in the past few decades: youth-oriented institutions, religious institutions, and community-based organizations (CBOs). Small entrepreneurship has created the financial base for the expansion of these institutions, which cater to coethnic clientele from all over.

The unusually high concentration of ethnic-based organizations in Koreatown calls attention to the significance of ethnicity in establishing a strong infrastructure for the individual and collective advancement of Korean Americans in Los Angeles. Youth-oriented institutions have been recognized to be particularly important because they may provide the institutional structure to either impede or facilitate the educational achievements and hence the socioeconomic assimilation of future generations of Korean Americans (Zhou and Li 2003). In recent decades, Koreatown has witnessed the emergence and proliferation of two types of institutions aimed at attracting youth from both within the enclave and outer suburban neighborhoods. The first is the Korean entertainment industry, which includes a wide range of social spaces, including Korean cafes, PC rooms, pool halls, karaoke bars, dance clubs, and arcades. These profit-making businesses offer high school and college youth an alternative place to spend their leisure time when their parents are not home. Such areas are often associated with gangs, smoking and drinking, and other negative activities that take youth away from their studies from the perspective of the Korean media and concerned parents. Although frequented mostly by younger generations of Korean Americans, adults, especially adult males, also take pleasure in re-creating the social and gendered nightlife in Korea.

Although these types of spaces do motivate parents to move to safer grounds outside of Koreatown, other institutions within Koreatown also offer substantial benefits to both lower-class and middle-class immigrants and their children. Among other things, Koreatown houses a multitude of private businesses and nonprofit institutions that cater to the positive academic, artistic, and leadership development of Korean American youth, including educational schools, music and art classes, martial arts studios, computer lessons, sports leagues, religious programs, and Korean American leadership workshops. In addition to after-school programs, churches and social service agencies offer community services for youth, such as counseling, recreational spaces, Korean-language schools, tutorials, and leadership programs.

Other characteristics related to the sociocultural interests of the Korean immigrant population have also played a part in the internal development of Koreatown. In particular, churches are one of the most important institutions of the Korean American community, with over 70 percent of Korean Americans in Los Angeles, Chicago, and Atlanta reported to be attending church on a regular basis. A much larger proportion of Koreans in Korea practice Buddhism, whereas only a little over 20 percent of Koreans in Korea are associated with Christianity (Min 2000). In stark contrast, the dominant majority of Koreans who have immigrated to the United States (about 65 percent) are reported to be Christians and mostly Protestant. According to one estimate, there is about one church for every 300 Koreans in the United States as compared with one church for every 730 Americans (Park 1997). The strong religious roots of Korean immigration in Christianity may explain the rise of countless religious groups in Koreatown, just as strong interest in youth education has spurred the growth of after-school programs and organizations.[3]

Indeed, an informal count of religious institutions in the 2003–04 Korean directory shows that there are well over 100 churches and temples listed for the zipcode region[4] of Koreatown, not to mention a host of religion-affiliated groups and organizations. Based on philosophies of Christian goodwill and humanitarianism, churches have been well known for providing not only a place for worship but also a place to foster coethnic networks, to preserve cultural traditions, and to access critical social services. In addition, many serve important functions as the social, cultural, and educational centers of immigrant life. Religious institutions, such as Christian campus ministries, continue to play a salient role in the ethnic identities and everyday lives of young Korean Americans who feel alienated from both immigrant churches and their white American counterparts (Kim 2004). By giving them the cultural and socioeconomic tools for adaptation to the new world, churches help to build bridges for immigrants and their children into mainstream American society.

Last but not least, the enclave community of Koreatown is most distinctive for its abundance of ethnic services and resources that cater to both the general and specialized needs of different interest groups within the community. Korean immigrants have been most noted for their propensity to join at least one or more ethnic associations in their lifetime (Hurh and Kim 1984). Table 2.2 shows a very rough estimate of CBOs and informal groups located in and outside the Koreatown zipcode area, based on a count of a 2003–04 Korean business directory and my own knowledge of CBOs not listed in the directory. CBOs include mutual aid organizations, social service agencies, political/advocacy groups, professional and business associations, and social/civic organizations. The data show that there are several hundred Korean CBOs located within the general Koreatown zip code area, out of which at least forty are well-known, established organizations.[5] Numbers alone do not convey the magnitude of the Korean community's institutional centralization: with some exceptions, the oldest, more-established, and largest of these organizations tend to locate in the central enclave, while institutions in outlying areas tend to be smaller branch chapters.

CBOs offer a diverse array of specialized services and programs, ranging from healthcare organizations that work to protect the physical and psycho-

Table 2.2 Estimated count of organizations within and outside of Koreatown

	Koreatown	Non-Koreatown
CBOs	107	66
Professional/Business	32	26
Religious	236	675
Recreational/Artistic	57	56
Alumni	132	111

SOURCE: Data from 2003–2004 Korea Central Daily Korean business directory and courtesy of author

logical well-being of Koreatown residents to political advocacy groups dedicated to specific ethnic-, class-, or gender-related causes. Representing the growing interests of grocers, restauranteurs, and other entrepreneurs within the enclave economy, a wide variety of business and professional associations have also sprouted to provide information, assistance, and in some cases, advocacy work for affiliate members within specialized industries and professions. Nor does this list include the hundreds of smaller friendship, alumni, recreational, hobby, kye (ethnic credit rotating systems), and service groups that make up the institutional vitality of Koreatown immigrant life, many of which are not necessarily included in the directory. Unlike CBOs that are strongly influenced by the new migration context, many of these more informal groups and organizations are extensions of premigrant networks and associations that enable immigrants to reconnect with their homeland roots.

The two most well-read Korean-language newspapers, the *Korea Times* and the *Korean Central Daily*, are both headquartered in Koreatown along with a host of major TV stations (for example, Korean Television Enterprises, Ltd.), radio stations (for example, Radio Korea), and journals. Because there is only one Korean language, the ethnic media is a key medium through which Koreans from all backgrounds and neighborhoods can stay in touch with the central Koreatown community. Some of the main newspapers have even created an English version for younger, non-Korean-speaking Korean Americans. This type of ethnic institution also plays a valuable role in providing culture-friendly information on both homeland and American events, along with tips on how to promote educational and economic goals. The media are also important forums through which the Seoul government and its organizational affiliates have swayed public opinion on different political matters.

In particular, these different institutions contribute to the maintenance of ethnic solidarity among Korean Americans through educational, religious, and political structures of support. While youth-oriented and religious institutions may cater to the social and cultural needs of the Korean American population, CBOs are particularly integral to the formation of ethnic political consciousness. In the words of one executive director, "Koreatown is not really the heart of the community, because most Koreans don't live there. But it's a place where people really try to participate in America 'cause they have their own physical space." Another second generation organizational staff member similarly explains, "It's hard to get a feel for Koreatown, 'cause it's loose and spread out. I mean, you know you're in it, but there's no central location where people feel like this is the center of Koreatown. I don't think we have a tight-knit community feeling. I think in terms of providing services, part of what we [organizations] do is build a community and have people take ownership." Service and advocacy work in the community help to foster ethnic solidarity by cultivating easily accessible networks to the community, consolidating collective resources, and creating a space for the politicization of ethnic consciousness.

Institutional clustering may be particularly advantageous for Korean Americans from the standpoint of ethnic politics. Socioeconomic mobility has allowed Korean Americans to move into more affluent parts of metropolitan Los Angeles, but the demographic distribution of the ethnic community has also been the Achilles' heel of Koreatown's political development. The apportionment of Koreatown into several assembly districts has further complicated their ability to vote as a single constituency. During the 2001 reapportionment hearings, Little Tokyo, Chinatown, and Philippine Town were able to keep most of their ethnically bounded communities contained within a single voting district with the help of organizations like the Coalition of Asian Pacific Americans for Fair Redistricting (CAPAFR). Yet despite pressure from various Korean and Asian American organizations since the 1992 riots, the Los Angeles Redistricting Commission decided to keep Koreatown divided into three assembly districts, with 50 percent of the region merged under the 46th assembly district and the remainder split in half.

What this means is that spread over several districts, Korean Americans lack the voting power to elect into office someone who represents their community of interest. In addition, Korean American interest groups must lobby and appeal to three different city districts in order to enact any legislative changes on behalf of their community. Although their electoral impact has been severely handicapped by their small numbers, residential dispersion, and electoral fragmentation, Korean Americans have maintained some semblance of political solidarity by consolidating their organizational infrastructure. Almost all of the major politically active organizations of the ethnic community are thus located in the enclave of Koreatown. An analysis of politics in developing immigrant communities cannot underestimate the impact such efforts may have on the future of ethnic politics—that is, in building the political foundations for communities that have very little to begin with.

Contested Boundaries

In the current era of immigration, it is becoming increasingly more difficult to identify enclaves that are defined by their ethnic homogeneity and social insularity as opposed to their multiple interactions with other racial and minority groups. Koreatown is no different in this respect. As mentioned, the 1965 Immigration and Nationality Act and the forces of global restructuring not only opened the doors to Korean immigration, but also immigration from other Asian and Latin American nations, transforming Los Angeles from a biracial to a multiracial city. The majority of new immigrants have settled down in traditionally Black urban areas where a process of ethnic succession has created a range of Latino-majority, biracial, and multiracial communities (Oliver and Grant 1995). The disintegration of these laws and the accompanying influx of immigrants after 1965 sparked white flight and turned enclaves like Koreatown into multiracial or Latino-majority neighborhoods. Social networks and increasing work opportunities for low-skilled Latino immigrants in these urban communities have contributed to the rapid growth of the population in these areas.

In light of the socioeconomic diversity of post-1965 immigration, even formerly White middle-class neighborhoods such as Monterey Park have not been immune to the effects of massive immigration during this period. Koreatown itself falls within four biracial and multiracial regions, including several highly clustered Asian-Latino spaces extending from Koreatown eastward into West Covina; one overlapping Asian-Black section around the Koreatown-West Adams border; one White-Asian area on the northern periphery of Hollywood; and a small multiracial area consisting of African Americans, Latinos, and Asian Pacific Americans (Oliver and Grant 1995). The enclave is situated next to the low-income Latino enclave to the east and the Black and Latino ghettos of South Central across the highway to the south. Because of the high concentration of Salvadorans and Guatemalans in Westlake (east of Koreatown), Central Americans are becoming particularly visible in areas of Koreatown, considering the small size of their overall population in Los Angeles.

The businesses and homes of Koreatown reflect the racial and class heterogeneity of its occupants. Low-skilled Mexican immigrant workers have been integral to the growth of not only major industries within Los Angeles but smaller, labor-intensive firms like Korean-owned businesses in Koreatown. Korean immigrant workers continue to occupy more visible and higher-level positions in Koreatown businesses as waitresses, salespeople, and managers, but Latino workers are becoming an increasingly important source of manual labor as movers, cooks, and busboys. During my time at KIWA, I came across Latino cooks who had learned to cook Korean dishes that rival those of the best Korean cooks in Koreatown. One such worker named all the dishes he could prepare, including soon-du-bu (spicy Korean tofu soup), sushi, ja-jjang-myun (Korean-Chinese black bean noodle dish), and other Asian dishes; he ended his list with the confession, "But I can't make American dishes."

An observational purview of bodegas and catering trucks selling Mexican food and Koreatown businesses toting Spanish-language signs also attest to the growing importance of businesses tending to Latino residents. Nevertheless, stores catering to Latino residents are relatively sparse in central areas of the business district and are more visible along the eastern and southern peripheries of the community. Although overshadowed by neighboring businesses, the residential sections of Koreatown are also occupied by everything from grand Victorian-style homes with manicured lawns to small apartment complexes. The phenomenon of "time-share churches," or churches that house separate Korean-speaking, Spanish-speaking, and English-speaking congregations, are also a common sight.

Racial diversity implies not only possibilities for conflict and cooperation among immigrant residents and Korean entrepreneurs within the locality, but also tensions with native minority residents in neighboring communities that are caught in the path of Koreatown's entrepreneurial expansion. Chapter 4 provides a more in-depth coverage of the nature of these conflicts, particularly between Korean immigrant entrepreneurs and native-born African American residents. Historically, the explosive proliferation of Korean-owned businesses elicited hostile reactions from non-Korean entrepreneurs and residents alike. The burgeoning population was followed by a sharp increase in rental and real estate values, especially on commercial property. Non-Korean business owners were wary about how this change would impact the success of their enterprise, while non-Korean residents expressed resentment over the proliferation of Korean signs and the negative effects of the intruding entrepreneurial community.

As interethnic tensions intensified, the municipal redevelopment agencies were compelled to voice the concerns of residents and regulate the growth of businesses (Light and Bonacich 1988). In a show of ethnic solidarity, representatives from the Korean community established their own organization to protect their interests, but the maintenance of zoning laws has slowed down entrepreneurial encroachment into certain residential areas. Yet even today, there is some evidence that the continuous extension of its boundaries into historically minority-dominated neighborhoods has sparked some tension with nearby non-Korean residents and business owners. Black and White residents of West Adams expressed some concern over the increasing presence of Korean businesses in their efforts to preserve the multiracial heritage of their residential Victorian homes. The growing presence of liquor stores and establishments that are granted liquor licenses have also been a major concern for local residents because of the unwanted clientele they attract, as well as more historically rooted efforts by African Americans to keep their youth off this addiction.

At the same time, the presence of the Korean American community may be seen as a mixed blessing. While ethnic-based networks and institutions rely on ethnic exclusiveness to maintain trust and internal stability, the benefits of a developed institutional structure do shape the lives of non–Korean American residents in the area to a certain degree. Strong relationships of trust and developed organizational structures can contribute to the overall welfare of the neighborhood community, the indirect benefits of which are felt by those who live in the area regardless of their membership in such networks. Compared to living in declining urban neighborhoods, for instance, low-income Latinos have at their disposal a variety of businesses and organizations, some of which cater to the Latino community. Latinos have even begun to attend a few of the after-school programs and churches I observed, although their presence is not proportionate to the size of the population.

In addition, some of these institutions may occasionally open their doors to non-Korean residents if they are able to pay the price. One study on educational institutions in the vicinity of Koreatown states that non-Korean residents have reaped some advantages from the highly developed educational structures of Koreatown that have spilled over into neighboring racial communities (Cota-Robles 2000). Nonprofit ethnic organizations that rely on government aid have begun to provide assistance to Latino youth and families since the 1992 civil unrest. A study of one Korean-Black coalition in Koreatown and the neighboring West Adams community also reveals the potential of communities of color to benefit from the political and financial resources of other groups (Chung 2001). This is of course not meant to understate the degree to which Blacks and Latinos have also been competing against and to some degree exploited by the ethnic entrepreneurial economy, but undoubtedly community development has elicited mixed reactions from residents and business owners within and around the expanding Koreatown community.

Over the course of its development, Koreatown has built a long-standing reputation as the business and institutional mecca of the Korean American community in Southern California. Entrepreneurial growth and corporate investment have helped to cultivate Koreatown's central institutions, which continue to attract Korean Americans who are no longer trapped within the residential boundaries of the original enclave. Among other things, the "institutional completeness" of Koreatown offers immigrants and their children a wealth of ethnic-based resources such as after-school programs, churches, social service agencies, and advocacy groups, all of which may facilitate their adaptation into American society.

Notwithstanding the significance of entrepreneurial activities, scholarly preoccupation with Korean immigrant "success" has neglected the ways in which ethnic-based social structures have evolved at the expense of disadvantaged subgroups within the enclave. Indeed, the more developed the resource base of ethnic enclaves, the more they rely on internal hierarchies that profit from the exploitation of coethnic and non-coethnic workers within the community. In this particular case, small business owners along with other traditional elite figures have firmly entrenched themselves as powerful constituents within the economic and political structures of the Korean American community. Within this context, upholding a sense of "ethnic solidarity" itself becomes an invaluable means to resolve pressing needs that cannot be addressed through mainstream channels, but it does so at the risk of essentializing the internal heterogeneity of both the Korean American and enclave populations. With this in mind, the next chapter will discuss how the dynamics of ethnic solidarity took shape within the residential context of traditional immigrant power structures in the early years of Koreatown's formation.

3 Convergent Destinies and the Ethnic Elite

LIKE THE POLITICS OF OTHER IMMIGRANT communities before them, Korean American politics evolved within the spatial confines of a traditional enclave that took shape in relative isolation from the rest of the world. Common interests rooted in the shared migration experiences, residential spaces, and day-to-day struggles of immigrants helped to foster a strong sense of ethnic political solidarity in the early years of its formation. Aside from individual competition for status and resources, Korean immigrant organizations took on a relatively homogeneous character that downplayed overt ideological differences and stressed common interests and cultural traditions. Such unity and isolation helped the immigrant community to create its own protective haven within which to operate and supervise internal affairs without much intervention from outside authorities.

Nevertheless, any analysis of ethnic political solidarity should not obscure the dynamics of power and inequality that allowed higher-status groups to control public discourse and become the official "spokespersons" of the broader ethnic community. Backed by the authority of the Seoul government, the ethnic elite were able to contain conflict and dissonance during the early years of Korean immigration through money, power, and status. In the case of Korean Americans, immigrant organizations for the most part represented specific factions within the population—namely, older, class-privileged male immigrants from Seoul, whose political agenda did not always coincide with the interests of all members of the Koreatown community. Furthermore, their social and physical isolation from mainstream society also meant they lacked influence outside the boundaries of the ethnic community—a situation that would have major ramifications on ethnic politics in years to come. Future events would transform the worldview of these ethnic powerholders, but some of the ideological and structural traits of traditional immigrant organizations have carried over into Korean American politics today.

This chapter explores the historical evolution and internal dynamics of ethnic power structures in early Koreatown, beginning with the emergence of the "ethnic elite," including church leaders, entrepreneurs and select Seoul-sponsored immigrant organizations. Although divided by constant struggles for individual status and resources, the ethnic elite maintained firm control over the political discourse of the broader community by emphasizing inter-sectional values and interests. Within this context, it is shown how the elite leadership structured its ideals around pro-Seoul, anti-Communist and pro-U.S. ideologies carried over from the homeland. This chapter briefly discusses the political evolution of each branch of the ethnic elite and the context for their empowerment.

The Early History of Korean American Politics

The picture of Koreatown politics in Los Angeles during the 1970s and 1980s was one similar to past Asian immigrant enclaves in its preoccupation with homeland affairs and extreme cultural and political detachment from main-stream society. The dynamics of community politics took on a distinctive characteristic though, because of the community's relatively shorter history in the United States, as well as Korea's development under colonial and post-colonial rule. Because of the small size of the pre-1965 Korean population and the sending nation itself, Koreatown, Los Angeles, has had a fairly recent his-tory as compared with other older enclaves such as some of its Chinatown counterparts. Although Korean Americans had been actively establishing as-sociations and political study groups since their arrival, the community devel-oped in isolation from other ethnic groups and remained minor figures at best within the broader arena of mainstream politics. Even as the much larger and well-established Chinese American and Japanese American communities in Hawaii began to send representatives to office throughout the 1960s, Korean Americans had yet to elect a politician to office on the state or national level until the 1990s (with one exception in 1962) (Cha 1994).

The nationalistic, religious, and entrepreneurial underpinnings of ethnic-based empowerment also offer an interesting contrast to that of Chinatown political structures where traditional elite status was based on real or imag-ined commonalities stemming from locality, dialect, and clan origin. Because of the small size of Korea and the greater homogeneity of Korean culture relative to China, elite groups had no compelling reason to carry over cultural or regional hierarchies from the homeland.[1] Even beyond commonalities based on the migration experience, the collective consciousness of the Korean community had been formatively shaped by a fierce sense of nationalistic pride and unity and a deeply-seated suspicion of outsiders, stemming from a long history of oppression under colonial rule, a war that tore the country in two, and foreign occupation in the homeland.

Nevertheless, members of the Korean ethnic elite created new lines of stratification based on the ideologies and material privileges of the Seoul elite in juxtaposition to nonurban South Koreans who were looked down upon as low-class farmers and laborers and North Koreans who were condemned as Communist infidels. The power structures of the community were partly shaped by the urban background of Korean immigrants, as well as the high proportion of middle-class and upper-middle-class members in the first major waves of immigration. Considering the hierarchical nature of Confucian culture and Korean society in general, it is also not surprising that top organizational positions were almost exclusively reserved for older, immigrant men well endowed with money and prestige. Within the confines of this power structure, three types of leadership comprised the core of ethnic politics: entrepreneurs, religious leaders from the Christian church, and the presidents of homeland-oriented immigrant organizations, the most important of which was the Korean Federation.

In the early years of Koreatown's formation, the three branches of the ethnic elite were able to dominate community politics as a result of the demographic composition of the immigrant-dominated population and the elite's control over the resource-rich social networks of the Korean American community. The three bases of empowerment within the immigrant community built its legitimacy around strong connections to the South Korean government, the Christian orientation of middle-class urbanites in Seoul, and the material wealth of immigrant business owners. Politics was thus largely conservative, ethnonationalistic, and oriented toward the interests of more privileged groups within the ethnic community.

The authority of the ethnic elite was nevertheless bounded by their marginal status as Korean immigrants and was thus mostly confined to the local Korean American community. Indeed, their social isolation partly stemmed from cultural and linguistic barriers that denied them access to outside institutions and their overall marginal status within American power structures.

For this reason, there was little incentive for immigrants to "air their dirty laundry" to the outside world. In the words of one forty-four-year-old first generation staff member:

> Problems that happen within the Korean community should be taken care of here [in the community]. If that doesn't work, we can bring it to Americans and if it gets resolved, it's good even if we get a little embarrassed. If it does not get resolved from within, we can let the media know but oftentimes we don't get any help from Americans anyway. We only lose face, and it doesn't do us any good. [Interview translated from Korean]

Within the context of cultural and political isolation, Korean immigrants were able to lay the foundations for ethnic political solidarity around their shared experiences as immigrants, especially in the 1970s and 1980s when the relatively small population was struggling with similar cultural and structural disadvantages, spatial isolation within urban neighborhoods, and a common political cause directed against Japanese colonialist rule over Korea (1910–45) and the perceived threat of North Korean Communism.

For this reason, community leaders devoted themselves to offering mutual assistance and addressing the more pressing needs of the general immigrant community. Many first generation community workers in the study expressed their desire to engage in humanitarian efforts because of the long legacy of war, poverty, and oppression that had formatively shaped their experiences in their native land, as well as the current hardships they were undergoing in trying to adjust to a foreign society. Korean immigrants have also been known to donate substantial sums of money to churches, organizations, and any humanitarian projects they feel make a worthy cause. More affluent business owners and church leaders can mobilize funds to revitalize institutions within the local community and start up new charitable projects, community events, and social services for immigrants that mainstream institutions would not provide.

Ironically, it is this sense of collective marginality that at the same time allowed the ethnic elite to dominate the political structures of Koreatown. For one, greater congruity in residential and eth-class interests helped to minimize more serious divisions among the ethnic elite and their constituencies. Few immigrants had the time, money, or interest to invest in protesting the political dominance of this leadership. In situations where their positions were threatened, the ethnic elite took advantage of their extensive networks and resources to stifle opposition and reassert their control over local community affairs. As we shall see later on, these tactics became particularly useful in subduing newer organizations that attempted to challenge their authority. Thus, members of the ethnic elite were able to dictate community discourse, leaving little room for major political dissent by internally marginalized groups like women and immigrant workers.

The general ideology of the ethnic elite was also firmly grounded in the notion of individual success and meritocracy—a philosophy that helped to foster an abstract sense of affinity to mainstream American ideals. Korean immigrants have much invested in what Cheng and Espiritu (1989) call the "immigrant ideology." That is, immigrants oftentimes arrive from a homeland that has been ravaged by the effects of economic or political turmoil and must make significant sacrifices in order to migrate to America in the hopes of making a better life. As a result, they are more likely to hold firmly onto the belief that America is the land of opportunity in the initial stages of immigration unlike native-born minority groups.

Although the traditional powerholders may have had more to gain in politically isolating themselves from mainstream America, they also had a vested interest in promoting the idea that anyone could achieve individual success and assimilate into American society through hard work and personal sacrifice. In Korean immigrant politics, such propaganda was used to raise the status of well-off immigrants and legitimize the nationalistic focus of the ethnic elite and their general intolerance for those they labeled as Communist sympathizers. Interestingly, North Korean refugees in the United States expressed even stronger support for the anti-Communist discourse of fellow Koreans because of their past persecution under the North Korean regime (Kim 1981). Although future events and hardships would cause some immigrants to reconsider the American Dream, the main area of criticism for later generations of leftist Korean leadership has been the elite's unyielding commitment to assimilationist rhetoric and the model minority myth, which in their minds merely reaffirm racial and class hierarchies in American society.

For this reason, the political hegemony of the ethnic elite and the shared interests upon which it was based helped to structure community politics around relatively homogeneous conceptions of ethnic political solidarity. Nevertheless, one must still differentiate between ideological consensus and structural unity. The immigrant elite was "unified" only in the sense that they shared similar norms and values, but this sense of solidarity did not necessarily facilitate well-integrated, cooperative actions among the various branches of the leadership. For one, the community lacked a central leadership that could coordinate the actions of the numerous ethnic organizations that constituted the broader political community. Thus, as reported in the *Los Angeles Times*, one poet remarks, "When three Koreans get together, they establish three organizations" (Kang 1992). As new leaders gave birth to more organizations, ethnic politics would increasingly become marked by bitter factionalism among various leaders—a problem faced by most racial and ethnic communities that fight over scarce resources.

Because of resource competition, socioeconomic marginality, and the general isolation of ethnic politics from mainstream society, the dynamics of alliance and oppositionality among immigrant organizations were mostly focused on individual status and secondarily on the distribution of ethnic resources within the immigrant community. The struggle for status in ethnic elite structures, whether it be over the different lay positions within the church or the presidency of the Korean Federation, continues to be a defining feature of Korean immigrant politics today. For instance, one study conducted on organizational leaders of various Korean associations found that Korean newspapers are replete with reports of political conflicts and alleged misconduct among the ranks of community leadership, a by-product of internal struggles for individual status and prestige, as reported in the *Korea Times* (Ahn 1992a, 1992b).

The highly competitive nature of ethnic politics can be attributed to several factors related to the historical background, cultural heritage, social status, and social networks of the Korean community. The first has to do with the historical context of Korea's political development under centuries of colonization and dictatorship. Eui-Young Yu (May 2, 2000 interview), an immigrant scholar who has studied and participated in numerous Korean American organizations, explains:

> In Korea, a few individuals dictate the whole society, because Koreans have a short experience of this democratic process. They lived for a thousand years under kings and some kind of dictator until very recently. So they're not familiar with this parliamentary rules [and] lack the skills of pulling together different ideas. They are good at working hard and achieving goals by just concentrating with a given task. But they are not good at reaching a consensus. Debate culture is lacking. So they fight so frequently in the Korean community meetings, because if someone says something against your ideas, they take it as a challenge to their authority and they get upset.

As stated, limited historical experiences with democracy and voluntary associations themselves have formatively shaped the internal structures of Korean immigrant organizations in America, which are usually subject to the unconditional control of a single leadership.

Furthermore, title and status are key components of Confucian culture, which has served as a guiding framework for the general social structure of Korean society. Until the twentieth century, Korean society was organized around a caste-like hierarchy between the "yang-ban" (upper-class elite), "jung-in" (middle-class), and "sang-min" (lower-class), in which age, education, and social status dictated the nature of social interaction. Aspects of this culture have carried over into Korean immigrant politics today. As one second generation male puts it:

> With the first generation, their status is tied to a title. That gives them automatic credibility. If he didn't have that title, he's just like any other doctor. I think in a Confucian culture where everything's based on a hierarchy system, if you have a presidential title, that gives you a lot of respect from other people. It also gives you power to do things that you want to do, that if you don't have that title, you won't be able to do.

For more Americanized Koreans, however, this emphasis on title is perceived to be problematic since it is inherently based on hierarchical understandings of society. The above interviewee goes on to say, "They have that kind of attitude. If you don't have that title, they won't give you respect. If you're not the right age, they won't give you respect. If you're not the right gender, they won't give you respect. Women have a hard time getting respect, you know?" Such cultural emphasis on status is said to underlie traditional attitudes toward women as well as Blacks and Latinos, who are seen to be at the bottom of the American hierarchy.

While culture may be one explanation, these differences also originate from structural inequalities that higher-end Koreans encounter upon immigrating to the United States. The struggle for social status and prestige within the hierarchical structures of the church may be attributed to the downward occupational mobility that Korean immigrants experience on their arrival. Inconsistencies between premigration and postmigration status occur when those with professional, managerial, and administrative backgrounds in Korea encounter disadvantages associated with language and cultural barriers and racial discrimination (Min 2000). Although they may be able to compensate for lower earnings through self-employment, owning a small business does not help immigrants to recover their social status in the sending country. As a result, presidential positions within ethnic organizations, which are relatively scarce, are highly coveted and take on particular significance for Korean immigrants from privileged backgrounds who do not have the means to pursue equivalent positions in American institutions.

As a result, everything from interorganizational relationships to political struggles to day-to-day interactions among the leadership is affected by the intricate dynamics of status, connections, and respect. One 1.5 generation leader claims that if you show them the proper respect, you can get the whole-hearted support of immigrant leaders without having to convince them about the issue. Another 1.5 generation executive director complains that at the same time, while immigrant leaders provide only 10 percent of the organization's financial support, they require about 60 percent of his time and attention.

Even beyond this, the internal structures of ethnic organizations are formatively shaped by their embeddedness within ethnic-based networks. Because of their isolation from mainstream America, CBOs rely heavily on financial resources garnered from within the Korean immigrant community; such dependency can aggravate internal resource competition and make a president's individual expenditures more difficult to monitor. As such, one young, second generation member points out that "they operate under completely different laws and regulations. As nonprofits, we have to be accountable for all the dollars that we spend, but they don't have to be. They're not as accountable to public entities."

Yet while greater accountability to mainstream institutions help to inhibit individuals from abusing and fighting over organizational resources, younger leaders have also come to recognize the benefits of soliciting unrestricted financial contributions from the immigrant population. As one immigrant leader sees it, "The first generation don't think about it; they just do it. They think that's good for the community; okay let's do it and give money and support." Such donations allow organizations to exercise greater flexibility in the types of programs they can offer and also help them to avoid some of the politicking and bureaucratic paperwork that can consume a significant portion of a nonprofit's time.

The Ethnic Elite of Koreatown

The following sections describe the historical origins of each ethnic elite group, the nature of their political involvement, the hierarchical structure and boundaries of membership, and the roots of their influence. The three branches occasionally overlapped in terms of their leadership, membership base, and access to resources but took shape within the context of their own distinctive interests and historical evolution. Someone who is successful in business may also be a deacon in his church as well as a president of some organization. This interconnectedness makes sense considering that power in these three institutions was very much based on how much money the person can contribute and how many connections he or she can cultivate. This framework was also used to justify the exclusion of women and workers from top leadership positions in the earlier years of organizational politics.

Immigrant Organizations

Over the years, a wide variety of Korean immigrant organizations have proliferated throughout Koreatown, representing everything from business interests to alumni interests to senior citizens in the enclave. However, Korean immigrants in the earlier years were primarily preoccupied with trying to make ends meet and creating an institutional infrastructure that would meet those needs from limited resources. Within this context, the most influential political spokesperson among the many CBOs during the late 1960s and 1970s was the Korean Association of Southern California (KASC). Founded in 1962, the mission of the KASC was to promote ethnic fraternity; provide informational, cultural, and educational resources to immigrants; and protect the rights and interests of the general Korean immigrant community.

Throughout most of its history, the KASC focused its efforts on organizing community events and providing limited mutual assistance for immigrants; it did not engage extensively in political advocacy work except on behalf of the South Korean government. The South Korean government has maintained an active interest in the political activities of these "gyo-po," or Koreans abroad, since military occupation, economic relations, and political interventions following the North-South division of Korea after World War II made the United States a powerful ally to the Seoul government and made North Korea its long-time adversary. For this reason, the Consulate General in Los Angeles became a critical channel through which these pro-U.S., pro-Seoul, and anti–North Korean sentiments would be fostered. In addition to performing important functions related to immigration, divorce, and economic trade, it played a direct hand in funding, sponsoring, and otherwise intervening in key organizational affairs within the community (Kim 1981). The community's dependency on the Consulate General in all areas of life allowed it to dampen any "unpatriotic" activities that were perceived to be a threat to the authority and influence of the Seoul government.

Because the Consulate General both discreetly and indiscreetly provided financial support for KASC, the organization acted as what Chang (1988) calls a "front" organization for pro-Seoul government sentiments and activities. Most other organizations during this period were still in their formative stages and often plagued by leaders who were preoccupied with competition for status. As a result, the South Korean government's integral involvement with immigrant organizational structures largely went unchallenged until the Kwangju Massacres in 1980. As one 1.5 generation leader put it, if you were not invited to attend events sponsored by the Consulate General, then you were not considered an important organization with the Korean American community.

Because most Korean immigrants regardless of residence or background rely heavily on the ethnic media, the Korean television, radio, and newspaper conglomerates were particularly formative in shaping public opinion on events within the community. The three main Korean-language newspapers—*Hankook Ilbo* (*Korea Times*), *Dong-A Ilbo*, and *Joong Ang Ilbo* (*Korea Central Daily*)—have been under the control of Seoul-based corporations and are thus indirectly censored by the South Korean government (Chang 1988). Kim (1981) states, "By informing geographically scattered Korean immigrants of community meetings and events, ethnic newspapers have emerged as a powerful means of provoking, leading, integrating, expanding and enlightening some selective community values or opinions. Ethnic newspapers seek a community consensus by reinforcing Korean nationalism and culture" (185). In this sense, they were also vehicles through which select CBOs gained political visibility, legitimacy and recognition.

Around the 1980s, the KASC changed its name to the Korean Federation and later to Korean-American Federation (KAF). Linked to a broad network of Korean federations in other major Korean American communities across the nation, KAF continues to be integrally shaped by homeland politics and its relations with the Seoul government. However, in its early years, KAF expressed little interest in mainstream politics aside from "symbolic" displays such as the official naming of Koreatown and the establishment of the Koreatown Parade (Park 1999). The organization was a powerful constituency within the ethnic political structures of Koreatown until the Korean-Black conflicts and the 1992 civil unrest weakened its stronghold. Since 1992, the organization has experienced some significant generational turnovers in the composition of its membership and leadership, with greater representation by 1.5 generation members; nevertheless, the interest base of the organization still firmly rests in the hands of the older immigrant elite.

The internal structure of larger-scale immigrant organizations plays an important role in shaping ethnic politics in Koreatown. These organizations do not operate under the kind of systematized democratic membership structure seen in American organizations. Instead, internal activities and affairs are primarily coordinated, organized, and financed by the president in a hierarchical manner (Chang 1999). Achieving the position of president confers not only social stature but a range of economic and political benefits stemming from strong personal connections with the South Korean government. Thus, the desire to be "hwe-jang" (president) often leads to bitter struggles over top leadership positions among the first generation.

Interviews with community leaders and Korean newspaper articles revealed many instances in which individual organizational representatives would fight over presidential positions, the misuse or appropriation of organizational funds, and views on how to run an organization. In explaining one scandal involving the misuse of funds by a Koreatown police association, *Korea Times* (Ahn 1992b) itself notes how many Korean CBOs are not approved for nonprofit tax-exempt status (501c3) and are therefore not equipped to run as a nonprofit organization. Individuals will write out checks to individual officers who come by to solicit personal donations instead of donations to the organizations they represent, and the use of these donations is not properly tracked. As a result, financial scandals like these are not an uncommon occurrence among immigrant organizations.

One older first generation female business owner explains how such lack of accountability and disregard for rules prompted her to make major reforms in her own organization, which led to a lot of criticisms about her leadership.

The past chairman did not follow the by-laws and I disapprove of that very much so before my two-year term is over—my term is over on the sixth of next month—so before my term is over, members who did not pay their *membership fees* and those people who do not have the qualities of a member, I kicked them out, five people. The reason is because those people didn't pay their membership fees. *They make a lot of trouble.* So if those type of people are in the organization, the organization does not work so even if those people talk behind my back, *I don't care. I want to keep the bylaw and we must keep the laws. So I am doing my work by the rules. There are bad rumors about our organization. I cleaned up those rumors.* [Interview translated from Korean; English statements in *italics*]

Political infighting among community leaders, corruption and bribery scandals in homeland politics, and the scarcity of alternative associations and activities in Koreatown have kept the majority of Korean immigrants indifferent to and skeptical of these types of political organizations. Politics aside, it is nevertheless important to acknowledge the amount of money and personal time that is required in operating voluntary organizations that lack an active membership. Furthermore, both immigrant and native-born interviewees involved in organizational politics consistently bemoan the general aura of disdain that surrounds volunteer work in a community that is more focused on achieving individual mobility and financial success—an obstacle that makes their efforts even that much more admirable.

The leadership and the bulk of organizational membership in larger political and business-related organizations have been dominated by male immigrants with prestigious, middle-class backgrounds in South Korea. Many of them also tend to be white-collar professionals, entrepreneurs, or in some cases church leaders. As previously noted, the occupational background is not so much the question as is the money that he or she contributes to operational costs, which also justifies the president's uncontested control over the organizational agenda. For this reason, working-class immigrants have been relatively absent within the ranks of these first generation organizations not only because they do not have the time to do volunteer work, but also because they lack the money, networks, and stature required to create and sustain an organization. In addition, immigrant women have been largely excluded from the top leadership positions of most organizations with some minor exceptions in smaller organizations associated with traditionally female professions, such as nurses associations, educational institutions, and a few social service agencies. However, they have still been able to make substantial contributions to the community "behind-the-scenes" through traditional gender roles, as will be discussed in later chapters.

The Church

Considering the predominance of Christians within the Korean immigrant population, one is compelled to ask what role the church has played within the political structures of the Korean American community. In African American communities, for example, churches have historically situated themselves at the center of American politics and movements for racial empowerment by producing active community leadership, mobilizing their congregation through politicized sermons, and cultivating indigenous networks of support. However, such interest in political affairs is not always a given, depending on how churches view themselves within the larger context of the ethnic community and American society.

During the era of Japanese colonialism in Korea, Christian church members and leaders exerted strong influence over the development of Korean community organizations. Since organizations at that time had few financial resources, religious institutions were one of the few places to offer employment to community activists from Korea (Choy 1979). As a result, churches in the United States became an important breeding ground for proindependence activities and were formatively shaped by political actors and events in Korea. As an example, some of the earlier denominational churches that branched out from the original Korean Methodist Church in Los Angeles came about as a result of ideological differences of political exiles like Syngman Rhee, the future president of the Republic of Korea (Choy 1979). In part, these political-religious schisms also prompted the emergence of a number of political organizations, such as the Korean Dong Chi Hoe of North America, Hung Sa Dang, and the Korean Ladies Relief Organization (Lee 1969). Yet most of these small organizations would not last through the end of the 1950s.

While attracting much of the human and financial resources of the Korean American community, it is generally agreed among most community leaders, including religious leaders themselves, that contemporary Korean churches in Los Angeles have failed to take a leading role in encouraging, supporting, or organizing political activities since the end of Japanese rule in 1945. Because of the evangelist roots of Korean Christianity, many Korean churches are considerably conservative both in terms of their theological convictions and their sociopolitical ideals. The withdrawal of churches from "secular" affairs may also be partly attributed to the end of Japanese colonialism, which eliminated a major political platform around which the community could rally. The proliferating number of Korean churches, strong religious factionalism, and the increasing size and diversity of immigration since the 1970s have further impeded the development of political unity within the religious sector. In addition, Korean churches do not have as strong linkages with the Consulate General as with other institutions within the community (Kim 1981).

In certain ways, churches have not completely stayed out of political affairs, at least on an informal level. On this issue, one senior pastor points out
that some of the larger churches have assumed a type of informal "advisory"
role to CBOs and the Consulate General.

> A lot of Korean organizations like Korean Community Center chairman are
> Christian so we give some suggestions like "Now that you have become the
> chairman, we want your politics to support this way." We give suggestions
> to better the Korean community and to better the service. If people like the
> Consulate General comes—"While you are here, treat the Korean community
> members honestly. *For example, last time, you favored particular Korean
> regionals, you got along with those from the Cholla province, but this time . . .*
> you should listen to all people." [Korean statements in *italics*]

However, as the above passage indicates, most of the church's focus has
been on humanitarian relief and affairs in Korea and not so much on the
needs and problems of the Korean community in the United States. Furthermore, their involvement in politics is certainly not comparable to the
central role that earlier religious institutions played in the movements for
independence.

My conversations with several ministers at one of the largest Korean
American churches in Southern California reaffirm that if at all, religious
leaders are more involved with events in Korea than with politics in the Korean American and mainstream American community. One pastor in the
study felt that the church should consciously keep its distance from politics
for the most part and that such issues should instead be left to designated Korean organizations; still, he concedes, it is the church's responsibility to take
a stand in the few instances the Korean government engages in "bad politics."
Little was said about intervening in American politics unless it pertained to
politics in the homeland. Another younger 1.5 generation pastor states simply,
"When you worship, then it's time to worship God. Politics does not belong in
the pulpit because our focus has to be God."

Despite their lack of involvement in politics today, Korean church leaders
wield substantial influence over local affairs and have the potential for effect-
ing major changes in the political consciousness of the community and its relations with other racial and ethnic groups. According to Min, Korean Americans outcompete most Asian Pacific Americans and other minority groups in
terms of frequency of church attendance and the amount of financial dona-

tions contributed to religious institutions (Min 2005). A study done on Korean American churches in Southern California found that about a third of the 149 churches surveyed reported an annual budget of $100,000 to $249,999, while a quarter reported a budget of $500,000 and above (Korean American Coalition 2003). With the dominant majority of Koreans attending service on a regular basis, Christian churches have access to substantial financial resources, as well as a large, devoted congregation of people. Because of this, a few CBOs I observed would solicit the aid of local churches in disseminating information and attracting warm bodies for key events. With a membership that is both sizable and diverse, churches can be considered one of the most significant institutions within the Korean American community. Moreover, their centralization in Koreatown makes these institutions a potentially ideal site for political mobilization, especially for an ethnic community that is both highly dispersed and ideologically fragmented.

In terms of its internal membership, the church is characterized by a rigid hierarchical structure that privileges first generation male immigrants in its decision-making bodies. A good number of Korean Americans are associated with the Presbyterian denomination. In Korean Presbyterian sectors, the church is usually structured around the power of the pastor, who often shares control over church affairs with a council of elders. Although the pastor represents the church, elders can be particularly influential because they have the authority to hire or fire pastors. Altogether, these leaders have almost absolute control over the internal operation and public representation of the church to the outside community. The next stratum of the church hierarchy is occupied by the deacons who take care of more mundane church matters, and then below them are various associate ministers who may run specific church departments such as youth ministry.

Some argue that the spread of Christianity helped to modernize and Westernize Korea away from the sexist orientations of Confucianism, but generally, Korean Christian churches continue to be "more sexist than any other social institutions in Korea at least in terms of hierarchical structure" (Min 2000, 380). In Korean immigrant churches, top clerical positions including the positions of deacon, elder, and even youth leader, are overwhelmingly dominated by men, even more so than those in Korea. At the same time, women comprise the majority of the church's membership and oversee day-to-day operations in the choir, Sunday school, and kitchen. The pastor of one of the larger churches in Koreatown also admits that women were the most active members of the church in terms of cooking, cleaning, and teaching, but they were not often entrusted with decision-making responsibilities. Thus, while generally inclusive in membership as compared with other ethnic institutions, the church is also structured around highly patriarchal relationships.

Although the church may be perhaps one of the more class-accessible institutions in Koreatown, the Christian religion has tended to appeal most strongly to urban, educated, and middle-class Koreans from Korea. The historical roots of Christianity come from the longtime presence of American missionaries in Korea who disseminated Western ideas among the urban middle classes and encouraged immigration to the United States. The founding minister tends to control most of the operations within the church, but professionals and big businessmen may also achieve the honored position of elder or deacon by contributing funds and professional skills. Because of the higher-income backgrounds of church attendees, Korean churches unlike earlier European immigrant churches focus less on providing basic economic necessities like jobs and housing and more on family and other problems associated with adaptation (Min 2000).

Immigrant workers and some business owners may not attend church as regularly as others, because of their loaded work schedules and, in the case of women and single men, the burden of household responsibilities. Research suggests that workers do not have as much prior exposure to Christianity in the homeland, as evidenced by the skewed class distribution of those members affiliated with churches in Korea. As for merchants, one important exception to this is the case of business owners who need to develop their networks with coethnic clientele by extending their loyalties to the local church (Kim 1981). However, religious institutions have also been known to provide significant sociopsychological comfort and support for business owners who work long hours under arduous conditions.

The conservative environment of the church and its merchant-dominated congregation reflect some of the inherent paradoxes of religiosity in the enclave economy, according to some workers and organizers interviewed. For example, one Korean waitress makes the following comment about an employer who mistreated her workers and refused to pay overtime: "The employer says she is a church-going Christian and cannot use bad words like I do, but she uses terms like "servant" to abuse me and other workers. I don't know what kind of praying she does at church, but she should criticize herself at home first. I feel those who are hurt and truly needed to be consoled are neglected by churches" [interview translated from Korean].

Individual pastors have occasionally tried to break the conventional mold, but the aura of conservatism that dominates the church has generally helped to stifle political dissonance among its members. For instance, one female organizer related to me how one pastor who had given a sermon on paying workers decent wages had been chastised for his statement by some congregation members afterwards—an anecdote that also underscores the difficulties of addressing workers' issues in the church setting.

The Ethnic Entrepreneurial Elite

The dynamics of ethnic politics were just as formatively shaped by the class-based interests and values of entrepreneurial elites within the enclave economy. Although Koreans had been engaged in small immigrant enterprise even before the emergence of Koreatown itself, their political power within the enclave has been considerably enhanced by their growing numbers and substantial financial resources since the 1970s. Because of the highly developed infrastructure of the enclave economy, the primary actors of this group in more recent years have grown to include more successful mom-and-pop store owners, larger-scale entrepreneurs such as wholesalers and importers, and representatives of transnational Seoul-based corporations.

A variety of local and national trade and business associations, such as the Korean American Grocers Association (KAGRO), Korean American Dry Cleaners Association (KADC), and the Korean American Garment Industry Association (KAGIA), were established to protect the specialized needs of different businesses in the area. These associations represented a newly emerging interest among immigrants to focus attention on problems and issues within the Korean American community as opposed to politics in the homeland and were therefore known to be more politically active within the community. In New York and to a lesser degree in Los Angeles, tensions with African American patrons and conflicting interests with suppliers, landlords, and government agencies helped to consolidate and mobilize Korean merchants into protecting entrepreneurial interests, thereby heightening ethnic political solidarity among immigrant business owners in the process (Min 1996).

While trade associations like KAGRO and KAGIA raised funds for organizations such as the KAF, they also made active efforts to maintain a distinct political identity apart from homeland-oriented organizations, especially after the 1992 Los Angeles civil unrest exposed the Federation's inability and lack of interest in negotiating relations with outside groups. In so doing, such business organizations significantly enhanced their political positioning within the ethnic community, more so than professional associations (Min 1996). Business associations have been very active in donating time and money toward projects by sponsoring scholarships for Koreans and non-Koreans, hosting seminars and conferences, organizing on the issue of liquor-licensing, and making financial contributions to the local police. However, these efforts have been largely focused on protecting entrepreneurial interests.

On a more individual level, the political power of immigrant business owners and corporate representatives rested primarily on their role as financial contributors, advisors, and political leaders within organizational structures. Leaders from CBOs like the KAF relied heavily on entrepreneurial support and access to financial resources in order to boost their standing within ethnic organizations. The 1975 KASC presidential elections demonstrate the crucial role entrepreneurs and corporations played in garnering support and exerting control within the community. Disillusioned with KASC, dissenting members formed the Council on Korean Community Affairs (CKCA) by building on widespread community support and challenges to pro-Seoul ideologies (Chang 1988). In the end, however, former KASC president Kim Hyung-il declared victory over CKCA founder Kim Ki-sung during the presidential elections and used ties to the Seoul government and Korean corporations to quell this reformist movement. Chang quotes from the *Korea Times*, "Candidate Kim Ki-sung lacked institutional or organization support whereas Dr. Kim received strong support from . . . Korea Trade Center, California Korea Bank, and Association of branch firms of Korean corporations, etc." (56).

The socioeconomic resources of this entrepreneurial class took on added significance for a culturally insular and politically marginalized community that relied primarily on ethnic donations for addressing the needs and problems of its immigrant population. Ethnic organizations used such financial contributions to support a variety of services, including those that would traditionally be provided by the city. The inferior quality or deficiency of law enforcement and public services in urban neighborhoods also prompted the community to come up with its own alternative service providers. The Koreatown and West Adams Public Safety Association (KOWAPSA) is one coalition that used donations from Korean church members and business owners to create a community policing substation to address problems with law enforcement after the 1992 riots.

The ranks of organizational leadership often include those individuals with entrepreneurial or corporate backgrounds, because of their financial backing and higher status within the community. With few of the younger generations engaged in either enclave politics or small enterprise, the entrepreneurial branch of the ethnic elite has been comprised primarily of first generation male immigrants. With some exceptions, Korean women do not own their own businesses or are recognized only as the working spouses of male business owners, even in the many cases where they are in charge of managing the businesses themselves—another factor that has kept them out of the inner circles of the ethnic elite. They are even less likely to work as representatives of large Korean corporations, which generally do not place women in key decision-making roles. The dual burdens of balancing home and work life have also prevented immigrant women from becoming more actively involved in professional or business-related organizations, with the minor exception of smaller women's associations like the Korean Business and Professional Women's Association.

Not surprisingly, immigrant workers had almost no voice and no advocates in Koreatown's political structures, partly because of the hegemonic influence of these entrepreneurs. Emphasis on hard work, middle-class values, and individual achievement helped to reaffirm the conservative slant of ethnic politics in the early years, according to one progressive 1.5 generation leader. He states:

> People who make up leadership are people with time and energy and those are usually successful small businesspeople, whose mentality's very much in line with republican conservative ideology, which says you know, with bare hand I became millionaire, so America's great, a land of opportunity and freedom. They certainly don't understand why ninety percent of others fail small businesses, pay low wages to workers, and so on. They don't speak about that experience of the community and so naturally it becomes conservative. Status quo ideologies are being enforced every day both by South Korean government, Korean media, which is supported by the small business, and so on.

The ethnic entrepreneurial elite of Koreatown exercises its political influence through financial capital and justifies their entitled status through ideologies of meritocracy and capitalism.

Most of the workers at KIWA said that they had never been involved with any workers' rights organization, much less any community-based organization, prior to their introduction to this organization. As with church attendance, workers do not have the time to participate in such activities due to the burdens of work and domestic obligations. In addition, many of them are not completely knowledgeable on the different kinds of ethnic community services available to them—a situation that reveals how exposure and access to social networks can also fall along class lines. As such, the interests of business owners often prevail over those of Korean immigrant workers, who are often neglected in the hierarchies of both mainstream and ethnic institutional structures. In most cases, unions are not a viable outlet for addressing workplace grievances since many organizers do not have the language capacity or cultural knowledge to deal with non-English-speaking Korean and Latino workers and the businesses for which they work.

In many ways, the traditional ethnic elite of Koreatown owes its standing to the geographic and social isolation of the enclave, which forced its members to come together around common ethnic and class interests. Aside from personal struggles for leadership status, overt political conflicts among Korean immigrant institutions during this early period were minimized in the interests of providing mutual assistance, strengthening solidarity against mainstream indifference, and addressing shared immigrant-based needs. Spatial confinement within the ethnic enclave enhanced this sense of cohesiveness and dependency among residents of this community. Of course, this is not to suggest that these institutions were structurally unified in any sense as demonstrated by the fragmented and unstable ties that bind the three branches of the ethnic elite. Nevertheless, common value systems, shared gender and class privilege, and overlapping memberships enabled these institutions to collaborate on a general level and avoid more serious clashes with one another. Under these conditions, government, media and corporate sponsorship from Korea became a key factor in reaffirming the political influence and social prestige of individual leaders in immigrant elite organizations.

At the same time, political convergence and cultural insularity did little to improve the status of the community in respect to mainstream power structures and, if anything, discouraged leaders from seeking new strategies for old problems and alternative sources of support that would take them beyond the status quo. Marginal groups within the community, including women and workers, had almost no political voice in an organizational structure built on the power and privileges of the ethnic elite. As the enclave continued to expand, the political situation in the homeland deteriorated, and younger generations of Korean Americans came of age, the ethnic elite began to face new challenges that would change the conditions for their political control. Some immigrant institutions would make minor changes to accommodate to these internal and external pressures through greater involvement in Korean American affairs, but for the most part there was little incentive or means to enact broader reforms. These adjustments were not profound enough to deal with three major events in Korea and the United States that would dramatically alter the political structures of Koreatown. As the next chapter explains, these events were catastrophic and extensive enough to prompt both ideological and structural transformations in enclave politics that might have otherwise taken several generations in other immigrant communities.

4 The Events That Shook the World

FROM A POLITICAL PERSPECTIVE, SCHOLARLY ATTENTION toward the ethnic elite is certainly warranted in light of their central involvement in tensions between Korean merchant–African American patrons, their substantial financial contributions to local and national politicians, and their role in building the entrepreneurial base of the ethnic enclave economy. Despite the fact that Los Angeles has a larger population of native-born Korean Americans as compared with other cities such as New York, another significant pattern to note is the numerical predominance of immigrants in both the Koreatown and Los Angeles populations—a dynamic that has profoundly shaped the inner workings of Koreatown political structures.

However, the growing population of Korean Americans born and raised in the United States is expected to transform the generational landscape of Los Angeles and thus the dynamics of ethnic political solidarity. A series of dramatic events throughout the 1980s and 1990s expedited this process by politicizing a new generation of Korean Americans and shifting the power balance between the first and 1.5/second generation leadership. Among other things, these political crises eroded the previously uncontested authority of the ethnic elite and introduced alternative resources and support networks, making way for new generations of American-born ethnic leadership to arise. Although past analysis has fixated on intergenerational tensions as the locus of contemporary ethnic politics, the chapter underlines the continuing dependency of the newly emerging leadership on the ethnic elite because of Koreatown's role as the institutional nub of the ever-expanding ethnic community. Torn between ideology and interest, the response of the younger generation to the political exigencies of the period has been both diverse and complex and characterized by patterns of conflict and accommodation with the immigrant elite.

The chapter focuses on those events that set the stage for the political incorporation of 1.5/second generation Korean American leaders and organizations, including the Kwangju Rebellions in Korea, the Korean-Black conflicts, and the 1992 Los Angeles riots. Among other things, the study shows how these events were particularly integral in weakening the political stronghold of the ethnic elite by challenging their pro-Seoul, pro-U.S. ideologies and unveiling their tenuous position within mainstream society. Building on their English-speaking abilities and stronger ties with mainstream institutions, a new generation of leaders and organizations from the 1.5/second generation gained political stature within the Korean American community, which prompted a dramatic shift in ethnic power structures.

Student Activism and the Kwangju Rebellions

As much influence as homeland affairs may have had on Korean American politics, such strong sentiments ironically allowed for a major event in Korea to shift the ideological tides against the Seoul government among younger factions within the ethnic community. With the end of Japanese colonialist rule in 1945, Korea struggled through years of political turmoil under a series of U.S. puppet governments that suppressed prodemocratic and prolabor activities by employing anti-Communist rhetoric, manipulating elections and legal institutions, and applying military force to impose their dictatorial policies. A former general of the Japanese military air force, President Park Chung Hee, ended a brief period of democracy in Korean history when he led a military coup and established himself as a civilian president in the early 1960s. Under his regime, Korea became a military state, which suspended constitutional laws at whim and enforced strict censorship of media, political activities, and any other forms of protest against the South Korean government.

Although the government was successful in suppressing dissident activities for decades, Korea's rule under state dictatorship, its rapid progress toward modernization, and its controversial ties with U.S. forces laid the groundwork for a series of uprisings that would ultimately lead to its democratization in the 1980s. Amid economic recession and increasing student and labor unrest, President Park was assassinated by the head of the Korean Central Intelligence Agency in October 1979. The move to establish martial law by General Chun Doo Hwan in the interim period incited a major uprising among prodemocratic student leaders, who demanded that the occupying party call for presidential elections and pave the way for democratic reform (Shin and Hwang 2003).

After a series of peaceful demonstrations and mass arrests throughout Seoul, the student demonstrators finally took to the streets on May 18, 1980, in the city of Kwangju, located southwest of the nation's capital. The movement was pivotal in bringing together students with other activists disenchanted with the repressive policies and actions of the Seoul government, which enforced uneven regional development and substandard wages and working conditions for workers. According to Edward Chang (1988), the ten-day struggle eventually led to "one of the bloodiest struggles in modern Korean history," as soldiers brutally attacked and shot at students and ordinary citizens who were protesting on the streets. Although there are no exact figures, the casualty rates ranged from between 200 (conservative government estimates) to 500 deaths (eyewitness accounts) and 380 to 3,000 injured (Shin and Hwang 2003).

The Kwangju Uprising of 1980 elicited an emotional outpouring among young Koreans in the United States against the cruel militaristic tactics of the Seoul government, which some believed was no different from the Communist dictators of North Korea that Seoul had so strongly denounced in the past. During this period of turmoil, the Seoul government attempted to place blame on Communist agitators, causing some to be further disillusioned by "red-baiting" propaganda that would also come to haunt select 1.5/second generation organizations in later disputes with the ethnic elite. In an act of solidarity with students of democracy movements within Korea, 1.5 generation Korean American students initiated sit-in demonstrations and blood donation drives to supplement shortages in Kwangju (Chang 1988). They established new branches of the Korean Student Association for Democracy in various places across the nation, including Los Angeles and Orange Counties, and later created the California Korean Student Association for Democracy (CKSAD). In an effort to challenge the strong influence of Seoul politics within existing immigrant organizations, progressive activists within the community fought for and eventually won over the leadership of the California Korean Student Association, which had previously worked in close relations with the Consulate General (Chang 1988).

As a sign of growing resentment against the ethnic elite establishment, the student organizations strategically planned to disrupt an annual entertainment event that was being scheduled by the Korean media (Chang 1988).

Although the plan was not carried through because of its cancellation after the Park assassination, the movement represented growing agitation among young activists against the power holders of the ethnic community. In the meantime, both the Consulate General and its front organizations remained publicly silent due to uncertainties about the political regime in Korea and some internal differences of opinion over the massacre.

In this sense, the Kwangju Rebellions would come to signify a new era in both South Korean and Korean American politics. For Korean Americans, the event was pivotal in weakening the political stronghold of the Consulate General and blurring the ethnic elite's ideological distinction between "good Korea" (South) and "bad Korea" (North). The Kwangju Rebellions also solidified links between student intellectuals and workers and, in the process, created a crucial forum for articulating a broader framework for leftist movements in the Korean diaspora. Many progressive 1.5/second generation organizations like the Korean Immigrant Workers Advocates (KIWA) and the Korean Resource Center (KRC) would emerge from the student activist base established by post-Kwangju politics. In addition, the rebellions opened the doors to growing discontent against the American government, which did little to protect Kwangju's citizens against the state's military aggression and even appeared to support the actions of the dictatorship. These and other future developments would fuel growing nationalist sentiment among future generations of Koreans and Korean Americans, who would come to challenge U.S. military occupation and call for greater efforts at reunification between the two Koreas.

Discontent among Korean student activists also helped to politicize the 1.5 generation, who were becoming a growing presence in Koreatown politics as a result of their intermediary role between the ethnic community and mainstream society. In this light, one thirty-nine-year-old, 1.5 generation activist relates to me how the Kwangju Rebellions shaped his political and, hence, his personal outlook on the situation of Korean Americans in the United States:

Nationalism is an interesting thing. You always have it, some level of interest or curiosity about your home country, even if you're second or third generation, just because of your friends or your family ties. But politically, my interest started in 1980 when there was [a] massacre in Kwangju. That's when history started to make sense under the auspices of [the] U.S. who came in really as liberator of our country and installed military dictators, who were brutally repressive. Basically there was no democracy, no freedom whatsoever. So I learned quite a bit about the modern history of South Korea at that time and became greatly concerned. I immediately identified with the democracy and unification movement in South Korea.

By politicizing what was initially deemed to be a personal curiosity in the home country, the Kwangju Rebellions gave him the conceptual framework with which to connect to the larger ethnic community.

Young leaders within the community began to recognize the need to demand greater attention to social inequalities and problems within the Korean American community as opposed to focusing on homeland politics. In fact, the leaders of many of these bridging organizations had branched themselves off from existing immigrant organizations, which they felt had consumed themselves with politics abroad to the detriment of Korean Americans at home. As one former activist from Young Koreans United (YKU) firmly states, "I believed that Korean Americans here or overseas really oughtta take the community matters into their own hands and not rely on Korea homeland politics to help solve them." Ironically, the events abroad would provide this opening by underlining the merits of disassociating Koreatown politics from the influence of the homeland government, casting doubt on Seoul's interest in serving the needs of Koreans in America, and turning the spotlight on a new generation of leaders. Although the uprisings did not completely destroy the structural underpinnings of ethnic elite structures, the ideological challenges put forth by 1.5 generation students undermined the legitimacy of immigrant power holders and created a new political framework for dissenting student activists among the 1.5/second generation.

A series of social movements and political events in the years following the Kwangju Rebellions further shifted the tides of public sentiment away from the rigid anti-Communist stance of former administrations and peaked general interest in the possibilities of North and South Korean reunification. As student and labor activists in South Korea continued to contest the pro-U.S., anti-Communist climate, the administration under the leadership of President Kim Dae Jung instituted the Sunshine Policy, which aimed to forge stronger lines of communication between North and South Korea through family reunions and cultural exchange programs.

These and other government policies led to the historic summit meeting in 2000 between South Korean President Kim Dae Jung, and North Korean president Kim Jong Il, during which the two presidents made a pact to reduce

tensions on the Korean peninsula and arranged for the reunion of families sep-
arated during the Korean War. In 2002, South Koreans responded in outrage
over the acquittal of two U.S. soldiers who ran over two thirteen-year-old Korean girls, with a 50-ton military tank—an incident that intensified hostility toward U.S. military occupation in South Korea. The aggressive anti-immigrant
policies and hostile actions of the Bush administration against North Korea
since the September 11 terrorist attacks raised more doubts about whether the
United States would act in the best interests of Korea. These events eventually
culminated in the 2003 election of current President Roh Moo Hyun, a former
human rights lawyer who had been active in pro-Democratic movements in
the past and was most known for his interest in continuing Kim's "sunshine
policy" toward North Korea with minimal U.S. intervention.[1]

The changing sociopolitical climate of South Korea in itself has also
shifted the ideological orientations of the first generation leadership toward
homeland politics. During this transitional period, new waves of immigrants
have started entering the United States with different ideas about homeland
politics that clash with the pro-U.S., anti–North Korea rhetoric of immigrants
who arrived before the twenty-first century. Although age may certainly play
a part, Chang (December 2004 interview) points out that this ideological shift
reflects more than a generational division based on age differences, but also
hinges on the immigrant's years of residence in the United States. Those who
arrived in the 1950s are more likely to hold onto an antiquated view of Korean
politics based on the strong anti-Communist society they left behind, whereas
those who immigrated in recent years are more likely to be moderate on the
issue of reunification.

As evidence of this, leaders of the Korean-American Federation (KAF) of
Los Angeles extended a goodwill invitation to visiting North Korean diplomats, only to be attacked by veterans of the Korean War whose bitter memories of the millions of Korean civilians and soldiers killed during the war
served as a barrier to any friendship with the Communist state (Marquez
2004). One 1.5 generation Korean American interviewee also remarked on the
stark differences he observed between the more conservative stance of the Korean American Veterans Association and the more moderate perspectives of
the Advisory Council on Democratic and Peaceful Unification, or *pyong-tong*,
the reunification council of the South Korean government.

Many Korean immigrant community leaders both young and old have
channeled their energies toward addressing the issue of reunification through
either new or existing institutions within the community. Reunification orga-

nizations have stratified themselves according to these political perspectives: they have ranged from younger leftist student/labor activist organizations such as YKU, Mindullae for Korean Community Empowerment, and One Korea L.A. Forum whose politics overlap with leftist organizations like KIWA to more moderate government-sponsored organizations backed by immigrant elite groups like pyong-tong. Both immigrant and 1.5/second generation organizations in major cities across the nation have sponsored educational and political forums on the current crisis in the "Koreas," held premiere documentary film showings on North Korea, disseminated news updates through mass e-mail listservs, and organized protest demonstrations and candlelight vigils. Both grassroots and corporate interest groups have chipped in by providing humanitarian relief to North Koreans and embarking on new ventures to boost the economy of North Korea. To be sure, most CBOs are not directly affected by the politics of reunification, especially since their main focus is on American issues, but the undercurrents of homeland politics have facilitated some of the larger changes that have taken place within the power structures of the Korean American community.

The "Korean-Black Conflicts"

The second event to shake the power structures of the Korean American community most directly impacted Korean immigrant entrepreneurs but also opened the doors to greater 1.5/second generation involvement in political matters. Conflicts among immigrants and native-born minorities had begun to climax throughout the 1980s and 1990s as more and more immigrants from Asia and Latin America made their presence known in the businesses and residential areas of formerly African American-dominated ghettos. The success of Korean immigrant merchants in these neighborhoods has not come without its own heavy toll. Hostilities between Korean merchants and African American patrons epitomize one type of competition that results from differences in the culture, politics, and economic interests of immigrant and native-born minority groups. Today, conflicts among African Americans, Latinos, and Asians in major metropolitan areas, such as New York, Chicago, Los Angeles, Miami, and Washington DC, continue to resurface over the increasingly scarce social, political, and economic resources of shared communities (Chang 1991; Johnson and Oliver 1994; Portes and Stepick 1993).

Although many immigrants choose to establish their businesses in the vibrant ethnic economy of Koreatown, a good number of Korean immigrants, seeking to avoid the cutthroat competition of serving coethnics, have established roots in poor African American neighborhoods instead. But some scholars argue that by distributing corporate products to low-income ghettos, these Korean immigrant entrepreneurs have assumed an inherently conflictual role in small enterprise as "middleman minorities" (Light and Bonacich 1988). As middleman minorities, small Korean entrepreneurs are used to distribute corporate products to low-income minority ghettos and thus play an intermediary role in providing large multinational corporations with cheap access to low-income markets. Corporations are able to pass the costs of directly working in urban neighborhoods, such as crime and labor costs, onto middleman minority enterprises. Because of their role between the "oppressed" and the "oppressor," Korean entrepreneurs are positioned in direct conflict with minority customers, other business competitors, and labor unions (Bonacich 1973). Their interactions with native-born residents are further exacerbated by language barriers and cultural differences, limited social interactions beyond the merchant-customer relationship, media sensationalism, and lack of multicultural education.

Within this context, African American residents and organizational representatives have raised various complaints about Korean merchants in their communities. They argue that these merchants have been notorious for overcharging customers, acting rude and suspicious toward African American patrons, failing to hire African American employees, opening up Korean-owned liquor stores in poor minority neighborhoods, and refusing to live or contribute to the community from which they profit. The overwhelming success of Koreans in small enterprise has been a major source of frustration for African Americans, whose discrimination from White-owned banks and insurance companies has posed a major obstacle in gaining access to this traditional avenue of mobility. In response, Korean immigrant merchants have argued that high criminal activities against such businesses, economic constraints in hiring practices, cultural misunderstandings, and unfair ethnic targeting have been the major source of problems between the two communities.

While hostilities between Korean storeowners and African American patrons in New York began as far back as the early 1980s, Los Angeles did not witness major confrontations between the two groups until 1991, with the exception of a few isolated incidents. Prior to that, minor boycotts such as the one staged by the Organization of Mutual Neighborhood Interest (OMNI) against Slauson and Inglewood Indoor Swap Meet were resolved within a short period of time (Chang 1992). Among other things, this may be attributed to the greater involvement of Mayor Tom Bradley in mediating Korean-Black disputes and the establishment of the Black-Korean Alliance (BKA) in 1986, which helped to minimize conflicts between the two communities (Min 1996).

Despite relatively low levels of confrontation between Korean merchants and African American patrons, escalating tensions within urban neighborhoods and in other areas across the nation motivated the Los Angeles County Human Relations Commission (LACHRC) to establish the African American-Korean Community Relations Committee (AAKCRC) in the hopes of preventing future conflicts. However, the AAKCRC remained inactive for the most part from 1985–86 due to a decline in interethnic incidents and convened sporadically until the spring of 1986. In April 1986, the AAKCRC (soon to be renamed the BKA) was revived when the shootings of four Korean merchants in South Central once again brought the issue of Korean-Black relations to the forefront (Chang 1992). Attempting to avoid involvement with mediation and crisis intervention, the BKA initially focused on proactive programs that included the "dissemination of positive information" and other preventive measures. Its membership consisted of representatives from human relations and dispute resolution agencies, small business organizations, religious organizations, and civil rights foundations, including the National Association for the Advancement of Colored People (NAACP), the Southern Christian Leadership Conference (SCLC), the Urban League, the Korean American Coalition (KAC), and the Korean American Grocer's Association (KAGRO).

In spite of these counterpreventive measures, acts of hostility and violence against Korean merchants began to increase throughout 1990 until they reached their culmination with the tragic shooting of Latasha Harlins by storeowner Soon Ja Du in March 1991. The incident arose when Du, suspecting Harlins of shoplifting a bottle of orange juice, engaged in a physical struggle with the fifteen-year-old African American girl, who threw several blows at Du in the process. Harlins finally left the bottle on the counter and turned around to leave, only to be shot in the back of the head by the merchant. Although initially charged with first-degree murder, Du was ultimately convicted of voluntary manslaughter by Judge Joyce Karlin and sentenced to a ten-year suspended sentence and five years of probation, in addition to community service hours and a small $500 fine in October 1991 (Yoon 1997). The sentence was upheld despite several appeals throughout 1992, but eventually

Harlins's parents were paid $300,000 in an out-of-court settlement through Du's insurance company (Min 1996).

The mild sentence elicited outraged responses and a series of protests by groups within the African American community. African American politicians such as City Councilman Mark Ridley-Thomas and Congresswoman Maxine Waters denounced the shooting and the court's decision as yet another "assault" on the dignity and lives of African Americans (Yoon 1997). As reported in the *Los Angeles Sentinel*, many called for the resignation of Judge Karlin, a Jewish American who for some represented the White-dominated judicial system that devalued the lives of African Americans (Mitchell 1992; *Los Angeles Sentinel*, June 25, 1992). The mainstream media fed the fuels of controversy by oversimplifying the conflict as the Korean merchant shooting of an African American teenager over a bottle of orange juice. Major TV news stations repeatedly showed security camera pictures of Harlins being brutally shot by Du with little context to the brawl that had taken place earlier. Articles from the *Los Angeles Sentinel* and *Money Talk News* throughout 1983 condemned Koreans for mistreating and exploiting the African American community (Chang and Diaz-Veizades 1999). Meanwhile, anti-Korean sentiments occasionally led to outbursts of violence, with more than ten other attacks against Koreans occurring within a month after the Harlins shooting.

Yet unlike other cities throughout the United States, the outbreak of racial conflict also elicited a quick response from other organizations within both communities. With the support of the LACHRC and the mayor's office, representatives from Korean and African American organizations such as the NAACP, SCLC, the BKA, and the Los Angeles Korean Chamber of Commerce convened during several emergency meetings and decided to steer people away from racializing the tragic event (Min 1996).

While the African American community was generally angered over the light sentence given Du, organizational response to the incident varied. Some perceived the shooting as yet another sign of the oppressive behavior of Korean merchants toward the community they served. The most organized efforts came from Danny Bakewell and the Brotherhood Crusade, which staged aggressive boycotts and protests in front of Empire Market where the shooting had taken place. Among other things, the protest leaders advocated the boycott of all stores, Korean and non-Korean, that "disrespected" African American residents and called for projects that would allow African Americans to build their own stores in local neighborhood communities. Oftentimes, the protests were used to support a broader effort to increase African American political and economic power through the promotion of Black entrepreneurship.

The response from the Korean American organizational community varied, with some outright supporting Du and others condemning her actions, but the response was not clearly delineated along generational lines. Some of the more well-known immigrant organizations in Koreatown did express some support for Du. The Korean Senior Citizens Association even donated $2,190 to Judge Karlin in her campaign to run for superior court judge (*Korea Central Daily*, April 16, 1992). However, it was not the specific circumstances of the shooting or some vague sense of ethnic solidarity that moved Korean immigrants to support Du in most cases. Rather, the general context of the Soon Ja Du controversy represented something greater for Korean storeowners, whose day-to-day struggles to make a living were aggravated by their vulnerability to repeated criminal incidents in the inner-city areas where they worked. While few would morally justify the actions of Du or Judge Karlin, many were quick to point out that the community's outrage over Korean merchants as symbolized by the Harlins shooting was taken out of proportion in light of the fact that more than a dozen Korean storeowners had been killed by African American robbers within the last two years (Ong and Hee 1993). Du herself had been the target of numerous crimes in the past.

Most other organizations saw the need to acknowledge the unjust nature of the shooting and racism within the ethnic community, while preventing outside groups from "demonizing" Du and ignoring the hardships associated with immigrant enterprise. As reported in the *Los Angeles Times*, one executive director of KAC stated, "We can relate to her as a Korean and we can pray that she does not suffer, but, on the other hand, just because we are Korean, that doesn't mean we wanted her to get off. There has to be justice" (Katz and Clifford 1992). Rather than expressing clear-cut public support "for" or "against" Soon Ja Du, different 1.5/second generation organizations "emphasized" certain aspects of the Korean-Black conflicts as it reflected on their relationship to both the immigrant leadership and mainstream society.

Consider the opposing viewpoints of two different 1.5/second generation organizational leaders in the following interviews:

> Our view on that is that our community exacerbates the situation by not having other viewpoints other than the leadership who comes from a mostly conservative business kind of perspective. In terms of Latasha Harlins and the

Soon Ja Du case, what the Korean community did was support the judge that gave Soon Ja Du a very light sentence—what a tragic incident to begin with—but we felt that the judge was being divisive by doing so. African American community organized to try and unseat that judge. Korean community, some of them so-called leaders, actually go and support the judge, which was not what a lot of key people and others in the community felt we should do at that moment. You can't ignore the fact that there are these two communities with this immediate, flaring issues.

It was a merchant-consumer issue that became a racial issue, but unfortunately, Soon Ja Du was a Korean woman and unfortunately, the media portrayed Soon Ja Du as a really mean-spirited Korean merchant, who don't care about them, has no respect for human lives and she killed this young beautiful teenage girl for just one orange juice bottle. That's the kind of image portrayed by the mainstream media. I'm not saying that what she did was the right thing or I'd give her a 100 percent support. But the media did not help us to have a place where we can talk about *our* opinions and *our* positions. I told many of the reporters that if you just stay at their store just one day and see what's going on, then you'll understand everyday life and what kind of situation [Korean immigrant merchants] are in. But the American media can care less about the Korean community. They don't care. And we're invisible. We're not creating any problems, and we don't have any political power, we don't have any media power. So they completely put us down and ignored us at the same time; they just took side with Blacks.

Both interviewees implicitly carve out their position on the issue around their view of immigrant merchants as either conservative or disempowered and consider how this may have serious ramifications on the ethnic community's relations with mainstream American society.

Some 1.5/second generation organizations acknowledged the need to change the racial attitudes and business practices of Korean immigrants and made efforts to mend relations with the Black community. Others stressed that they were being unfairly targeted as a group by "political opportunists" and biased media coverage and worked to solidify the political position of Korean Americans. These leaders challenged the way the media repeatedly showed edited scenes of the Du-Harlins struggle that left out the context for the shooting and failed to cover the political opinions and general hardships of Korean immigrants throughout the tragedy.

A few months later, a second fatal confrontation again sparked hostilities between Koreans and African Americans, but this time the context for the incident elicited different responses from within the Korean American community. While the confrontation had arisen from a senseless shooting of a teenager over a suspected shoplifting incident, the second one occurred when a forty-two-year-old African American man allegedly tried to rob a Korean-owned market in South Central. The grocery owner, Tae Sam Park, shot and killed Lee Arthur Mitchell, who had beaten Park's wife and threatened to shoot her with what turned out to be a fist in his jacket. Because the shooting was determined to be an act of self-defense, the police did not charge Park for the shooting. After learning about the event, Bakewell and Reverend Edgar Boyd of Bethel AME Church spearheaded a major boycott against the store-owner that lasted for about three and a half months.[2]

The Korean American community's response to the Park-Mitchell incident is particularly telling, because it initially unified both first generation and 1.5/second generation organizational leaders within the community but ultimately led to deeper internal schisms in the end. As Bakewell and his constituencies launched their campaign against Tae Sam Park, various leaders within the Korean American community decided to take a more active stance on this issue. To this end, they established a new organization called the Korean American Race Relations Emergency (KARE) fund, which would serve the dual purpose of providing financial support for Park during the boycotts and facilitating better communication between the two communities. The organization was led by younger 1.5/second generation leaders of the community, including Korean members of the BKA, and financed by immigrant organizations such as the Korean American Grocers Association (KAGRO) and other community donations. Within the first few months, KARE was able to raise almost $60,000 from its nationwide fundraising drive (Yoon 1997).

Tensions that arose among Korean and Black leaders within the BKA over this issue provide some insight into the Korean community's initial reasons for rallying behind Tae Sam Park. One 1.5 generation male who had been involved with both BKA and KARE recalls:

We were attacked by everybody. African American members [from BKA] were attacked by Danny Bakewell or people from the community as a sellout to the African American community, and that's when the position of each community hardened. Korean merchants were saying, if we give in it will happen again in another store so there were worries about rippling effect, so they wanted to maintain their own position. The African American community also said, look this is a continuous attack on African Americans by Korean Americans who doesn't value African American life highly. That meant the end of BKA, because you're taking the position of representing only Korean voice, right? Many of the BKA African American members were upset about this. Obviously, they were upset. But at the same time, we were upset at African American members, because they weren't willing to take a public stand against Danny Bakewell and the demagogues. We felt that the purpose of BKA was to do that, during the crisis, we would form alliance and try to stand together but the coalition was fragile. And that's why we set up our own KARE.

Accountability to the ethnic communities that each coalitional member represented was one factor that would lead to the ultimate demise of the BKA.

Consensus would eventually dissolve into political turmoil as the two generations of leadership clashed over how they would use the donations. On one side, second generation leaders argued that although Park would receive a portion of the funds, the remainder should be set aside to create a dispute prevention center, whereas first generation leaders felt that the entirety of the donations should be given to Park. Eventually realizing the divisive effects of the KARE campaign, second generation members withdrew from the organization and the decision was made to terminate the group, which later facilitated negotiations with African American representatives. With the help of Mayor Bradley, KARE, KAGRO, and the Brotherhood Crusade reached a compromise to suspend the boycott temporarily, during which time the community would seek an African American buyer and if that failed, a Korean buyer. The agreement also included a stipulation that the new owner would not sell liquor, that both communities would attempt to set up a dispute resolution center, and that they would write up a code of ethics for business owners. Both the dissolution of KARE and the final compromise elicited strong criticism from members of the Korean immigrant community, who perceived the leaders as having sold out to African American leaders and used up funds with little results.

Unequipped to deal with the confrontations of the past couple of years, the BKA officially disbanded in November 1992.[3] A few organizations such as the Asian Pacific American Dispute Resolution Center and the Martin Luther King, Jr. Dispute Resolution Center continued their efforts to help mediate conflicts between the two communities in the years immediately before the

1992 civil unrest. Nevertheless, continuing tensions between the two communities set the backdrop for the subsequent massive destruction of what some call the "Los Angeles riots" and others the "Los Angeles civil unrest" of 1992.

The 1992 Los Angeles Civil Unrest

From Wednesday, April 29 to Friday, May 1, 1992, Los Angeles witnessed an outbreak of rioting that led to the loss of more than 50 lives, thousands of arrests, and almost a billion dollars in property damage (Ong and Hee 1993). The upheavals originated in the streets of Hyde Park in South Central, shortly after the acquittal of four White Los Angeles Police Department (LAPD) officers who had been charged of a brutal attack on an African American motorist. The civil unrest began as a political expression of pent-up frustration and anger by African Americans, but both the nature and the demographic profile of the rebellion eventually shifted as violent political protest gave way to the fulfillment of socioeconomic needs, especially by low-income Latino looters. The rioting eventually spread northward toward the mixed African American and Latino neighborhoods of West Adams between the Santa Monica Freeway and Pico Boulevard; by Thursday, rioters had invaded stores in Koreatown as far north as Santa Monica Boulevard (Morrison and Lowry 1994).

Without the political leverage to make such demands, Koreatown suffered the worst effects of the civil unrest, as looters and arsonists destroyed their stores without check. The police were egregiously absent in the lower-income neighborhoods of South Central and Koreatown, where many Korean business owners worked. It was reported that the Chief of Police Daryl Gates failed to make adequate preparations for defending these areas despite strong advice to that effect from other officials (Cho 1993). Once the riots broke out, officers were deployed to protect the higher-income neighborhoods of the Westside, while they were held back in lower-status areas until order had been fully restored by the National Guard. As a result, many of these merchants felt it necessary to arm themselves with guns, institute neighborhood patrols, and solicit individual volunteers to defend their businesses with the help of Radio Korea. Yet when Governor Pete Wilson finally dispatched the National Guard on Friday, there was little left to salvage among the ruins of charred and damaged business establishments.

In stark contrast to the Watts rebellion of 1965, the Los Angeles civil unrest is distinguished by the multiethnic composition of both its participants and its victims and its most devastating impact on mostly inner-city neighborhoods already blighted by urban poverty. Of the 5,438 people arrested between April 30 and May 4, there were 2,764 Latino, 2,022 Black, 568 White, and 84 classified as "Other" (Navarro 1993). Approximately one-third of the casualties during this time were also Latino, with 19 of the 58 people killed from this group only second to Black fatalities (Navarro 1993). One young Korean American was also shot during the riots. Although the figures may vary depending on the source, it is generally agreed that the group that was financially hit hardest by the riots was Korean merchants with 1,867 Korean-owned businesses suffering at least an estimated $347 million in damages, according to more conservative figures (Kwong 1993). Data gathered from the Los Angeles Department of Building and Safety and the City Clerk's office indicate that Korean merchants incurred about a third of the losses from the 1992 civil unrest, as compared with 12.1 percent of Hispanics, 8.7 percent of other Asians, and 25.0 percent of "Other" (Tierney 1994). However, an estimate of businesses that sustained 100 percent damage shows that almost half of them (46.4 percent) were Korean. In contrast, only 9.9 percent were Hispanic owned, 8.4 percent were other Asian owned, and 19.1 percent were Other owned. There is major disagreement on the reasons for this imbalance, but it is likely that a combination of racial tensions and the visibility of Korean-owned businesses in low-income urban neighborhoods may help to explain their overrepresentation.

Although the rioters vented their frustrations on small retail stores and other properties, these actions were expressions of general disempowerment, which was aggravated by the racial and economic discrimination of White-dominated institutions. Harlan Hahn (1996) describes the 1992 civil unrest as a "politics of last resort," initiated by a socioeconomically devastated population that had been excluded from or disenchanted with the traditional means of political expression, including electoral voting, litigation, lobbying, and protest demonstrations. The brutal police beating of Rodney King and the subsequent acquittal of the four officers symbolized a long history of brutality and injustices inflicted upon racial minorities. Headlines in the city's largest African American newspaper, the *Los Angeles Sentinel*, proclaimed, "King Case Just One Example" (*Los Angeles Sentinel*, April 8, 1993). African Americans in the United States had long expressed their disillusionment with the police, which had been infamous for committing countless abuses against racial minorities yet failing to provide adequate protection of their neighborhoods from rampant crime. All in all, the volatile elements of police brutality, urban poverty, growing violence, and political disenfranchisement in inner-city areas finally culminated with the explosive outbreak of violence in neighborhoods that did not have the political or economic means to demand protection from traditional sources of authority.

In contrast, the general Korean immigrant community had always believed that they would receive the proper protection and services by the government if they worked diligently, obeyed the rules, and contributed financially to political incumbents. As a relatively new immigrant group, Koreans were also unable to apply pressure on politicians or police departments for improvement in law enforcement protection. In the years preceding the riots, select organizations would make financial contributions to politicians and the LAPD that enabled them to gain minor favors and concessions on issues, such as liquor store licenses and other business-related concerns, but future events would show that donations could not compensate for lack of political voice and representation in local politics. Social, cultural, economic, and political insularity had rendered Korean Americans out of touch with the realities of a multiracial society, as well as leaving them virtually voiceless and disempowered in America. Even prior to the civil unrest, the LAPD clearly did not place priority on the protection of low-income, minority neighborhoods, yet Koreans did not feel compelled to mobilize against these problems until after the riots as a result of cultural and language barriers and general apathy.

Tensions were exacerbated by sensationalized portrayals of the 1992 civil unrest by the mainstream media. The stereotypical depiction of Korean immigrant merchants and African American residents and activists in the "Korean-Black Conflict" overlapped in many respects with the coverage of the civil disturbances. In newspapers such as the *Los Angeles Times* (Dunn 1992) and in television reports, shocking scenes from the Latasha Harlins shooting were intermingled with suggestive photos of Korean American vigilantes standing menacingly on roofs with guns during the rioting. In other articles, a mass of unruly Black and Latino looters were pictured ruthlessly wreaking havoc on the hard-earned stores of "model" immigrants.

Korean American community organizations like KIWA did their part in attempting to control media distortion of these events during the three days of mayhem. As one middle-aged 1.5 generation organizer recalls, "When news reports came out, we had volunteers around go check it, verify it, see if it's true or not, and if it's not, then we challenge the media to correct themselves, cause all kinds of b.s. like those happening caused more pain for lot of the people who were really in desperate situation." Addressing media distortions in the Harlins case, headlines in the *Korea Times* demanded, "Koreans Want an Equal Treatment from the Mainstream Media" (Lee 1994). In addition, the *Los Angeles Sentinel* heatedly contested the tactics of the media, which "sought to exploit and reinforce longstanding racial stereotypes while inflaming racial tensions" (*Los Angeles Sentinel*, June 25, 1992).

If the trauma and financial losses during the upheavals were not bad enough, Korean immigrants faced the even more daunting and heart-wrenching process of rebuilding their lives in the aftermath of the civil unrest. A survey by the Korean American Inter-Agency Council (KAIAC) stated that three-fourths of the 1,500 victims reported financial difficulty and had not yet recovered from the financial and psychological impact of the riots ten months after the riots. Of the businesses that were partially damaged or looted, only 27.8 percent of the respondents were able to reopen their stores by March, 1993.[4] A majority of victims also suffered from posttraumatic stress disorder, ranging from moderate to severe symptoms. Based on survey and case management studies, KAIAC found that assistance from both the public and private sector proved to be ineffective and inadequate to meet the specialized needs of this victimized ethnic population.

Korean American churches, CBOs, and other ethnic institutions did what they could to provide short-term relief for victims of the Los Angeles riots by offering free legal aid, social welfare consultation, and food supplies. In coordination with 1.5/second generation Korean American leaders, other Asian American organizations and minority coalitions such as the Asian Pacific American Legal Center (APALC), the Multicultural Collaborative (MCC), and APANLA also pitched in during the relief efforts by providing supplies and information for riot victims, assisting in filing complaints against the LAPD and insurance companies, setting up loan funds for business owners, establishing leadership programs with other racial and ethnic communities, and pressuring the media and LAPD to diversify their staff (APALC newsletter).

The governmental program that was supposed to offer more long-term assistance in the post–Los Angeles riot period emerged in the form of Rebuild Los Angeles (RLA), a private nonprofit agency whose main purpose was to direct investment into impoverished inner-city neighborhoods. The proposal for this organizational program centered almost exclusively on the head of RLA Peter Ueberroth's attempt to persuade major corporations to voluntarily contribute to neighborhood reconstruction (Smith 1997). Although it was able to raise pledges of up to $485 million from major corporations, RLA did not live up to many people's expectations.

Among other things, critics pointed out that RLA took credit for changes that would have occurred anyway and made very little impact in terms of initiating major economic restructuring in urban communities. From the perspective of Korean American organizations, the most problematic feature of the agency had to do with its lack of accountability to the community. As an example of this, Ueberroth's visit to a Korean American church elicited outraged responses from the gathered contingency of merchants who were told that they would not be given money for recovery (Smith 1997). As evidence of their invisibility in Los Angeles politics, Korean Americans were nowhere to be found among the chairs appointed to the committee. When the organization decided to diversify their leadership, they appointed Linda Wong, a Chinese American, as the "representative" for Asian Americans (Park 2001). Thus, after undergoing several changes in leadership and strategy, RLA proved to be disorganized and largely ineffective in producing tangible results to cover the major damages of the civil unrest.

Generational Politics in the Aftermath

The 1992 civil unrest is the one pivotal event that has helped to transform the politics of Korean American communities across the nation in a profound way. Although efforts to improve interethnic relations began with the outbreak of Korean-Black tensions in the 1980s and early 1990s, the Korean immigrant community has been instilled with a new sense of urgency to ensure that what happened in 1992 does not repeat itself. These types of efforts have come from both first generation and 1.5/second generation community members, although with different strategies and goals in mind. Strategies for ameliorating tensions have ranged from cultural and educational programs to issue-based coalitions to long-term development projects.

In addition, a variety of coalitions such as the MCC and the African American Korean American Christian Alliance (AAKACA) were established in the wake of the Korean-Black conflicts and the 1992 civil unrest. The immigrant leadership made its own contributions through Christian-based coalitions with Black churches, food donations to needy residents, funding to local politicians and the LAPD, and sponsored trips to Korea for African American high school students. More importantly, the growing presence of Latinos as both residents and workers in Koreatown has pressed a handful of organizations to move beyond a Black-Korean understanding of race and ethnic relations in Koreatown.

Despite substantial changes, it is doubtful that community projects will be completely effective without the assistance of mainstream institutions and power holders in rectifying more profound structural inequalities within disintegrating urban neighborhoods—a situation that has underlined the growing need for bridging organizations. For many, the "triple scapegoating" by looters, the local government and police, and the media during the civil unrest made the community painfully aware of the price of political powerlessness (Cho 1993). In protest, roughly 500 Korean Americans set up a demonstration outside Radio Korea during President George Bush's photo-op visit to Koreatown and organized a series of rallies in front of city hall in June 1992 (Chang 1995). Yet despite these acts of solidarity, the organizers were unable to gain any substantive concessions from either politicians or law enforcement officials because of their politically marginal status and lack of alliances with other active groups.

Disappointment over the Korean government's failure to provide significant political support led many Korean immigrants to realize that preoccupation with the internal affairs of their native land did little to better their situation in American society. The riots also had an impact on other generations of Koreans like the following 1.5 generation male community leader, who explains:

> Before the riots, I really didn't think much beyond the Korean community. My focus or scope was pretty much fixed to the Korean American community. And I thought we, Koreans, had great working relationships with local politicians cause we gave a lot of money and we were close buddies with the LAPD. And so when the riot broke out, there was a call for a community meeting about organizations in Koreatown. So I went to the meeting and there were about forty representatives from other organizations. And out of the forty, there were three of us who were considered young people. We were the only three that advocated for peace for means of resolution, where we shouldn't pick up any arms cause LAPD will be here. [So] we placed calls and we did what we thought was proper thing to do. And we were left out to burn. We were left out to burn for three days. All the city councilmen and you know LAPD and captains and deputy chief didn't matter, cause Koreans didn't matter to them.

So that was a very difficult lesson. That's when I learned that we can not just own this community. We have to recognize and be respectful with others in this community.

As the last two sentences indicate, many Korean Americans in Los Angeles experienced a profound change in attitude as they realized that the community upon which their livelihoods depend is multiethnic and must be dealt with if they are to progress as individuals and as a collectivity.

As a sign of this growing awareness, Korean Americans engaged in several protest demonstrations to demand attention and services from mainstream institutions that had abandoned them during the rioting. In one of the most remarkable displays of ethnic solidarity, 30,000 Korean Americans of all ages, generations, and backgrounds convened at a spontaneous, massive demonstration in Koreatown on May 2, 1992 in what Elaine Kim called, the "largest and most quickly organized mass mobilization in Asian American history" (Kim 1993, 229). Instead of blaming the looters for the destruction of their stores, the demonstrators accused American institutions, such as the media, the police, and the government, for inciting tensions, reinforcing economic and political inequalities, and indirectly instigating urban violence. For the first time, many Korean Americans began to see themselves as "victims of White racism"—a perception that signified a critical departure, even if temporary, from past conservative views. Having been abandoned by law enforcement officials during their time of crisis, these demonstrators also denounced the injustices committed against Rodney King and the verdict that had reinforced the current power structure.

The following twenty-three-year-old, second generation female activist describes how the demonstrations had affected her political consciousness by showing her for the first time what Korean Americans can do within the community.

But then I remember that one day I woke up and my parents were like, "We're gonna go into L.A. into Koreatown." And I was like, "What the hell's wrong? What if the riot is still going on?" Cause you weren't really sure how long it would go on. But they drove me and my brother into the city and then we saw all the burned shops. They didn't even tell us where we were going, but they were taking us to a peace rally when Korean Americans were having all these peace rallies. So we went to one of them and I actually saw my parents feel secure in standing up for themselves. You know they came with their friends and that was the first time I heard Korean American speakers that were actually speaking on behalf of the community, and very strong figures like Angela Oh and you know all these other people. That was the first time I saw her speak. As a high school student, you never see that before, because you never had like a Korean American teacher or Korean American anything except like maybe your pastor, your priest and your parents. And they've never really stood up for themselves, so that was kind of a defining moment. And so I grabbed my little sign that said, "Honk for Peace" and we all sang, "We Shall Overcome."

The interviewee also explains how the civil unrest became the first opportunity for younger people to develop a greater sense of political awareness from their personal experiences, which had been largely absent from the home and the church before the riots.

Organizational politics itself has been thoroughly transformed by new questions about the "American Dream," the growing presence of second generation Korean Americans, and an overall consensus on the need for greater political involvement in mainstream society. For this reason, the *Korea Times* appealed to Korean American leaders to put aside their political differences in the interests of establishing a single Korean American organization to represent the needs of the Korean American community. More importantly, the riots and the mass demonstrations had a transformative effect on the political consciousness of young second generation Korean Americans, many of whom would become more actively involved in community work in the aftermath. For the first time in their lives, the second generation could empathize with the plight of their parents' generation whom they felt had not only suffered the trauma of the rioters' attacks but had also been abandoned and abused by mainstream America. American-born Korean youth wrote letters to major English-language Korean newspapers, expressing their sense of solidarity with first generation Koreans.

At the same time, to state that the Korean American community became united as a community would be a gross overgeneralization of what occurred in the period after the civil unrest. As Angela Oh, one second generation Korean American who would gain enormous status in mainstream politics, remarked in an interview with the *Los Angeles Times*, "In terms of the people that were directly affected and suffered losses, I feel a tremendous amount of frustration because there was a very brief window of time in which I think that ethnic Koreans from all walks of life came together and then—as happens in all communities, I think—there was a breakdown" (Hall 1997). As sign of this political fragmentation, an emergency meeting of Korean American leaders called together by the Korean-American Federation (KAF) a month after the riots disintegrated into heated debates as the presiding members struggled over the political visions of the postriot community (Park 2001).

Just as the riots helped Korean Americans of different backgrounds to realize how their fate was intertwined, it also made the more politically active members aware of more profound differences over time, in terms of what their ultimate goals should be, how they should go about achieving them, and who would be the ones to do so. Internal conflicts were accompanied by ideological shifts in the power structures of the ethnic enclave. As younger generations of leadership gained a greater voice in ethnic and mainstream politics, they brought with them new political perspectives on a variety of issues in the post-civil-unrest era. At the same time, not all 1.5/second generation organizations aligned themselves in opposition to immigrant interests and values, nor did they come to a consensus on many of the issues to arise during this period. In particular, the community's response to two controversial issues in the post-civil-unrest years demonstrates the fluctuating nature of ethnic political solidarity within the Korean American community.

First, tensions with the African American community resurfaced when Korean merchants tried to rebuild damaged liquor stores after the riots. The concentration of liquor stores in inner-city neighborhoods had been a sensitive issue for African American residents and leaders long before the advent of the 1992 civil unrest. Inner-city areas such as South Central had attracted an unusually high concentration of liquor stores, which has been the subject of great concern among residents and leaders of the African American community.[5] From this vantage point, the oversaturation of liquor stores in marginalized neighborhoods was partly accountable for increasing rates of crime and alcoholism within the community. In addition, liquor stores were generally known to be magnets for graffiti, trash, and negative elements such as gangs, prostitutes, and homeless, which decreased the overall quality of life for neighborhood residents. According to the California Black Commission on Alcoholism, the proportion of liquor stores in South Central relative to the population was nearly double that of White-dominated neighborhoods in the 1980s (Light and Bonacich 1988).

In this light, the destruction of approximately 200 liquor stores during the 1992 civil unrest provided an opportune moment for African American activists to contest the reconstruction of such businesses within minority neighborhoods. Needless to say, the overwhelming majority of these stores were owned by Korean immigrants—a situation that caused enormous friction between the two communities to arise once again. Led by local African American politicians Mark Ridley-Thomas, Rita Walters, and Marguerite Archie-Hudson, African American leaders and liberal White and Latino politicians spearheaded a "Campaign to Rebuild South Central Without Liquor Stores." The organizers were able to implement a conditional use variance process that would require business owners to undergo a public hearing before reopening liquor stores and to submit to several provisions including limited store hours, uniformed security guards, and parking lots for customers. The required conditions proved to be too much for business owners so that less than a dozen of the 175 Korean-owned liquor stores were able to reopen two years later (*Los Angeles Times*, July 21, 1994).

While some business owners agreed that there were too many liquor stores in these communities, many felt that it was unfair to revoke their fundamental right to engage in free commercial enterprise, especially without adequate compensation. Aside from the costs of relocating and retraining, the greatest expense came from the loss of liquor licenses, the average value of which ranged from $10,000 to $15,000, according to Ong and Hee (1993). As one 1.5 generation proponent of this movement argues:

> Well it's not fair. Let's say your liquor store completely burned, and then you try to rebuild but they're saying no, you have to reapply. Now they're using all these you know hearings and then protest to stop you. So it's like, you lose your liquor store but they successfully block you in rebuilding it. So that's not fair. They can not just issue it and then tomorrow, after you spend an entire tens of thousands of money that you have invested and now you come to them, oh you cannot do it? They invest because you said it's okay. Now you say it's not okay. Hey, then pay me back whatever amount of money that I've wasted for this project. They say no, you just cannot do it. How unfair!

As another second generation advocate argues to the *Korea Central Daily*, the incident highlighted the need for Korean Americans to stop relying on political donations alone to attract the support of mainstream politicians, but also, to exert its political influence by organizing against politicians who go against the interests of the Korean American community (Min 1994).

Finding support within the ranks of the Republican Party, conservative factions within the Korean American community, including both immigrant and 1.5/second generation leaders, mobilized together to override the new city council ordinances by appealing to the state legislature. With the assistance of

Republican Paul Horcher, the KAGRO and the 1.5/second generation Korean American Republican Association (KARA) drafted the AB1974 bill, which would essentially overturn the city ordinance. In the end, the group failed to pass the bill but was able to reach a modest compromise with the help of the Asian Pacific Planning Council. In it, the city council would agree to allocate $260,000 toward a program to help former liquor store owners convert to laundromat businesses (*Los Angeles Times*, July 21, 1994). Still, not all Korean Americans were satisfied with the resolution.

Indeed, the Korean American community was not united in its position on the liquor store issue. While aware of the sacrifice that would be required by Korean business owners in giving up the liquor trade, some 1.5/second generation Korean Americans also understood the deeper social meaning that this issue had for the African American community and recognized the futility of resisting the movement to prevent their reestablishment. The alliance of other 1.5/second generation Korean American leaders with an African American-led coalition to convert liquor stores into laundromats sparked tensions with the ethnic elite. In their defense, one second generation male activist reasons:

> Now what the first generation's understanding of that was that they sold us out. Now the problem with that logic is that they're not understanding the political landscape, okay? Of course you could say that you could practice any type of business that you want but it does affect the Black community. There's no doubt about it. Now their understanding of the political landscape is that well, there's no way that the Koreans are gonna win. We got three Black city council people, okay? It's not gonna happen. So if you know the Korean community's not gonna win, then at least we should try to help Koreans set up other businesses. And that's a very key thing to understand when dealing with first generation: when they don't have the political understanding, it's all about what's right or what's wrong. And sometimes, that's not really the best way to go about things.

The above passage reveals the way in which the 1.5/second generation members in support of liquor store conversion were situated in opposition to immigrant leaders based on a broader understanding of American politics. In particular, it demonstrates how the political and historical understanding of some Americanized Koreans may collide with the capitalist values of first generation ethnic elite groups.

The second area of controversy to emerge during this period involved the distribution of donations collected from various fund-raising campaigns across the nation and from South Korea. Koreans from the United States to homeland Korea empathized with the plight of their brothers and sisters in Los Angeles who had suffered tremendously during the rioting. As a result, the ethnic community was not only able to provide emotional and political support but also raise significant financial contributions for victims as well. Almost ten million dollars in donations were raised from individuals to churches to large Korean corporations.

However, the money garnered from this national and international act of solidarity again led to internal conflict among the political leadership over how to use and distribute the funds. The Korean Riot Victims' Association (KRVA), one of the organizations designated to collect and allocate the funds, had a difficult time getting intermediary organizations like the media and the Consulate General to release the money they had accumulated for this relief effort. In addition, community leaders struggled over the appropriate criterion they should use for allocating funds to riot victims since some had suffered only minor damages during the riots while others lost their businesses altogether. Funding disputes compelled several individuals who had been excluded from the final list to seek redress through the courts, which ultimately led to 200 of these merchants being appropriated $2,500 each (Min 1996). Leaders of several professional associations felt that part of the donations should be used to set up a community center that would have a more long-term impact on the Korean American community. In opposition to those who felt the entirety should go to riot victims, the organizational leaders were able to set aside $1.8 million by April 1993 to begin a community center (Min 1996).

Another area of dispute focused on the fates of hundreds of employees who lost their wages and in some cases their jobs as a result of the riots. According to one KIWA organizer, the people in charge of the funds made a general announcement that they would be distributing funds to riot victims but did not inform the community that they would not be giving any to workers. As he describes it:

So thousands of victims showed up and they didn't even announce the policy earlier, so all the workers who lost their job were told, only criteria they had was [if] you're a worker, you don't get it. And so they get pissed off. Most of them gave up you know, said screw you, it's not that much money, I could live without it. About fifty, sixty die-hard workers said, no way, this is unjust. We want our equal share. We're victim too. When people gave money, they wanted to be given out to all peoples, not just storeowners. Well, the worker who lose his or her job, now have no more livelihood. So it was grossly unfair but it was expected because until that point, workers had no say in any of this.

In response, KIWA organized forty-five workers to demand their share of the postriot funding and won about $109,000 in total. The movement to secure funds for victimized workers was a major turning point for KIWA and workers in general since it symbolized the first time that the needs and problems of workers were made publicly known to the larger Korean American community. Consequently, more than fifty workers were granted their share of the postriot donations, yet not without resistance and growing resentment among members of the ethnic elite.

In the early period of Korean American history, the three branches of the ethnic elite were able to dominate enclave politics as a result of their stronghold over the social, financial, and human resources of the ethnic community. However, the Kwangju Rebellions, the Korean-Black conflicts, and the 1992 civil unrest exposed the vulnerable position of the immigrant elite in American society and opened the doors to a new wave of leadership among the 1.5/second generation who had the language skills, cultural knowledge, and institutional networks to articulate the needs of the Korean American community to mainstream power holders. The perceived plight of Koreans in America and their isolation from mainstream society renewed a strong sense of ethnic consciousness among younger Korean Americans. At the same time, the new wave of leadership brought with it diverse political perspectives and ideologies about the situation of the Korean American community that oftentimes clashed with those of the traditional ethnic elite, leading to periods of conflict amid ethnic solidarity.

As opposed to creating a clear-cut divide between the new and the old, these events underscore the diverse political perspectives that shape relations between the newly emerging leadership and the traditional immigrant elite. Despite their steadily declining status in the new era, the immigrant elite still continue to exert some influence over the political development of this evolving power structure, because they control the people and resources of the institutionally complete enclave community. The next few chapters will take a closer look at how 1.5/second generation organizations have strategically adapted to the immigrant ethnic elite and how they have achieved their divergent political agenda based on their unequal relations with the ethnic community and mainstream society.

5 The Politics of Incorporation and Marginalization Today

IN THE AFTERMATH OF THE 1992 CIVIL UNREST, ethnic organizations old and new have struggled to reposition themselves in order to take advantage of political opportunities both within the ethnic community and mainstream power structures. On the one hand, 1.5/second generation organizations have felt compelled to challenge the conservative homeland orientation of the immigrant leadership and recenter organizational structures on the diverse needs of the Korean American community. On the other hand, they must also decide how to do this while maintaining linkages with the traditional elite, who continue to dominate the major resources and support of the Koreatown immigrant community. Efforts to accommodate conflicting agendas to ethnic power structures have laid the foundations for fluctuating cycles of intergenerational conflict and cooperation.

In this sense, scholarly focus on the generational divide only goes so far in understanding what has taken place since the 1992 civil unrest. The lines of political conflict and cooperation arise not only from cultural differences between immigrant and more Americanized ethnic leadership but also from the scarce and unequal distribution of resources within the ethnic community, which ironically gives the leadership a reason to band together. Despite intermittent tensions, immigrant and 1.5/second generation leadership have struggled to find ways to work with one another in an effort to address the social and political needs of their ethnic constituencies. The resulting expansion of the community's resource base has also opened up new opportunities for organizations to represent marginalized and underserved segments of the ethnic enclave population.

This book describes the reorganization of contemporary political structures around multiple bases of ethnic political solidarity that do not simply reflect generational differences between the "assimilated" and the "unassimi-lated," but rather, specific political initiatives based on diverse relationships with the ethnic elite in the post-1992 era. Issues arising from the Los Ange-les civil unrest initially triggered conflicts between the old and new guard, as the 1.5/second generation attempted to assert its position within existing power structures; yet in the process, both sides began to discover the potential benefits of working with one another. This goal of accommodation has also changed the ways organizations relate to one another based on new political roles and hierarchical relationships. While intergenerational relationships are an integral feature of ethnic politics, this chapter reveals internal heterogene-ity and divided political loyalties among 1.5/second generation organizations themselves, which must compete over scarce resources, conflicting political viewpoints, and unequal status within the ethnic structures of Koreatown. Because of continuing power differences, bridging organizations have forged new interracial partnerships with local organizations that allow them to over-come the limitations of working within a geographically circumscribed com-munity dominated by the interests of the ethnic elite.

At the Crossroads of Intergenerational Politics

Increasing ideological tensions among generational leadership in the post-1992 era preceded a broader shift within the larger power structures of the ethnic enclave community. Throughout the Korean-Black conflicts and the 1992 civil unrest, the first generation leadership whose structures were bounded by culture, language, and homeland ties was unable to deal with the myriad of problems faced by the Korean American community. As explained, the traditional power structures of Koreatown were completely disconnected from the institutions of mainstream society—a status that set the stage for the 1992 riots. At the height of turmoil, the ethnic elite leadership lacked the skills, knowledge, and networks to either address or challenge the claims of other racial and ethnic groups, the political visibility to demand support from American power holders, or the resources to work to address the cultural and structural roots of the problem by themselves.

In the months following the riots, the Korean-American Federation (KAF) received harsh criticism from those who felt it had done little to help actively with the rebuilding process or represent and publicize their grievances to out-side groups. While the general socioeconomic resources of the ethnic elite gave them claim to political power *within* the structures of the ethnic enclave community, they lacked the skills and resources they needed to deal with out-side groups. Although the Seoul government would provide some support in the form of relief funds, it was not in a position to apply direct pressure on the U.S. government or lobby on behalf of the political interests of Korean Americans.

In their place, a new generation of leaders and organizations positioned themselves to vocalize the needs and grievances of the ethnic community to the public, the media, the government, and mainstream institutions across the nation. Thus, the 1992 riots transformed ethnic politics by directing main-stream attention toward 1.5/second generation Korean American leaders best able to articulate the concerns of the ethnic population. During the rebuilding processes, this new wave of community leaders became the intermediary be-tween the immigrant population and mainstream institutions by employing English-language skills, greater knowledge of American politics and culture, and their outside networks to demand better political representation for Ko-rean Americans.

As a result of greater sensitivity to the plight of racial minority groups, these leaders were also better able and more willing to forge coalitions with other Asian American and minority communities through organizations such as the Asian Pacific Americans for a New Los Angeles (APANLA), the Black-Korean Alliance (BKA), and the Multicultural Collaborative (MCC). APANLA for instance came about through the efforts of Asian American leaders who were demanding greater Asian American representation in Re-build Los Angeles (RLA). MCC also began as a multiethnic effort to address some of the structural roots of interethnic conflicts that were raised during the Korean-Black conflicts. With the active assistance of Korean American leaders like Bong Hwan Kim and Marcia Choo, these Asian American orga-nizations used their linkages with the mayor's office and city council to help Korean immigrant merchants recover some of their losses and call for better Korean American representation in local institutional structures. One of the outcomes of these coordinated efforts was the hiring of a Korean American, K. Connie Kang, as a reporter for the *Los Angeles Times*.

Another distinguishing feature of the new leadership has been its greater inclusion of women and immigrant workers in both leadership and staff positions, which represents a significant departure from the elite male-dominated political culture of the past. Women have figured more promi-nently in the new organizational structures of Koreatown as individual advocates, community workers, board members, and leading representatives of various ethnic organizations. They also constitute at least half, if not the majority, of staff members in many of these newer organizations. In fact, it was Angela Oh, a second generation Korean American lawyer, who became one of the first prominent spokespersons to articulate the frustrations of the Korean immigrant community on a nationwide level. Her debut appearance on the TV program *Nightline* marked the first time a representative from the community was able to vocalize the plight of Korean Americans on national media (Park 1998). Oh would later serve as an Asian American representative for President Clinton's Advisory Panel of the Presidential Initiative on Race. In addition to Oh, both liberal and conservative Korean women leaders such as Laura Jeon (Korean Health, Education, Information and Research Center [KHEIR]), Susan Lee (Korean American Family Service Center [KAFSC]), and Marcia Choo (Asian Pacific American Dispute Resolution Center) have made their way into the top leadership positions of several major organizations, although proportionally their presence in top-ranking positions is still somewhat disproportional.

Although these leaders generally recognized the need for greater political empowerment and solidarity within the community, the process of coming to a consensus took tremendous effort on the part of both the immigrant and 1.5/ second generations. In the years immediately following the riots, first generation organizations began to acknowledge the potential benefits of utilizing the political expertise of 1.5/second generational leaders on outside matters and to this end attempted to incorporate some of them into their organizations. In the case of the KAF, however, this effort proved to be futile when differences in cultural perspectives and the politics of operating an organization resulted in bitter struggles between the two sides. According to one second generation leader, the tensions began when discrepancies over finances compelled the new 1.5/second generation members to question the organization's president on financial matters, who taking this as a challenge to his authority, ended up kicking them out on questionable pretenses.

The rigid, autocratic approach of first generation leaders has been a continuing source of tension for 1.5/second generation members, who are accustomed to the democratic style of operating American organizations. As one 1.5 generation leader describes it, immigrant leaders place emphasis on preserving personal relationships, while the second generation is more concerned with cultivating working relationships. Furthermore, most 1.5/second generation leaders do not subscribe to the deferential values of Korean immigrants, arguing that they are too easy to criticize the hard work of second generation leaders while actually doing little of the grunt work themselves. One second generation activist complained, "How do you work with the first generation organizations where their understanding of 'let's work together' means 'I will work the whole thing and you just do the work for me?'" In response, the ethnic elite defends its rights to dictate the agenda based on the Confucian-rooted belief that money determines control and legitimacy in the political arena. A 1.5 generation Korean American explains that the first generation mindset is such that "When you do most of the work and when you raise most of the money, you make most of the decisions." In turn, newer immigrant leaders interpret the assertive, critical, or informal mannerisms of younger, native-born Korean Americans toward older immigrants as signs of insolence or at best ignorance about their cultural roots and cherished value systems.

The issue of political representation has become a particularly poignant issue for the Korean American community with the increasing prominence of 1.5/second generation leaders within mainstream politics. In the years following the civil unrest, government agencies began to streamline substantial resources into 1.5/second generation organizations. This unequal funding allocation fed resentment among the old guard, who felt that the younger generation were completely disconnected from the immigrant-dominated community and were profiting from postrecovery and social service funds meant to help immigrants. Thus, the key role that these leaders played in bridging the Korean American community with mainstream society has not always been greeted with a warm reception.

An example of this tension arose when Angela Oh's invitation to the White House elicited a critical letter to President Clinton from the head of the Korean American Grocers Association (KAGRO) which read among other things, "Those who speak English and acted as our spokespersons of our community such as Ms. Oh could not convey our opinion adequately to the outside world because they do not speak Korean" (*Los Angeles Times*, April 29, 1996, A-1). The content of the letter was later retracted in a second letter that attributed the misunderstanding to "language barriers."

However, disenchantment with the political representations of English-speaking Korean Americans emerged once more in a series of scathing letters written by a well-known Korean staff member of the *Korea Times* (Lee 1997a, 1997b). In it, she critiqued English-speaking Korean Americans for taking advantage of their mainstream political status, which she claimed was achieved on the backs of riot victims. As an example of their opportunistic tactics, she referred to a conference that was organized by the University of California Los Angeles (UCLA) Asian American Studies Center, the Korean Immigrant Workers Advocates (KIWA), and the Korean Youth and Community Center (KYCC) to discuss the 1992 tragedy in Los Angeles. She described the conference as "a show without the main cast" because it did not include riot victims, and she attacked their simultaneous use of the word *riot* in Korean and *civil unrest* in English. In the *Korea Times* she stated bitterly:

> Korean victims who lost their businesses believed that those who looted and burnt down their life-long investments were not average citizens who stood up against social injustice but rather hoodlums and vandals. The fact that English-speaking Korean Americans use terms other than riot to refer to the economic holocaust indicates how removed they are from the community and how unqualified they are to deal with this most pressing Korean American issue...Korean American community leaders and intellectuals...who intentionally avoid calling Sa-ee-gu a riot, are traitors to their people and history. (Lee, 1997a, 3–4)

The letters argued in no unclear terms that political representation required accountability to the immigrants who had been most devastated by the riots, without which younger Korean Americans became mere opportunists and "traitors" to their ethnic community.

In response, Angela Oh delivered an impassioned speech at the conference declaring that 1.5/second generation leaders would persist in doing what they could to establish a Korean American presence in mainstream America and not be put off by accusations about political opportunism and disingenuous motives. Interestingly, Edward Park (2001) finds that this exchange, although highlighting tensions within the community, could also be interpreted as an implicit affirmation that the 1.5/second generation should and would prove its devotion to the immigrant community and commit to working together despite political and generational differences. As he states, Oh's speech avoided the narrow tactic of promoting a liberal agenda by focusing on 1.5/second generation commitment to the Korean American community, thereby taking "the moral high ground of inclusion rather than appearing as either a community gatekeeper or a partisan advocate (302)." Her presentation was met with a standing ovation by almost all 1.5/second generation attendees, regardless of their political leaning.

Unequal access to government funding has also been a source of inter-generational tension. In an effort to find remedies for problems that ignited the 1992 civil unrest, governmental agencies funneled massive funding into community organizations that had prior links to the government, hence re-affirming the rising status of new ethnic organizations that were most likely to have these connections than their first generation predecessors. The situation generated more resentment among immigrant leaders, who claimed that these so-called "community representatives" used the money to develop their own organizations rather than assisting smaller immigrant organizations that "lack the administrative savvy and connections to compete for funding" (*Los Angeles Times*, May 13, 1994, B-3). By being out of touch with these organizations, they argued, Americanized Koreans were not capable of adequately representing the interests of the immigrant-majority community and were thus not deserving of this funding.

Yet despite the growing political influence of the 1.5/second generation leadership since the 1992 civil unrest, first generation leaders still maintain a stronghold over political affairs within the Korean American community due to the numerical predominance of immigrants and their general control over the socioeconomic resources of the ethnic enclave community. In spite of intergenerational struggles, most of my 1.5/second generation interviewees have emphasized that the two generations must ultimately come together if they want to address the problems that plague the community.

When asked why the younger generations still need to work with first generation immigrant leaders despite their newly found political power in mainstream society, the following 1.5/second generation male community workers focused on the need to connect with immigrants who constitute the majority of the Korean American community.

> First generation community *is* the community. We're there to service them. We're not there in spite of them; we're there because of them, you know? I didn't realize that before. I thought we were just on our own and then I realized that through [my] youth work, it had everything to do with their parents. And it's their parents that made up this whole community. So without really having a capacity to work with first generation, we're not effective. We're just a very isolated small piece that really doesn't matter.

> Because they're definitely part of the community. I think KAGRO [the Korean American Grocers Association], no matter how they operate, they do really good work with the merchants. And I know that there's a lot of other first

generation organizations that are doing really, really good work. You gotta give them respect for that. So you definitely have to work with them. A lot of our parents' generation, they're storeowners. A lot of our parents' generation have very different issues. The thing is that the 1.5, second generation, they have the political know-how, they know what to do. The first generation don't.

Another 1.5 generation female program manager reaffirms these assertions but also emphasizes that representing the ethnic community is a necessity in a society that views groups along racial and ethnic lines.

I think politically that it would be wiser for the subsequent generations to be mindful of the first generation, because I think that only when you can be truly community-based and speak to your community as a whole can you have any validity out there, partially because U.S. is a racist society and we are being seen in racial and ethnic terms and we cannot avoid that. I'm not gonna be able to walk out there and say I'm American and somebody not questioning me where are you from *really*?

Second generation leaders acknowledge that first generation organizational leaders have a greater understanding of these types of immigrant issues than younger Korean Americans.

The first and second interviewees also argue that the two generations are dependent on each other in another way. One dimension to this is pragmatic in that the first generation has the money whereas the second generation has the skills and the "political know-how." Although diminished in recent years, immigrant organizations, churches, and entrepreneurs still constitute the "ethnic elite" bases within the community as a result of their access to the socioeconomic resources and human capital of the community. For this reason, the executive director of one 1.5/second generation organization and a first generation Korean American scholar both affirm,

So when you think of Koreatown, you really have to bring up small businesses. We have thousands and thousands of small businesses here and I think that's our strength. But at the same time, small businesses would be more united if our community were more united in our vision. I think this would be much more powerful community. See we have a lot of resources here. We have a good combination of first generation as well as you know second generation people, not living in the community but still here working together. So we've come a long way.

The second generation depends on the first generation because basically financially they are not yet strong to stand on their own. Most of the second generation community organizations like KYCC and KAC [Korean American Coalition], they need support from their own. First generation lack those kind of skills, but they have that very strong ethnic identity and love of the community. In that sense, you cannot beat that. Second generation has skills, but they lack the passion for the community. The first generation has the passion, but they lack the skills.

Thus, the first generation has direct linkages to the resources of Koreatown community, while the 1.5/second generation are able to draw on mainstream resources and act as political representatives to American society. By working together, they would be able to complement each other's resources and different sources of empowerment.

Another theme that emerges from the second passage involves the different types of relationships the immigrant and native-born generation have with the ethnic community they each represent and service. Although the claim that the first generation is more committed to the ethnic community has been hotly debated, what is important to draw from these passages is that leaders from each generation foster a different type of connection to the ethnic community they represent. Part of this may have to do with the fact that second generation members are more residentially scattered and acculturated into the individualist culture of American society so that they are likely to have weaker connections to the ethnic community than immigrant leaders. At the same time, they recognize the need for Korean Americans to garner broader political support outside the ethnic community. In contrast, the first generation can claim to have a deeper connection with the community because of their common experiences as immigrants, their collectivist orientation as Asian immigrants, and their dependency on ethnic-based networks and institutions in a society that is not always mindful or aware of their interests. As a result, it is easier for immigrant leaders to mobilize people and resources within the ethnic community.

The following anecdote by one twenty-nine-year-old, second generation community leader demonstrates how the different capabilities of both generations can work to the overall benefit of the Korean American community:

I remember way back when welfare reform was going on, we had a task force in the Korean community. We had first generation and 1.5/second generation involved with this. And basically what happened was that the first generation said that we don't know what we need to do. So it was the second generation that came up with the strategy, okay? There was five of us that came up with a strategy. You know what happens? The senior citizens, they went out and got all these petitions signed. They got these letters signed and they came back with almost like three thousand letters, you know. So I was very surprised. To me, it blew my mind away. But that's basically it—that the senior citizens, they'll work really hard because welfare reform can impact them. Back then, when they thought that the SSI was gonna get taken away and if the SSI is taken away, then Medical gets taken away too. So they had a vested interest in this. Um, that the younger generation we came with the plan and the first generation, they implemented it.

In addition to the importance of mobilizing on the different strengths of both sides, the excerpt makes another revelation about the interests of senior citizens, who comprise a significant percentage of residents in Koreatown. Direct interest in the political issue mobilizes these first generation leaders in a way that could not happen for younger, suburban Korean Americans disconnected from the day-to-day realities of living in an immigrant enclave community.

For some organizations, mainstream institutions may offer more in the form of financial resources, particularly in the post-civil-unrest era. Nevertheless, ethnic-based networks contribute to institutional development by conferring upon organizations other valuable forms of support, including political legitimacy and community backing, immigrant clientele upon which their programs depend, and financial resources that are not subject to strict federal or institutional regulations. Geoethnic organizations that directly service the neighborhood community must also maintain strong relations with the local immigrant population in order to receive federal grants and develop a strong clientele base. With the out-migration of native-born Korean Americans to outlying areas, the majority of clientele come from the immigrant-dominated population of Koreatown. A second generation youth program director notes, "When the mainstream government thinks about community, they mostly think about geographic community, not necessarily the ethnic community." When there is a disjuncture between the two, bridging organizations must find ways to ally with those institutions that represent those immigrant interests.

Because the more disadvantaged segments of the Korean American population are foreign born, organizations like KYCC and KIWA would be unable to justify their social service contracts or even their political mission without some support from the first generation. For this reason, a former executive director of KYCC notes:

> [Organizations] need community backup in terms of moral and financial support in addition to the community grant. And see, if you're getting the grant, you also have to show that you're getting a certain amount of financial support from the community, and you have to show that 20 percent of your total budget comes from the community and 80 percent from the grant. I think the grant people look at it more favorably instead of getting 100 percent from the grant.

In addition, several interviewees have remarked that the limitations of government contracts motivate them to seek other sources of financial support within the Korean immigrant community. As one social service worker notes, "I think a lot of times the way the program's designed is not culturally sensitive to the Korean American community. Some of the things that [funders] want us to do with our clients is very difficult—you know like financial screening. Koreans hate that."

Moreover, the ethnic elite itself has undergone tremendous changes and made some adjustments internally in order to accommodate to the new political climate of Koreatown. In 1993, the *Korea Central Daily* (Park 1993) featured a front-page article discussing the major generational shifts that had taken place in Korean immigrant organizations, as evidenced by the growing number of 1.5 generation Korean Americans working as board members, executive directors, managers, staff and interns. New bilingual and bicultural leaders among the ethnic elite have helped existing immigrant associations to pay greater attention to local issues and foster relationships and projects with groups outside the Korean American community. KAGRO for instance was active in protesting the revocation of liquor licenses after the riots and city laws that require liquor business owners to implement expensive security measures in their stores. The Korean Federation changed its name to the Korean-American Federation [KAF] in 1996, elected bilingual/bicultural Korean Americans to its presidency, and organized a variety of crosscultural and mediation programs with outside groups in the years following the riots. In addition, coalitions between Korean immigrant leaders and Black residents such as the Koreatown and West Adams Public Safety Association (KOWAPSA) came about only as a result of the shifting political climate of postriot Koreatown.

In the end, the lines of factionalism are not clearly drawn between the first and 1.5/second generation as would be predicted by assimilationist theory. Instead, interest groups have emerged along multiple lines of stratification, particularly among newer organizations that have arisen in the aftermath of the riots. The executive director of one prominent bridging organization says, "In the beginning, they criticized us as elitist group and geon-bang-jin [arrogant] young people but now, I think they appreciate us, what we have done. Whenever we do projects there, they're 100 percent behind us." Intergenerational relations are hence characterized by periods of conflict and cooperation in which the same immigrant leadership that struggled with certain American-born leaders in the past may find themselves working together for the same political cause. For example, collaborative projects between the Korean Resource Center (KRC) and the KAF in recent years would have been inconceivable only ten years ago. In fact, it is rare that you will find a major 1.5/second generation community-based organization that does not incorporate or collaborate with immigrants as advisors, board members, clientele, or organizational allies.

Even organizations that seem to butt heads with the ethnic elite on a wide range of issues can claim strong roots within a particular segment of the immigrant population. Because these immigrants come from more marginal and invisible segments of the population, the existing leadership does not always recognize their presence and accuses these organizations of detaching themselves from the immigrant community. The most obvious instance of this would be KIWA, whose networks extend way beyond the reaches of the ethnic community but whose organizational structure firmly centers on the needs and interests of Korean and Latino immigrant workers. Other examples of crossgenerational solidarity include organizations such as Chingusai of Los Angeles and Korean Coalition for Lesbian, Bisexual, Gay, and Transgender Rights, which also boasts a strong membership of first generation gays and lesbians, according to one active member. Leaders of the Korean American Republican Association (KARA) claim that because of the strong liberal bent of 1.5/second generation organizations in Koreatown, some of its staunchest allies come from the older generation of Korean immigrants who lived through the Korean War. Conversely, other efforts by native-born leadership to address urgent immigrant-related issues without widespread support from the immigrant community, such as the BKA in the 1980s, ultimately fail to produce any substantive outcomes.

Important political events also play a role in bringing together a wide mix of immigrant and 1.5/second generation Korean American organizations, many of whom had denounced one another in the past. One example of such collaboration took place after the suicide of Mr. M. S. Lee, a Korean immigrant who had allegedly been harassed and discriminated by co-workers and employers at a Japanese corporation called Nippon in the years before his death. Recognizing the urgency of the situation, a conglomerate of immigrant and native-born leaders joined forces to publicize the tragedy in ethnic and mainstream newspapers and organize protests outside the company. A twenty-three-year-old, second generation organizer just starting out with KIWA commented on how this experience taught her how to work with the diverse leaders of the Korean American community: "M. S. Lee brought together the Korean American community as a whole and not just the progressive Korean Americans. So I think the one thing I learned was really how to deal with people and how to work effectively in that type of coalition. Because you know everybody's in there for a different reason. We might have the same goal, but then there's personality issues too."

Although not without its tensions, KIWA worked alongside church leaders, immigrant organizational representatives, and more conservative 1.5/second generation leadership, with whom they had struggled with in the past. The contribution that each organization brought to the table was also especially telling. KIWA was responsible for making brochures, translating M. S. Lee's journals and suicide note, manning the registration tables, and arranging protests in front of the Nippon's corporate building. Immigrant elite leaders from the KAF and the Council of Korean Churches and more prominent organizational representatives including the KAC took center stage at Lee's wake, protest demonstration, and accompanying funeral by leading the public eulogies, making presentations to the press, and communicating with family members of the deceased. Though it is apparent the allocation of duties was uneven, both sides came together to work for a common cause and did what each did best.

Similar political issues such as Proposition 187, Koreatown redistricting, Korean reunification, voter registration drives, and the "comfort women" issue[1] have helped to foster provisional alliances between the ethnic elite and 1.5/second generation leadership not commonly known to work together in the past. Despite the significance of interorganizational alliances, immigrant and second generation leadership have been better known to collaborate with one another on a more informal level, because such flexible relationships are easier to sustain in the face of cultural differences. In this sense, 1.5 generation leaders, or those who were partly educated in Korea and partly in the United States, are especially crucial in mediating relations between traditional and newly emerging organizations. Because of their bilingual abilities and socialization in both Korean and American culture, 1.5 generation leaders are more aware of how mere differences in communication style and cultural perspectives can cause intergenerational tensions to seem bigger than they are. Organizational mediators must also be aware of internal immigrant politics down to the details of knowing which immigrant leaders they should not seat next to whom at fundraisers because of past and current rivalry.

One such mediator in KARA states that overcoming these minor obstacles allowed them to come together around the more important interests they had in common:

> I tried to communicate with the second generation and first generation how we sometimes misunderstand due to the miscommunication. I had to tell Korean second generation, listen. These first generation, what's important is we gotta show our respect toward to them, because they're elderly and we're younger people. Just like how you respect your parents. So when they come, whatever they say, show them respect. It's not that they're angry at you, but they tend to talk loud. That's how they are and it's very normal to them, we just have to understand their culture. I go to first generation and say, you know second generation Korean Americans these young people, you know they don't like when people tell them what to do. So you kind of have to respect them in that term, try to communicate, you know just think of them as your grandchildren or your sons and daughters then it's gonna be good. So these are the main points that each party has to understand. It's not the language that they'll unite together. It's the value and then great communication skill. And because of that, we had no problem.

Similarly, another fifty-three-year-old immigrant board member who works for a second generation organization explained how the organization relied on him to negotiate relations with the immigrant community.

> Yeah, I submitted a resignation but they don't let me go, because among those board directors, I guess they choose me as one first generation guy who speaks good Korean and can relate to Korean community, the il-se [first-generation]

community. So they don't let me out. But at the same time, I found out my role whenever there's an issue with the press, there's an issue with Korean Consul General, you know the so-to-speak Korea side, I could manage. *If there are too many second generation only getting together, then they don't know the problems of the first generation.* The second generation don't read Korean newspaper and they don't watch Korean TV and they don't aware how people move, what they thinking, what they done. And local Korean politics, they don't know, I'm the one [who's] supposed to share and say, look this is what happened. And in order to raise funds and deal with the media, I know who to talk, where to go, but sometimes they don't know. [Korean statements in *italics*]

Indeed, younger generation, lower-level staff members are only vaguely aware of immigrant support and participation in some cases, because 1.5 generation staff members higher up on the organizational chain tend to take care of the logistics of dealing with the immigrant leadership. Yet as I shall argue, the extent and nature of this collaboration varies depending on how they choose to navigate traditional ethnic power structures.

Organizational Hierarchies

As stated, one of the consequences of the newly found attention in the post-civil-unrest era was the establishment and strengthening of organizational networks outside the ethnic community. The sudden availability of mainstream funds in the aftermath of the 1992 civil unrest did much to facilitate the expansion and specialization of ethnic organizations within the Korean American community. The greater the resources, the greater the capacity of ethnic organizational structures to cater to an internally diverse population, including marginalized groups within the Koreatown community. Drawing on both ethnic and mainstream resources, 1.5/second generation ethnic organizations have been able to broaden their programs to include activities that go beyond the traditional entrepreneurial, cultural, and mutual aid focus of their predecessors. The diversification of ethnic organizational structures has helped to offset some of the constraints of homogeneous immigrant organizations by offering alternative spaces for political expression and new opportunities for mainstream exposure. Indeed, one of the difficulties that the KAF faced had been in trying to do everything for everyone, even as more specialized organizations with more resources began to emerge within the community.

Table 5.1 Table of select 1.5 and second generation-led organizations in Koreatown, Los Angeles

Type	Organization	Year of founding
Political	Korean American Republican Association (KARA)	1992
	Korean American Democratic Committee (KADC)	1992
	Korean American Coalition (KAC)	1983
Advocacy	Korean Immigrant Workers Advocates (KIWA)	1992
	Korean Youth and Student Union (KYSU)	1992
	Korean Resource Center (KRC)	1983
	Young Koreans United (YKU)	1984
Social service	Korean Youth and Community Center (KYCC)	1975
	Korean Health, Education, Information and Research Center (KHEIR)	1986
	Korean American Family Service Center (KAFSC)	1983
Coalitions	Korean American Inter-Agency Council (KAIAC)	1994
	Black-Korean Alliance (BKA)	1988
	Multi-Cultural Collaborative (MCC)	1992
	Asian Pacific Americans for a New Los Angeles (APANLA)	1992

NOTE: Some of these organizations (e.g., KAFSC, KYSU, and BKA) have become defunct since the study began but were well known during their existence.

SOURCE: Courtesy of author

Table 5.1 shows some of the more well-known community-based organizations (CBOs) that have gained political visibility within Korean American and mainstream communities since the 1980s. These organizations cover a wide range of political/advocacy groups and social service agencies serving the diverse social, cultural, economic, and political needs of the Korean American population. Note that many of the organizations were also founded around the time of the riots. Other well-established 1.5/second generation organizations have been less politically active but have helped to cultivate ethnic political solidarity, including cultural associations like the Korean American Museum (KAM) and the Korean Cultural Center (KCC) and professional associations like the Korean American Bar Association (KABA) of Southern California. As noted in the table, Korean American leaders of the 1.5/second generation have also become involved with a number of important alliances with other Asian Americans and racial/ethnic groups in the past few decades.

Ethnic nonprofit organizations are defined as those "nongovernmental associations established by and for [a particular ethnic group] for the specific purpose of delivering services—social, economic and cultural—and/or acting as advocates on behalf of community" (Rodriguez-Fraticelli, Sanabria, and Tirado 1991, 34). Such organizations are to be distinguished from governing nonprofits specifically designed to broaden the civic involvement of a community, coordinate the agenda or platform of a political party, or participate in some aspect of governing processes. This distinction has become a crucial one in minority immigrant communities that have been historically excluded from formal electoral processes but have come up with indirect ways of participating in civic society.

The contributions of 1.5/second generation CBOs go way beyond the simple delivery of social services or advocacy around select political issues. Because of the absence of strong governmental organizations and leadership within most developing Asian immigrant communities, social service and advocacy groups have acted as surrogate governing bodies and politicizing agents for marginalized minority populations. For various reasons related to historical exclusion and discrimination, cultural and linguistic barriers, electoral fragmentation, and political corruption in homeland nations, Korean Americans, like their foreign-born Asian American counterparts, have tended to shy away from direct and active involvement in electoral issues and political candidacies. Although critical in spreading political knowledge and experience, government and party-affiliated organizations in the broader Asian American community have generally lacked the kind of support and funding necessary to sustain regular, coordinated efforts within the community. Thus, organizations such as KARA and the Korean American Democratic Committee (KADC) though growing in membership and influence are only beginning to gain recognition and expand their range of activities within the Korean American population.

Instead, political activism in the Asian American community has been conducted through indirect channels of influence, political discourse, community activities, and nonelectoral institutions. Despite its major shortcomings, financial contributions to local and national political campaigns, for instance, have been a subtle yet noteworthy opening for political participation among new Asian immigrants who lack familiarity with the inner workings of American politics. Unfortunately, the 1992 riots taught many Korean Americans that financial contributions would not carry much weight during times of crisis if they were not backed up by political representation and influence within mainstream society. Rather than "institutionalizing" their political membership through citizenship and other formal channels, minority groups have created informal ways of expressing and mobilizing around their political interests through civic and cultural institutions within the community.

In particular, both social service agencies and advocacy groups have been highly active within the political structures of the Korean American community in terms of creating networks with politicians and political organizations, promoting and raising awareness on various political issues, and organizing and mobilizing younger generations of Korean Americans. Although relatively disengaged from the core of ethnic politics, professional associations and cultural centers have also set the backdrop for the politicization of the community by raising social and political consciousness, strengthening ethnic-based networks, and acting as feeders to more politically active organizations. The political roles of these different CBOs will only continue to expand since funds for grassroots activities remain scarce in immigrant communities and the need for bilingual and bicultural social services and advocacy work grows.

In addition to established organizations, 1.5/second generation Korean Americans have created informal political spaces within which to educate, train, and mobilize future generations of ethnic political leadership. This includes political study/language groups where young Korean Americans can brush up on their Korean fluency by speaking and reading about labor struggles and reunification movements in Korea. Womens Organization Reaching Koreans (WORK) was created to address the growing need of Korean American women to foster social connections and for some a political niche within a community structure dominated by men and male interests. Some have channeled their political energies and opinions toward artistic, cultural, and technological forums, such as literary journals, Asian American theater, spoken word performances, bible study groups, internet websites, and e-mail listservs.

It is just as difficult to generalize about the political orientation of contemporary Korean American organizations because of the complex ways 1.5/second generation organizational leaders must promote their political agenda within the confines of immigrant hierarchies and federal nonprofit statutes. Based on votes during the 1996 gubernatorial and 1998 presidential elections, one study conducted on Asian Pacific American voters in Southern California reports that Korean Americans generally lean toward the Democratic Party and are getting stronger in that area (Lien 2001). In terms of organizations, however, the lines of political partisanship are more blurred. I have heard as many claims from leftist groups that the new Korean American leadership is too conservative in outlook as I have heard conservatives decry the hidden liberal agenda of 1.5/second generation Korean American organizations. One conservative 1.5 generation leader commented on the community's inability to reconcile the wide political disjuncture between the leftist ideologies of second generation Asian American organizations and the conservative values of the Asian immigrant population they are purported to represent. Conversely, other leftist 1.5/second generation interviewees argued that the community was being overtaken by the traditional, conservative values of elite leaders who were neglecting the interests of marginalized groups within the community, reaffirming their model minority status in the eyes of mainstream society, and heightening tensions with other racial and ethnic communities.

What is apparent however are the clear-cut political divisions that have emerged between Republicans and Democrats within the community that both reflect and transcend the generational divide.[2] The 1992 civil unrest further polarized the community along partisan lines, with some factions seeking to pursue their interests with the Democratic Party and others with the Republican Party. From the perspective of more progressive Korean Americans, inequalities based on race, class, and gender continue to shape the social structures of American society yet are obscured by rhetorics of color-blind meritocracy and the model minority myth. Within this context, the Los Angeles civil unrest represented a misdirected rebellion against decades of oppression and diminishing resources within the inner city. As such, the ultimate goal of social justice can be achieved only through alliances with progressive Whites and other communities of color.

Conservative Korean Americans on the other hand play more strongly to the interests of immigrant entrepreneurs and professionals who dominate the ethnic community and whose class interests they feel are best protected by the Republican Party. From this standpoint, hard work ethics and Christian values are the key to advancing in a society that promotes both democracy and equal opportunity for all. Thus, the plight of the underclass stems not from systematic inequalities, but cultural deficiencies and failures in the welfare approach, which prevent certain groups from moving up the socioeconomic ladder. From this perspective, Korean immigrants were continuously the victims of political scapegoating by African American activists and rioters—an injustice that could only be rectified by strengthening law enforcement and ties with mainstream power holders.

In Koreatown, 1.5/second generation Korean American organizations have also stratified themselves along two interactive but divergent circuits of power, including one based on resource-rich networks with the ethnic elite and established mainstream institutions and the second based on other marginal Korean American organizations and diverse leftist groups outside the ethnic community. While loosely connected to one another, each circuit draws on different networks of support from inside and outside the ethnic community. Location within each organizational circuit depends on how individual ethnic organizations negotiate their political/ideological agenda within traditional immigrant power structures. Indeed, the hierarchical nature of ethnic organizational structures may be attributed to the varying quantity and quality of information, resources, and support derived from these different circuits. At the crossroads of intergenerational conflict and cooperation, most 1.5/second generation Korean American organizations fall somewhere in a continuum between the two ideal types of ethnic CBOs.

On the one hand are those organizations that have established relatively stable (albeit not conflict-free) relations with immigrant elite groups, partly because they share certain fundamental eth-class values based on the middle-class American Dream and also rely on them for political legitimacy, resources, and other kinds of support from the immigrant-based population. The more bureaucratic and larger the organization in terms of its financial base and internal structure, the more likely it will work to maintain such linkages with the immigrant elite. Financial support and legitimacy among well-endowed immigrant leadership and mainstream institutions are critical to the growth and survival of larger organizations such as these. The rigid and hierarchical nature of internal structures in turn allows such organizations to provide resources for their upwardly mobile staff members and to manage their political image among their key coethnic and mainstream supporters.

On the other hand, the Korean American community has also witnessed the political emergence of more progressive and ideologically driven organizations whose values do not always coincide with those of the ethnic elite and who must therefore draw on stronger networks outside the ethnic community, including transnational, Asian American, or labor-based organizations. However, this flexibility does not detract from their ethnic focus. As one second generation Korean American organizer explains, "All of us are Korean Americans with obviously Korean American families and interest in the Korean American community but who are approaching issues from all these different angles you know. Just because you don't work *with* the Korean American organizations doesn't mean that you don't work *in* Korean American issues." These groups tend to be smaller in number and more informal and flexible in structure because of their greater emphasis on ideology over funding. The organizational structure allows for greater democratic decision making among the staff, which chooses to take on programs, services, and events that they believe will achieve their broader goals for social justice. Such malleable organizations are also better equipped to respond to the blacklisting tactics of their resource-rich opponents and to adapt to the conflict-ridden environment within which they work. Such organizations maintain the political loyalties of their membership through ideological conviction, more so than resource opportunity.

The influx of mainstream resources and networks has had two main effects on the internal structures of these two tiers. First, it has allowed more established organizations like KYCC to extend and diversify their services to the surrounding area, thus increasing their influence both within and outside the Korean American community. As the best example, KYCC used the governmental connections it had cultivated through social service contracts to attract much of the postriot recovery funds that were channeled into the Korean American community as a result of the devastation inflicted on Korean immigrant merchants. Within a matter of years, KYCC went from a small, drop-in community center to an agency working on a three million-dollar budget and well recognized within both the Korean American community and the outside world.

And second, it has helped smaller, lower-tier Korean American organizations like KIWA that had until then suffered from lack of ethnic elite support to begin to build a progressive base within the community and mobilize disempowered Koreans. By offering an alternative source of support with which to challenge the status quo, outside networks helped to provide the funds, knowledge, and manpower KIWA needed to make its message be heard by immigrant leaders within the ethnic community. Through its incorporation of Korean and Latino immigrant workers and progressive Asian Americans, KIWA has worked to represent and advocate for the oft-neglected interests of marginalized groups within the Korean American population. As a result, KIWA could not have expanded and emerged politically to the extent that it did without the support it received from these mainstream groups.

How They Relate

It was stated in the previous chapter that the dynamics of competition and cooperation among the traditional immigrant leadership have been largely shaped by struggles for individual status/title and conflict over the distribution of ethnic resources. However, when an ethnic community is forced to open its doors to the outside world, the exposure results in the infusion of new resources and ideological perspectives that changes the dynamics of alliance and oppositionality among ethnic organizations. Relative to immigrant organizations of the past, 1.5/second generation Korean American organizations have become more heterogeneous in terms of internal structure, service provision, political visions and ideologies, support networks, and their relationship with the traditional ethnic elite partly as a result of greater access to resources, diverse paths of acculturation, and heightened political visibility after the 1992 riots.

Although status and title are still relevant among the immigrant leadership, the incorporation of 1.5/second generation Korean American leadership and resulting diversification of organizational structures have restructured the bases of intraethnic conflict and cooperation around new axes of ideology and interest. The basis for interorganizational conflict and cooperation thus depends on the organizations' ideological orientation, resource distribution, service provision, and political representation.

Ideological Orientation.   Ideology refers not only to political partisanship, but also, different ideas about where the ethnic community should be headed and how it should go about achieving its goals. For instance, even among those organizations that are considered to be "progressive," ideological differences about the definition of individual and collective empowerment and the means by which ethnic groups can achieve such success may vary dramatically. For some organizations, this means working within the mainstream system of electoral politics to enact social change and reform, while for others it means questioning this very system and using more militant tactics to demand social justice. Some leaders work toward running their organization like a business corporation, while others envision it as a politicized space in itself where individuals must practice what they preach. The organization's ideological approach will thus determine what support networks they will solicit and how they view the practices of other organizations in the community.

Resource Distribution.   Internal struggle over funding sources has been heightened by the multiple resources, networks, and services that have been made available with the increasing visibility of Korean Americans in mainstream America. Sometimes resources are shared among organizational constituencies, while other times they become sources of conflict due to their inequitable distribution. For example, organizations that work on healthcare issues, such as KHEIR, KAFSC, and KYCC, draw on support from similar funding sources to service the health needs of youth and family—a situation that can potentially pit one against the other. As mentioned, immigrant leaders have also demanded their share in mainstream financial resources directed at the Korean immigrant population.

Service Provision.   Related to this, as organizations begin to expand and diversify their services, the new leadership has been concerned over the possibility that the clientele, programs, and agenda of social service agencies and political organizations will overlap. Some organizations have taken steps to prevent future conflict, although competition for resources and clients continues to feed internal "turf wars." Turf generally refers to the territorial claim that an organization may have on a certain area of service provision. Sometimes turf wars can arise between various Korean American organizations that cater to the same stratum of clientele. Other times, these turf wars surface with organizations outside the community, as in the case of some traditional labor unions whose industries overlap with those Koreatown-situated businesses that KIWA has targeted.

Political Representation.   Competition to claim political representation of an ethnic community within mainstream society is the result of increased awareness of the importance of political empowerment among immigrant organizations and the emergence of second generation representatives in the American media and politics. Conflicts can arise on ideological grounds, as in the case of first generation accusations that English-speaking 1.5/second generation figures, who are touted as leaders of the community, have not properly represented the values and interests of the Korean immigrant population. Political representation may determine not only how the community is represented to the outer world but also how status and resources will be distributed among the existing leadership. Thus, it is also a source of political empowerment within the Korean American community.

Despite the greater availability of resources since the civil unrest, ethnic organizations are still dealing with a limited number of contracts, resource, and representatives that are allotted to the Korean American and Koreatown communities. In addition, the growing number of ethnic-based interest groups whose agendas or support networks overlap has aggravated competition among these groups.

As a result, many of these organizations have experienced considerable internal growth and diversification in services and have hence run the risk of infringing on the jurisdiction of other ethnic organizations. When limited funding sources focus on specific ethnic groups or the media seeks out political "representatives" in Koreatown, ethnic organizations must also assert themselves to become that one "ethnic representative" of the community. This situation limits the ability of organizations to adequately address the diverse interests of the population. As a result, those contemporary 1.5/second generation organizations whose interests and ideologies align may find that they are each other's greatest rivals, as well as their strongest allies. When asked whether Korean American organizations work together, one female program manager responds, "Sometimes we do, sometimes we don't, sometimes we fight each other for the same pot of money."

Nevertheless, the past leadership's inability to respond systematically and effectively to the 1992 riots and the failure of mainstream institutions to address the needs of Korean Americans have compelled such organizations to strengthen their relationship with others of their kind. Furthermore, greater accountability to institutional funders and government agencies have laid the basis for more regular and sustained relationships among different CBOs, in contrast with the immigrant organizations before them. Under the rubric of coethnic cooperation, congruities in interest have compelled them to create informal rules of engagement to prevent one organization from stepping on the toes of others. As the organizations grow, these instances of cooperation may solidify in the interests of ethnic empowerment, but may also allow upper-tier organizations to dominate informally the agenda of intraethnic alliances.

In an effort to coordinate their resources and prevent conflict over future turf issues, executive directors for six of the major 1.5/second generation organizations had been regularly meeting for informal dinners to discuss community and organizational affairs. Out of this type of collaboration, a number of 1.5/second generation organizations launched a large coalition in the aftermath of the riots called the Korean American Inter-Agency Council (KAIAC) through relief funds given to KYCC. As one director commented, the formation of KAIAC allowed Korean American organizations to respond more effectively to the Northridge earthquakes of 1994. While they have certainly made inroads in terms of enhancing generational solidarity through intragenerational coalitions like KAIAC, more subtle power differentials continue to play out among 1.5/second generation ethnic organizations.

For the most part, internal hierarchies remain intact even among the new political leadership. Part of this difference has to do with where these organizations primarily derive their resources and support within the ethnic community and mainstream society. Those who have stronger networks with the ethnic elite leadership as well as mainstream corporations and governmental institutions have tended to wield greater influence over political affairs than do those with weaker networks in these areas. Observation of alliances and political interactions among different 1.5/second generation organizational leaders indicates that how resources are distributed and collaborative strategies are formulated among representatives within the coalition depend largely on who has the strongest influence over these types of intragenerational efforts. Of course, other features, such as the strength of the organization's leadership, also factor into the power equation, but nevertheless organizational support networks lay the foundations for determining status in ethnic stratification systems.

In a gesture that symbolized the power of interorganizational cooperation and hierarchies, five 1.5/second generation-led community centers—KAC, KAM, KAFSC, KHEIR, and KYCC—recently purchased a building to create a "one-stop community center" for the Koreatown community, called the Koreatown Organizations Association (KOA). As one participating board member explains it, "Because these agencies have grown, the close proximity to each of the offices will eliminate duplication of services and maximize resources" (*Korea Times*, September 19, 1997). Interestingly, these five organizations also happen to be the more prominent, upper-tier organizations of Koreatown and are perhaps not so coincidentally housed in the same building as the immigrant elite organization, KAGRO.

The opening ceremony of the KOA building was attended by many of Koreatown's current power players, including the five organizations, the Korean media, the Korean Consul General, and various corporate sponsors. According to the speakers, financial contributions for KOA came largely from grants from the City of Los Angeles, as well as the Y. S. Mae Foundation and the *Korea Times*. During the presentations, a first generation board member of KAC praised the spirit of cooperation he had witnessed between the first generation and second generation in launching this project, as evidenced by the "quiet" contributions of immigrant representatives from Nara Bank. Another

1.5 generation leader emphasized the pivotal decision the organizations had made in deciding to adopt "Koreatown" as the title of the association instead of "Korean American," in order to reflect the increasing diversity of Koreatown. He proceeded to express the hope that the association would eventually include other non-Korean service organizations in the community. In addition, the five executive directors, two of whom were women, proceeded to introduce themselves and the organizations they represented.

Despite these strong displays of support, sources indicate that all organizations have not participated in these coalitional forums on equal grounding, as shown by the leaders who were involved in the KOA project and those who attended the ceremonies. In the case of KOA, the most telling sign of this differential status involves the exclusion of groups like KIWA from the building project. One inside source has attested to their intention to incorporate KIWA along with Latino organizations in the future but notes that there is a general fear that if KIWA becomes involved, KOA would lose support from the first generation. When asked why these five organizations were selected for the building project, another outside community worker replied:

> Well it was partly a matter of politics. I mean, these five organizations, other than the museum, are the four most credible, oldest, reputable, you know sort of conservative Korean organizations. So all these executive directors have sort of a working relationship with each other. And these organizations have a certain political leaning and know each other and you know they really look down upon the work that KRC and KIWA does and in fact has looked very suspiciously on these two organizations.

Considering the political inequities that are at play, it may not be a coincidence that KIWA has just recently spearheaded a similar effort to start a "Koreatown Community Center" for leftist organizations in the area. Among other things, the leased office space would consist of conference and study rooms, a library, audiovisual and computer space, Korean language and culture classrooms, and an auditorium that would be used to host organizational and community events. As the fundraising flyer describes it:

> Our building will provide important working space for those who work on Korean homeland issues and on building a healthy Korean community, as well as to provide a space for the future Korean American and Koreatown activists. This will be a space for educating and organizing the next wave of

activists; a place for dreams; and a lively place where the Los Angeles Korean progressive movement can come together and be seen as one. Let us gather our efforts to establish a Koreatown Community Center that will serve as our main headquarter for raising the consciousness of future generation activists, for the reunification of our homeland, and for building a progressive Korean American community.

Just as KOA implicitly limited its affiliates to the higher-ranking Korean American organizations of the community, the envisioned Koreatown Community Center would initially house "progressive individuals and organizations" but open itself up to other participants in the future. The flyer welcomes most progressive organizations, both Korean and non-Korean, into its fold and also underscores its ties to leftist activists and progressive causes within Korea itself. Signifying their passion for this cause, all staff members decided to donate almost $30,000 in back wages owed them for pay cuts they took when KIWA was facing financial difficulties. At the time of this writing, KIWA was just beginning to raise funding for this project.

The individual influence and perceptions of executive directors also seem to play a role in determining how much he or she can do within such coalitions. One second generation staff member for instance has related to me one example in which the leader of a dominant organization in KAIAC used his powerful position to take over a major government-funded project that a more marginal organization had expressed interest in partaking. The same kind of turf-related power play surfaces over and over again between core and peripheral organizations, as well as among different elite organizations competing for claims over various projects—from riot-related funding to management of the Census 2000 data to the creation of daycare centers in Koreatown. These internal dynamics underline the ways in which relations among 1.5/second generations are just as cooperative, competitive, and hierarchical as those across generations.

Cooperation and Incorporation: The Case of Latinos

Although more and more organizations have incorporated crossethnic activities into their broader political agenda, newly emerging Korean American organizations among the 1.5/second generation stand apart from their immigrant predecessors in terms of their deep and wide-ranging interactions with outside communities. Coalition building allows bridging organizations to harness resources both within and beyond the spatial confines of the ethnic enclave community. Collaborative partnerships with other racial and ethnic groups that actually live within Koreatown enable ethnic organizations to overcome some of the limitations that arise from representing an ethnic community that is scattered across various neighborhoods. In addition, strong networks with outside groups serve as an alternative source of political empowerment that extends beyond the boundaries of a community dominated by the narrow interests of the ethnic elite.

For these reasons, younger organizations are more inclined to engage in political partnerships with a wider spectrum of racial and ethnic groups, including Blacks and Latinos, based on lessons learned throughout the 1980s and 1990s. In some cases, such crossethnic activities have gone beyond occasional coalitional activities and programs to more involved mergers that have substantially transformed the internal political cultures of such organizations. In terms of their diverse clientele, membership, and program offerings, both KIWA and KYCC represent some of the internal transitions that may take place among organizations that attempt to bridge the political divide between Korean Americans and other racial/ethnic groups in multicultural Koreatown. As noted earlier, both organizations have not only offered programs to Latino residents and workers but have also included them in all levels of management.

In part, the leaders of these organizations have instituted these internal reforms in response to the demographic patterns and structural inequalities that have come to characterize what some call "ethnic" but is in actuality the "multiethnic" enclaves of Los Angeles. As stated, Koreatown is distinguished by the growing demographic presence of Latinos, who lack the kind of developed institutional support system that Korean Americans have developed within the local community. The neighboring region of Pico-Union houses a few major Latino CBOs like the Central American Resource Center (CARE-CEN), El Centro Del Pueblo, El Rescate, and the Coalition for Human Immigrant Rights L.A. (CHIRLA), as well as mainstream agencies such as the Young Men's Christian Association (YMCA) that cater to the social, socioeconomic, health, and political needs of the local Latino population. Although they may serve the general Latino population, many of these organizations were initiated by Central Americans, particularly Salvadorans, whose extensive experience in political and labor organizing in their homelands laid the foundations for some modest organizational development.

Nevertheless, Latino organizations in Koreatown and the neighboring areas of Pico-Union, for the most part, do not have the kind of specialized services and overall capacity needed to target the diverse demands of this sizable, low-income immigrant population. Latinos still cannot claim a strong organizing base in Koreatown upon which to mobilize and empower themselves beyond service provision because of their weak financial base and lack of institutional resources. As a Korean community organizer from KIWA explains:

> In fact, some of the Latino organizations refer Latino workers to us. They don't have the capacity to handle it. Even in the Latino community, there lacks an organization that specifically handles worker cases. I mean, the closest they come is, there are immigrant advocates that have a worker-organizing component, but nothing like us. Like this is all we do: it's just worker-specific. And so I think a lot of times, these organizations either get overwhelmed with cases or they're not equipped to handle them. So the word's kind of gotten trickled out that we have the capacity to handle Latino workers so they kind of have us on a referral sheet. Then they get a call or if someone walks in, they can just send them over here.

Recognizing this leadership gap after the 1992 riots, more established leaders from East Los Angeles began outreach efforts to immigrants and organizations in South Central and downtown regions as reported in the *Los Angeles Times* (Lope, Renwick, and Seo 1993). Korean American organizations have filled some of these institutional gaps for the time being.

Latinos face a number of structural disadvantages that prevent them from building a strong institutional base in the downtown regions of Los Angeles, especially one that is as well connected to mainstream institutions as the Korean American community. Among other things, the population primarily consists of low-income immigrant wage-earners, many of whom entered the country without legal documentation. Even if they could find the time, money, and interest to build organizations, many of them would be particularly vulnerable to outside pressure because of their illegal status. The population has been able to utilize social networks to acquire jobs, housing, and employment and to provide ethnic support systems for new immigrants, but these types of networks do little for the community beyond facilitating day-to-day survival, because they are not yet well connected to politicians or the middle-class elite. Although they have the potential to sway elections through numbers alone in coming decades, the community as a whole with some exceptions has had little experience in American politics and has not fine-tuned its grasp of protest politics in their efforts to fight against social injustices. This is primarily the result of the short and sporadic presence of Latino immigrants throughout U.S. history, as well as disadvantages associated with their nativity, such as language barriers and citizenship. Many of them also maintain stronger ties with the homeland and perceive their stay in the United States as temporary.

Despite these structural disadvantages, Latinos offer bridging organizations in the Korean American community an even more powerful opportunity to engage fully in the future of ethnic and multicultural Los Angeles politics. Looking at numbers alone, Latinos are expected to dominate local and statewide elections as the new "majority-minority" population in most major cities of California. The rise of Latino city council representatives, mayors, and congressmen/women, such as Lucille Roybal-Allard, Gil Cedillo, Linda Sanchez, and Antonio Villaraigosa, in recent years is a testament to the growing influence of the Latino vote in California. Some organizational leaders have come to realize the potential for creating linkages with this expanding political base—a goal that will take much longer and be much harder to attain for the smaller Korean American population alone even in the distant future. One thirty-nine-year-old, 1.5 generation male leader who has worked for both immigrant and 1.5/second generation organizations notes:

> It's becoming more critical as we look in the political scene in California. I think by now, the assembly, and the senate is dominated by Latino politicians. And I think things will come when L.A. area politics will be the same, both county and the city. We have an opportunity to forge a working relationship with the Latino community and start fighting for political power in California. And if we miss that, we're not gonna have that opportunity ever again.

Thus, on a practical level, the interviewee has taken advantage of the chance to expand the future political influence of the Korean American community by investing in the growing Latino community today.

As a result, more politically minded bridging organizations led by 1.5/second generation Korean Americans have used this time to act as institutional springboards for the local Latino population by offering an array of social services; taking them on board as interns and staff members; and in some cases organizing, mobilizing, and intervening on behalf of Latinos in disputes with Korean power holders. The growing presence of such institutions have also played a part in mitigating tensions with other local racial groups by offering mutual aid support, mediating tensions, or even suppressing internal political opposition through the power of institutional influence. Although there are various ways of explaining the more positive interactions between Koreans and Latinos, it should be noted that these kinds of mediating ethnic infrastructures are relatively absent in Black ghettos where Korean-Black conflicts have been more frequently known to erupt.

Looking at it another way, the diversification of organizations in Koreatown has also helped to counter the ethnocentric effects of elite dominance that could potentially heighten bitter conflicts between Koreans and Latinos within the local community. The effects of institutional inequality and heterogeneity were recently played out in a controversy over the naming of what was previously known as Ardmore Park in the heart of Koreatown. The small park is primarily used by Latino residents and only a small number of elderly Koreans for private outings, soccer games, family gatherings, and children's playspaces, except on rare occasions when the leadership of the Korean American community organizes major political functions and events at the site. However, Korean immigrant leaders successfully spearheaded a campaign to change the name from Ardmore Park to Seoul International Park, with some minor protests from Latinos in the neighborhood. The move did however raise voices of opposition from within the Korean American community, including the executive director of KIWA who expressed his dissent in *Korea Times.*

Among other things, the incident underscored the key role that younger Korean American organizations would play in helping to voice and protect the interests of Latinos in the community while in some cases giving them the tools to create their own collective base of empowerment. It was clear that Latinos had little say in the naming of the park because of the lack of leadership and institutions that could speak on their behalf. However, the growing influence of organizations such as KIWA has provided an open political space within which to contest the ethnocentric focus of Korean immigrant power holders. The different alliances and political voices that emerged throughout the controversy reaffirm the diverse ways that 1.5/second generation leadership can involve themselves within the local community depending on their relations with the ethnic elite.

At some level, all bridging organizations within the Korean American community have sustained some sort of working relationship with other racial and ethnic groups in their efforts to link the ethnic community to mainstream American society. However, not all of them have used this opportunity to engage actively with Latinos in the local community to the extent of incorporating them as clients and staff members. In part, these differences can be attributed to the distinct ideological and political orientations of the organization's governing leadership. Some leaders are clearly more responsive to the demographic diversity of Los Angeles, while others feel that there is more potential in focusing their energies on the ethnic community.

However, diverse interactions with the local population may also be the result of the different ways organizations have negotiated their political agendas with the spatial peculiarities of the Korean American population. Because Korean Americans do not have a strong residential presence within the local neighborhoods, racial inclusiveness opens up significant political and financial opportunities for organizations that rely on the geographic community more so than the ethnic community for outside support. Working with Latinos can be a particularly empowering strategy for organizations seeking to expand their political resources either through government grants or general support as long as they are able to include them without losing sight of their political mission.

Translocal ethnic organizations such as the KAC derive a substantial amount of their support from not only government officials but also young professionals, the ethnic elite leadership, and large-scale corporations so that they are not as highly dependent on the local community to sustain and expand their internal operations. Although KAC is involved with coalitional projects with other racial and ethnic communities, allowing these bridges to change the internal mission and structure of the organization would spread thin their focused interest in politically empowering Korean Americans in the wake of the 1992 Riots.

In contrast, geoethnic bridging organizations like KYCC have much more to gain from extending their services to the local community population and are able to do so as part of their underlying goal of community service and political leadership for Korean Americans. In the hands of a progressive leadership and growing government contracts, KYCC began to recognize the potential for expanding its programs and services and hence its political influence through its diversifying clientele base. The resulting influx of resources and outside support has enabled it to expand the type of assistance it can provide to a so-called model minority community whose social needs alone cannot justify substantial financial support in the eyes of outside institutions.

KIWA's evolution was much more inevitable yet nonetheless groundbreaking in the way it built on the concept of worker solidarity to overcome the problems of interethnic competition in the workplace without losing sight of its interest in Korean Americans. Learning from the lessons of its predecessors, KIWA realized that organizing against Korean business owners on behalf of non-Korean workers was a risky proposition, but it also allowed them to help Korean immigrant workers deal with the divide-and-conquer tactics of entrepreneurs and to expand its range of political influence in the process. Making use of its insights on the Korean immigrant community, KIWA cultivated a powerful bridging relationship between Korean and Latino workers that could overcome the protected power of ethnic enclave business owners in a way that no mainstream labor union could rival. In so doing, both KYCC and KIWA have succeeded in not only achieving their mission of servicing, organizing, and empowering Korean Americans, but also making their presence felt in other racial and ethnic communities.

Although crossgenerational relationships have certainly been a defining feature of contemporary community politics, differential empowerment may create the conditions not only for intergenerational conflict, but also intergenerational dependency, such that some 1.5/second generation organizations must still work within the constraints of immigrant power structures. Despite intensifying competition and divergent political ideologies, a new generation of political elite leadership has found greater potential in building on the resources of the immigrant population, which complement their own contributions. Even organizations like KIWA that have drawn negative attention from the ethnic elite and the Korean media have built a visible base of support within the immigrant worker and youth populations. Furthermore, relations *among* the different 1.5/second generation leaders, although more stable than relations with first generation leaders, can be just as contentious because of ideological dissonance and resource competition. On the other hand, this is not to deny that lower-tier organizations have pursued more confrontational forms of interaction with the traditional power holders of the ethnic community in order to fulfill their political mission. If anything, it is more useful to conceptualize the foundations of political loyalties as being organized around unequal relations with the *traditional ethnic elite* than immigrants overall depending on the organization's political agenda.

As opposed to simply supplanting one ethnic power structure with another, generational transitions in the political leadership of the ethnic community have been accompanied by the diversification of ethnic organizations that are now able to cater to a wider range of needs, including those of previously marginalized subgroups within the Koreatown population, such as women, workers, and Latinos. Although organizations have worked to manage turf conflicts among the proliferating organizations, political growth and specialization have also been accompanied by the creation of more subtle interorganizational hierarchies. Within this context, the next half of this book will take a closer look at the internal development of these organizations, with an interest in understanding how organizations attract their membership despite the spatial, ideological, and socioeconomic fragmentation of the Korean American population. Based on two case studies, KIWA and KYCC, the chapters will explore the processes through which organizations have negotiated their political agenda within existing ethnic hierarchies and how this has affected the identities of staff membership, their internal structures, and their political activities within the ethnic community.

6 The Historical Evolution of KYCC and KIWA

POLITICAL CONFLICTS PARTLY REFLECT the rapidly changing geography of the Korean American population over the past few decades. Despite the concentration of ethnic institutions in Koreatown, most Korean Americans are no longer settling down in one place, making it more difficult for organizations to cater to the shifting needs of a geographically dispersed ethnic clientele and raising new questions about their responsibility to non–Korean Americans in the surrounding neighborhoods.

While the need for ethnic-based services and programs has not waned, heightened class polarization has also diversified the interests of the Korean American population and exerted more pressure on political leadership to articulate and justify the clientele they represent within the context of the broader community. Moreover, we have seen how generational transitions in leadership have been characterized by cultural and ideological clashes between immigrants and the American born, between conservatives and liberals, and between elite power holders and peripheral political activists. Amid ideological accommodation and dissent, efforts to coordinate the political agendas of different organizations have been further hindered by the kind of competition and power play that arises in communities with limited access to resources and few arenas for political representation.

As the first half of the book has shown, the contours of political discourse have been largely shaped by these various points of contestation and conflict, making it increasingly difficult to reconcile the notion of "ethnic political solidarity." Although the book has touched on why solidarity persists despite these conditions, the question remains *how* organizations are able to attract and maintain their ethnic constituencies while accommodating to this new ethnic power structure. With this in mind, the following chapters explore how 1.5/second generation organizations have been able to harness the social energy nurtured by the events of the 1980s and 1990s and construct a political framework that helps bridge the gap between young and old, between woman and man, and between Korean American and non–Korean American. To attain the elusive goal of ethnic political solidarity, they must navigate the bumpy terrains of shifting ethnic hierarchies, as well as constraints imposed by their dependency on support networks outside the community.

To this end, I concentrate on two 1.5/second generation organizations, the Korean Youth and Community Center (KYCC) and the Korean Immigrant Workers Advocates (KIWA), that have tapped into different bases of social support within the upper and lower tiers of ethnic and mainstream power structures. In the initial stages of organizational development, 1.5/second generation organizations must draw on preexisting resources and networks with non-Koreatown organizations in order to establish themselves as respectable political contenders within this immigrant-dominated community. However, the two case studies show that how they deal with the elite of the traditional ethnic community will vary depending on the historical context of their emergence as well as their internal leadership and ideological orientation. This chapter explains how KYCC and KIWA both began on the peripheries of traditional hierarchies but strategically used their available resources and opportunities to situate themselves at different ends of the ethnic power structure over time. It is important to note that regardless of their approach, both organizations recognized the need to deal with the pervasive influence of the immigrant elite and have developed their agendas accordingly.

KYCC: Creating a Political Base from Within

From AA to KA

The KYCC has evolved into one of the largest community-based organizations (CBOs) in the nation to provide social services to Korean American youth and families. With approximately fifty-five full-time and twenty part-time employees and a $5 million budget, KYCC is one of the largest Korean American social service agencies in California focused on youth and families. The agency offers six different types of programs, including (1) counseling for youth and their families (for example, individual/group counseling, support groups); (2)

educational programs (such as after-school tutorials, Scholastic Aptitude Test workshops); (3) employment assistance (for example, job placement, training programs) and business development (including loan assistance and information); (4) youth development (such as youth and multiethnic leadership, gang awareness); (5) community education (such as HIV/AIDS and tobacco education); (6) and an environmental division (including water conservation, graffiti removal). More recently, KYCC has focused its energies on raising money for two new daycare centers in Koreatown that will provide quality childcare services for over a hundred infants, toddlers, and preschool-age children at an affordable rate.

Considering the expansive and bureaucratic nature of the organization today, it is surprising to know that the origins of KYCC were quite humble and more analogous to smaller organizations such as KIWA in terms of their internal structure and peripheral status within the ethnic community. KYCC began in the mid-1970s when the community was still small and overwhelmingly immigrant and struggling to root itself in the face of marginalization within American society. As such, ethnic organizations at the time were compelled to accommodate to the existing leadership and work together for the greater good of the Korean American community.

However, the institutional support of a government-linked Asian American social service agency and the Christian orientation of its first and 1.5 generation founders allowed the organization to gradually expand its resources and maintain an uneasy alliance with the ethnic elite. This relationship has had its ups and downs depending on the political visions of the organization's leadership. Organizational leadership refers to the top members of an organization who have the most influence over the mission, structure, and ultimate direction of the organization. In the case of KYCC, this function has mainly rested upon the board members and executive directors of the agency.

Interestingly, it is primarily with the support of outside Asian American agencies that emerging 1.5 generation leaders of KYCC were able to find an entrance into the closely protected power structures of the Korean American community. KYCC began as a program created under the Asian American Drug Abuse Program (AADAP), a well-known social service agency in South Central whose main purpose is to provide substance abuse prevention and intervention services to Asian American youth in the Los Angeles area. Problems with juvenile delinquency and gang activities among Korean American youth emerged as early as the 1970s and peaked throughout the 1980s. Several of the older members of KYCC informed me that Korean youth at that time were mostly immigrants and thus dealing with the difficulties of adjusting to a foreign environment, including schooling, acculturation, and interethnic tensions with other youth. As a result, many Korean immigrant youth began to join gangs, such as the American Burger and the Korean Killers (Yu 1987).

With incidents of juvenile delinquency on the rise among the growing Korean American population throughout the 1970s, AADAP began to recognize the need for a separate division that would deal with the specialized problems of Korean immigrant youth. On February 14, 1975, the agency created a program directed at Korean youth and formed an advisory committee to oversee the program. The committee included several second and third generation Asian American representatives from AADAP and first and 1.5 generation religious leaders, government officials, and young professionals from the Korean community. However, as Koreatown rapidly expanded, the committee members realized that the population would be better served if the program split off into its own independent entity and consequently formed a small center, which was then called the Korean Youth Center (KYC). Over time, the Korean members of the board brought in more coethnic members, thereby allowing the organization to take shape under a Korean-dominated leadership.

Under the guidance of a minister in its earlier years, KYC primarily functioned as a Young Men's Christian Association (YMCA) type "drop-in center," where youth could hang out and engage in various recreational and educational activities. To this day, the ideological orientation of the organization can be attributed to its strong roots in Christian philosophies of service among its Korean leadership, many of whom were in some ways connected with ethnic churches in the community. When the organization was taken over by a new first generation leader, the center shifted its attention to intervention/prevention counseling for more troubled and disadvantaged youths and their families. The director, who had been associated with the center since its inception, devoted his earlier years to visiting local parks, schools, and nightclubs in order to assess the needs of Korean American youth in the area and recruit gang members, other juvenile delinquents, and their parents into the program. He states, "I didn't want it to have a YMCA function. I wanted to see the real problem. I will go to jail, I will go to meet the gangsters, who are fighting in the street and then bring that into the center."

As veteran members recall, the KYC began in the back spaces of a small office building and was operated by a handful of staff members and volunteers and a minuscule budget taken from individual and community donations and some city funding. The financial supporters listed in KYC's earlier newsletters included small donations from select Korean banks, restaurants, business owners, immigrant organizations, and churches. However, one former executive director recalls that the benefits of having such a small, low-budget organization was that the staff became like a "family," all committed to helping the poor and the disadvantaged and willing to overlook the insubstantial pay.

Furthermore, with virtually no organization of its kind in Los Angeles during that time period, staff members and volunteers were bonded by their marginal status in an ethnic community that showed little interest in the psychological problems of youth over other immigrant community agendas. As a thirty-nine-year-old, 1.5 generation male board member explains, cultural emphasis on age hierarchies and the educational achievement of youth were prioritized more highly than the emotional needs of youth. A former director also adds:

> We were an organization that really focused on the grassroots efforts and really reaching out to population that were not supported on a widespread basis. At that time, things were quite different because I think Korean community was just starting. People didn't want people to find out about the problems that we were facing and even kids or families themselves, because it's such a shameful thing that you don't share with other people. So initially when we were trying to reach out to the Korean community for support, it was quite difficult, because I was criticized by quite a few people saying, "Why are you trying to really focus on negative aspects of the Korean community? We have to solve the problems within our community and we shouldn't really let other people know, because people have negative stereotypes of Koreans and we are immigrants and we have to really give good images." So it was quite difficult in the beginning to get the support, especially the financial support.

This statement underlines how the interests of ethnic solidarity overruled all other internal divisions partly because of the community's low status within mainstream society.

Because of its relative exclusion from immigrant-dominated political structures, KYC relied heavily on the support of other non-Korean, Asian American community organizations, such as AADAP, Little Tokyo Service Center, and Search to Involve Pilipino Americans (SIPA). Thus, the early history of KYC shows how panethnic organizational networks are particularly important when the peripheral status of an ethnic organization excludes it from tapping into the internal resources of its own ethnic community. This is not to say that the organization had adopted an adversarial approach toward other first generation leaders, but rather that the organization had to struggle to gain recognition and visibility among the political elite. KYC had to maintain a nonconflictual image in order to become an accepted part of the Koreatown establishment, even though building alternative bases of support did allow them to become more autonomous once they became well known. The mission and generational composition of the organization distinguished it from other Korean organizations of the time, but the nonpolitical, Christian bent of the organization prevented it from directly clashing with the interests of ethnic elite leaders, who themselves were strongly tied to Korean churches. In this respect, we can say that KYC first began as a small, informal, and grassroots youth center on the invisible margins of ethnic power structures.

In 1982, KYC became incorporated as an independent, nonprofit organization and designated Jane Kim, one of its young female program coordinators, to become its first female executive director. Although lacking some experience in the beginning, she received guidance from a non–Korean Asian American mentor in AADAP, which allowed her to eventually take the organization to another level. Under Kim's leadership, the organization adopted an air of professionalism, expanded its staff and programs, and progressed rapidly into an independent agency. Having immigrated to the United States as a teenager, she was able to interact well with the organization's largely immigrant clientele as well as its ruling board members.

As the number of 1.5/second generation youth in the population grew, the community began to express greater concerns over rising rates of juvenile delinquency and increasing generational tensions within the family. At the same time, the organization was able to focus more on the educational needs of youth through various educational and after-school programs, which drew the attention of parents in the immigrant community. In the early years of its development, KYC provided training and parenting seminars at various church sites and received financial support and clientele from churches in return. By the 1980s, KYC's programs had diversified such that it was offering not only individual, family, and group counseling services, but also programs such as crime prevention, school outreach, club activities, employment assistance, and education. As the organization's programs converged with the interests of the community, the organization began to garner more and more support from the media, small businesses, and churches within Koreatown, but only a few donors outside the ethnic community.

Managing Organizational Growth and Dissent

In the next stage of its evolution, the organization underwent dramatic transformations, which can be attributed to the ambitious visions of its new director, major demographic shifts within Koreatown, and most importantly the outbreak of the 1992 Los Angeles civil unrest. This transformative era is perhaps the most crucial for three main reasons. First, the organization experienced its most dramatic growth and program diversification during this period, which allowed it to become a corporate entity and improve its social standing with the ethnic elite leadership. Second, as part of its commitment to extend its services to the community, the agency, encouraged by the visions of its new executive director, began to recognize the need to deal with the growing Latino residential population through the incorporation of new community programs, clientele, and staff members. And finally, controversy over the political visions and actions of the executive director offers critical insights into the organization's accountability to the community's immigrant leadership.

As stated in Chapter 4, the Korean-Black conflicts and the Los Angeles civil unrest were influential in transforming the political consciousness of Korean Americans and the power structures that had unconditionally governed the enclave until this point. Events in the aftermath of the riots raised KYC's status by not only allowing 1.5/second generation leadership to "represent" the ethnic community in mainstream society but also funneling massive funding into the community through organizations such as theirs. It is said that the agency was the greatest beneficiary in the Korean American community to receive postriot funding from government agencies and other mainstream institutions. One 1.5 generation board member attributes this to their previous ties with government agencies. As he describes it:

> The riot I think gave an opportunity for an organization like KYC to bring in resources that it didn't have access to before, because during that time, the federal government wanted to bring in a lot of money into L.A. area to remedy some of the problems that it thought it understood, but you can't just give money away. There has to be a system in place and KYC had a mental [health] contract with the county, and the federal government decided to use

the mental health system as the means to distribute funding. The good part was that that started bringing in a lot of funds and then KYC became more well-known in other funding organizations so we had more opportunities to do more funding.

With the assistance of AADAP, KYC had been able to generate some funding from governmental agencies in the early years of its development. In this case, preestablished links with the government through mental health contracts gave KYC a distinct advantage over other organizations in the enclave so that when the crisis hit the agency was best positioned to receive incoming government resources as the designated "ethnic representative" of the community. As a result, KYC became a well-respected social service agency that began to attract more and more financial resources. From these contracts, the board was able to implement new programs focused on race relations, community organizing, and political leadership within the community.

However, money alone cannot explain all the tremendous changes that KYC experienced during this period. Leadership was also critical in enacting change not only in the internal structures of the organization but also the role it assumed within the broader ethnic and mainstream communities. In 1988, Bong Hwan Kim assumed the mantle of leadership of the KYC. As a second generation Korean American in his late twenties, Kim was relatively unknown within the traditional circles of Koreatown, Los Angeles, but politically active in other Korean and Asian American organizations in the San Francisco Bay area. For Kim, the opportunity to work with a large Korean American community had initially drawn him to the organization but proved to be a greater challenge than he had expected. For one, he assumed his position as executive director during the height of the Black-Korean conflicts. Working across racial and ethnic lines was not a new experience for the second generation director, whose political background originated in Oakland, a city with a minor Korean population but sizable non–Korean Asian American and Black American communities. Nevertheless, Kim related to me, "When I came down, I was pretty focused on the Korean and Asian American community, but the [Latasha Harlins] incident really expanded my focus and network of relationships. That's not something I really expected."

Regardless of their later views on his leadership, many of the people I spoke with described the director as being a charismatic leader, well connected with the mainstream community, and fully able to articulate a broader political vision for the organization. Kim himself envisioned the organization as taking a major part in the movement for progressive politics and social justice in Los Angeles, and key figures within the executive board generally supported the notion of nurturing ties with other racial and ethnic groups in light of past events. To this end, he placed strong emphasis on leadership development and advocacy training for youth and worked actively toward establishing relationships with other racial and ethnic minority groups through involvement in coalitional work, controversial stances on political issues, and the implementation of several new community-oriented programs. In many ways, the progressive vision of the director would bring the organization much closer to the ideological orientations of KIWA. However, strengthened by their connections with both the ethnic elite and American professionals, KYC's strategic approach for developing this vision was still based on corporate and political leadership over grassroots organizing.

Along with postriot funding, Bong Hwan Kim, with his strong knack for outside fundraising, helped to increase the organization's annual budget from $300,000 to $2.2 million. With this funding, KYC was able to develop several new divisions, including the business development unit (for example, loan assistance, education, information, and outreach for business owners) and the racially diverse environmental unit (such as water conservation, graffiti removal, and tree planting). This move was one of many that represented a new postriot philosophy predicated on servicing, employing, and creating linkages with other racial and ethnic groups within and outside the Koreatown community. As suggested, financial support from mainstream institutions factored largely into the organization's ability to reach out to other populations, because they could not draw such substantial resources from their traditional ethnic elite providers. Taking its first step to officially recognize the diversity of the community it serviced, the board members voted to change the name of the organization to Korean Youth and Community Center (KYCC) in October 1992. In 1992, KYCC had about forty-one staff members, and by 1995 it became known as the nation's largest social service agency for Korean Americans. The rapid growth and internal development of KYCC was symbolized by the construction of a larger facility that included a nineteen-unit housing complex for low-income residents. With growth came the expansion of social networks linking the ethnic community more closely with mainstream institutions through the conduits of KYCC.

Although organizational growth put KYCC at the forefront of ethnic politics in Koreatown, some of these major reforms were met with sharp criticism from the Korean immigrant community and eventually from the board itself. No sooner had the organization announced the grand opening of its new building when first generation community leaders publicly expressed their resentment over the way mainstream funds were being used to benefit an organization that they believed could not voice the needs of Korean immigrants.

The executive director himself was at the core of heightened discontent among many first generation leaders, whose immigrant mentality clashed with the second generation mindset of Kim. For instance, certain cultural norms on the deferential treatment of elderly male leaders did not coincide with the director's more Americanized belief that one had to "earn respect" in order to get it. These types of cultural tensions placed the organization in direct conflict with the ethnic elite leadership of Koreatown, a situation that became increasingly unsettling for KYCC's more generation-conscious board members. At stake was the agency's dependency on the resources and support of the immigrant community. On hindsight, Kim explains:

> This community is much more immigrant-driven so one of the lessons I learned is that people are slow to change and that you have to work with that pace of change, but also be sensitive to the cultural nuances of the community. And that again takes a lot of thought and you know lining up your allies and really kind of being very deliberate about trying to go and change an organization or community.

Yet even beyond cultural schisms, the political actions of the new executive director disconcerted many immigrant leaders—a sentiment that became most apparent during his controversial stance on the liquor store conversion project. While previous executive directors of KYCC had more or less refrained from entangling themselves with controversial political issues, Kim evoked antagonism among the traditional ethnic elite when he became an active participant in the campaign to convert liquor stores. KYCC joined the Community Coalition for Substance Abuse Prevention and Treatment, Asian Pacific Planning Council (APPCON), and Asian Pacific Americans for a New Los Angeles (APANLA) in a city-funded movement to convert liquor stores in South Central into coin-operated laundromats after the civil unrest. In part, this decision was a logical one considering his progressive background and broader political vision to unite with other racial and ethnic groups around issues of social justice. Some believed that Kim had not "sold out" to the Korean immigrant community but was salvaging what he could for Korean immigrants based on his deeper understanding of American politics. Believing that the Korean community did not stand a chance against the campaign of Black activists to shut down liquor stores, Kim attempted to assist the storeowners in setting up new businesses for themselves as an alternative to fighting a losing battle. Nevertheless, immigrant business owners interpreted his actions as sacrificing the welfare of the ethnic immigrant community in the interests of raising his own political status through coalitions with other racial and ethnic groups.

As conflicts with immigrant community leaders increased, disagreements began to emerge between the board and Kim, the executive director, over the role of the organization within the community. Interestingly, dissension over the way Kim handled the organization often cut across generational boundaries. Some were concerned that the organization was shifting its attention away from the needs of Korean American youth and families toward broader community goals. One 1.5 generation member states, "It started to grow into areas that were not planned and it started to dilute our concentration and focus on youth. We grew to a point where we couldn't manage funding and we couldn't manage contracts. It sort of lost its focus, because it was not a planned growth."

Others perceived this division as a conflict in political vision and the willingness of organizational members to compromise some of these broader visions in order to maintain stable relations with immigrant community leaders. Another long-time, American-born board member explains:

[The board] wanted to see Hispanic, Black, Asian populations woven together, distinct but woven together, but we saw the agency as just one of the threads in this weaving together and we thought that it was the mission of the organization to make sure that we took our thread and we wove it through that tapestry in a way that was appropriate, but we didn't take a role in weaving the entire tapestry. In order to keep our thread moving through the tapestry in a way that we would want it to, we feel that it is really important to maintain absolutely strong ties with the first generation Koreans. And where those first generation Koreans may not see the importance of the overall tapestry, then we might just back off just a little bit in order to keep them as part of our thread. I think Bong Hwan was more of the opinion that no, we should force the tapestry together and that might mean offending or not trying to bring the first generation along with them. I think he was looking at the broader tapestry and saying how can we weave this whole tapestry together.

It becomes clear that both the board members and the executive director were interested in playing their part in improving relations with other racial and ethnic groups. However, according to the interviewee, one side wanted to be mere participants in the movement toward racial equality, whereas the other felt that the organization should take a more proactive leadership role. The passage also shows the different degrees to which each side was willing to compromise their relationships with first generation Korean leaders in order to participate in political movements with other racial and ethnic groups in mainstream society.

As a result of these ideological differences, Kim resigned from the executive director position in 1998. The internal conflicts ultimately reflect the firm entrenchment of KYCC as an organization within the elite networks of the Korean American community. Although initially starting out at the fringes of ethnic politics, KYCC eventually strengthened its ties with other immigrant community leaders in its ascension within the power structures of Koreatown. Indeed, KYCC has achieved a certain level of prominence within the enclave community because of its political expertise, newly found financial resources, and strong ties to "desirable" mainstream institutions, such as law enforcement agencies, government officials, and large-scale corporations. However, the development of KYCC remains intimately intertwined with the ethnic elite networks that support them. Although the board members saw the organization as having benefited from Kim's ability to cultivate linkages with American society, it was clear they were no longer willing to do so at the expense of losing support from the immigrant community.

Currently, the organization is under the management of Johng Ho Song, a new 1.5 generation executive director, who has dedicated fifteen years to serving the organization in different staff and managerial positions. According to several interviewees, Song's cultural understanding of both Korean and American culture as a 1.5 generation person allows him to better interact with the board while maintaining stable relations with the staff. In addition to cultural awareness, his ability to work the media and his withdrawal from mainstream politicking have brought him a step closer to the ethnic elite of the community. Under the new leadership, KYCC has reshifted its focus toward quality of services over program expansion and youth and family services over community politics and programs, returning the organization to its original focus and mission according to some. It also seems that this internal emphasis on program quality and the desire to make KYCC more palatable as a career option has strengthened the corporate underpinnings of the agency.

Best describing his philosophy, Song states, "This is a business. It's a business of serving people and I think lot of times other nonprofits lose sight of that. You know, we're nonprofits; we're just supposed to do good. They don't necessarily understand about the capacity, their own infrastructure that they need in order to do good."

On the other hand, tensions based on generational differences clearly show that KYCC has not always had a stable relationship with the immigrant elite leaders of Koreatown nor consistently maintained their dominant status within ethnic hierarchies. When entrepreneurial interests seriously conflict with the specific concerns of youth and their families, the organization has also been known to stand up against the ethnic elite. An example of this is a debate that arose between KYCC and a large hotel in Koreatown when the Los Angeles Unified School District announced plans to build a high school at the hotel site. In an opinion article on this issue published in the *Korea Central Daily* (Song and Kim 2000), the current executive director advocated firmly for the construction of the school and argued that businesses should temporarily put aside their interests for the development of schools, bookstores, and libraries. However, it is notable that the article did not contest the benefits of growth in the economic sector but instead requested that business owners make attempts to harmonize their interests with the educational interests of youth and family, which Song felt would only lead to greater economic prosperity. Furthermore, the debate took place in the orderly forum of the ethnic media. Thus, KYCC's ideological orientation had developed within, and not in opposition to, ethnic elite power structures.

KIWA: On the Margins of Ethnic Politics

Building an Ethnic Strategy

Partly because of its ideological orientation and its evolution under the guidance of one executive director throughout most of its existence, KIWA has not experienced as drastic a change as KYCC in terms of internal structure. Generally, their staff has consisted of roughly ten full-time organizers and case managers and a handful of Korean and Latino lead worker organizers to run the affiliate workers' organization. KIWA has also brought in student interns to assist with research, organizing, and case management from time to time. The organizational budget in 2005 was approximately $600,000. If anything, KIWA has grown more in terms of their political vision and to a limited degree the types of networks they have tapped into in order to fulfill their expanding ideals. KIWA has recently focused its time and energy on the Market Workers Justice Campaign in addition to working on case management, summer activist training, and coalitional efforts with ethnic, interethnic, and international organizations.

The evolution of KIWA has also been significantly determined by its relationship to the ethnic elite within the Korean American community, although in ways very different from KYCC. KIWA emerged right before the Los Angeles civil unrest when the second generation was beginning to assert its leadership, ethnic organizations were proliferating and competing for newly emerging funds, and the community was beginning to realize the need to deal with racial and ethnic groups other than their own. As such, conformity was not the norm. Unlike KYCC's Christian immigrant origins, KIWA until recently evolved under the guidance of a 1.5 generation executive director with strong political visions and ideologies about the power structures of Koreatown and the role of the organization within it. Because of its leftist leanings, the organization followed a different trajectory than that of KYCC. Ideologically, KIWA has more or less positioned itself against the traditional leadership of the ethnic community, thus compelling it to draw on alternative networks of support. However, KIWA is also acutely aware of how it must deal with the influence of a conservative entrepreneurial elite that is more than willing to use its ethnic resources to protect its interests. Because of conflicts with these elite groups, KIWA has had to employ different political strategies than KYCC to service the needs of marginalized immigrant workers.

The predecessor to KIWA was the Korean Labor Association (KLA), which was founded in the mid-1980s by activists from Korea. Aside from offering case management services to Korean workers, KLA worked together with American labor unions on a few major labor campaigns. Eventually, the organization was able to launch two of its own campaigns against corporations that had been accused of exploiting their Korean-majority workforce. However, both of the campaigns fell apart when the owners replaced the protesting Korean workers with Latino workers. Without the capacity to organize Spanish-speaking workers, KLA's labor campaigns ultimately failed and the organization dissolved.

Although not directly linked to KLA, KIWA was able to draw some lessons from the mistakes of its predecessor. Officially founded in March 1992, KIWA was most formatively shaped by the ideals and experiences of one of its early 1.5 generation cofounders, Roy Hong. With a background in Asian American political activism from the San Francisco Bay Area, Hong developed a strong consciousness around the power of mass leftist movements, the deficiencies of mainstream institutions, and the importance of youth activism early on in his career. According to Glenn Omatsu (September 23, 1999, interview), he became actively involved with traditional labor unions in order to gain the knowledge, experience, and networks he would need to start his own labor organization in the Korean American community.

While recognizing the value of labor unions, Hong understood that the specialized needs of immigrant minority workers could not be met simply by employing the bureaucratic labor organizing strategies of traditional American unions within enclave communities such as Koreatown. As one female KIWA organizer explains it:

> Unions tend to go after big corporations and very established workplaces. You don't hear much about unions in ethnic enclave community so we are out there organizing workers where unions are not. We are rooted in the community and we know the politics of Korean community issues. It's very different from the mainstream. And also we can bring community pressure. That's why I think we're able to function well and do our work well, because we are rooted in the community and we have ties with the union and different labor organizations.

To this end, the future cofounder of KIWA envisioned the creation of a grassroots community organization that could incorporate ethnic immigrant workers into the framework of social activism and economic justice. Just as significant was the organization's guiding philosophy to provide a progressive voice within the conservative domains of Koreatown politics, which had up until this point been monopolized by elite immigrant leaders and business owners.

Prior to founding KIWA, Roy Hong had been a member of Young Koreans United (YKU), a leftist advocacy organization founded by political exiles of the Kwangju massacres, who dedicated themselves to supporting movements for peace, human rights, and social justice in South Korea. Here he met the future executive director, Danny Park, a young 1.5 generation activist who had been actively involved with the prodemocratic student movements in Korea and was more familiar with the politics of the Koreatown community of Los Angeles. Disenchanted with the homeland focus of most Korean organizations at the time, both organizers decided to start an organization that would not only redirect attention toward the situation of Korean Americans in the United States but also provide a progressive political space for young activists within Koreatown.

Like KYCC, the cofounders were motivated to seek alternative sources of support from labor groups and other Asian American communities because of the relative absence of a progressive base within the Korean community of Los Angeles. However, because the mission and ideological vision of the organization and its founder directly conflicted with ethnic elite interests, KIWA preserved only tenuous connections with the traditional leaders of Koreatown throughout its history as compared with KYCC, and it was more likely to have relationships with smaller progressive organizations like its own within the Korean American community. Nevertheless, KIWA's strong roots in non-Korean bases of support do not indicate that the organization was "ethnic" in only an incidental way, but rather that the organization developed a more flexible and broader understanding of ethnicity. Although focused on the issue of workers rights and economic justice, the organization has also recognized the ways in which other progressive struggles, such as women's rights and fights for racial equality, are intertwined with those of workers within the context of ethnic and mainstream power structures. In this sense, KIWA's focus on class issues has had a strong ethnic component in terms of how it perceives the plight of Korean immigrant workers.

With his partner, Hong prepared the groundwork for the organization's conception by seeking the counsel and support of various progressive Korean, Asian, and labor organizations both within and outside the enclave community. Following the footsteps of their predecessor, the KLA, the two organizers began by providing workers' counseling services with the strategic purpose of securing their position within the power structures of the Korean American community. Hong explains:

> We knew that the business community dominates the leadership of the community, the media, and so on and were gonna be leery of the fact that a worker organization was starting. On the other hand, we knew there was really a need for an organization like ours who would really dedicate their work on their interest. So we started with certain set of strategy where we start with service so that we're not a major threat to anyone and make it easy for workers to talk to us and get service and then advocating more community-wide issues that relates to civil rights, immigrant rights, women's rights, worker's rights— not necessarily so much within the community than without. Now we feel

like we have enough bases of support in the community to be able to become bolder about our demands for change in the community, and we're not just red-baited or completely silenced by the media to the point where we become completely defective.

The above quote underlines the intricate strategizing required in order for a marginalized organization set against the interests of the ethnic elite to ease its way into the enclave community. By providing nonconfrontational services to workers, the organization quietly built up a strong support network and resource base among progressive groups with which it could challenge the ethnic elite.

Barely a month had passed when the 1992 riots hit Los Angeles and devastated the Korean American community. The civil unrest had two effects on the organization. First, the crisis initially enhanced a more universal sense of ethnic solidarity among KIWA's members, who decided to temporarily put aside its specific interests in order to assist Korean American victims with postriot recovery efforts. KIWA was among the many ethnic organizations to help victims of the riots that were neglected by mainstream institutions—from writing letters for non-English-speaking victims to helping to check inaccurate portrayals of the riots by the media. In addition, KIWA joined other social service agencies and political advocacy organizations within the Korean American community to help launch the Korean American Inter-Agency Council (KAIAC) coalition.

However, the crisis that pulled together Korean Americans of all backgrounds would not last for long. As noted in the previous chapter, the unequal distribution of relief funds prompted KIWA organizers to launch a campaign on behalf of victimized workers, called the 4.29 Displaced Workers Justice Campaign, which put the organization in the community spotlight for the first time. Although the size of the monetary concessions was somewhat significant, the campaign was more symbolically important for its effective use of direct action tactics against the power holders of the entrepreneurial community. The campaign was the first in which KIWA exercised its political strength to protest the hegemonic practices of both entrepreneurs and their conservative supporters. By using such aggressive approaches, the community could best publicize the needs and problems of Korean immigrant workers to outside groups where their strongest bases of support lie. Using less militant tactics would keep the issues contained within the ethnic community and hence fail to challenge internal power structures. Furthermore, direct action strategies are most effective for groups with minimal financial resources or few ties to resource-rich organizations, because it requires more manpower than money.

Although KIWA would have mostly likely reached this point on its own, the second impact the riots had was to reaffirm the organization's commitment to reach out to other racial and ethnic communities. Throughout 1993 and 1994, KIWA began to engage in a number of coalitional movements that helped to strengthen its bases of support outside Koreatown. As part of the Bus Riders Union campaign, the organization teamed up with other grassroots organizations to demand that the Metropolitan Transit Authority allocate more funding to the bus system, which primarily serves low-income minorities in urban areas. In addition, KIWA joined other groups in educating Korean American voters on the potentially damaging impact of Proposition 187, the proposition that would deny undocumented immigrants access to specific public services. In the Jessica McClintock Garment Workers Justice Campaign, KIWA actively supported the Asian Immigrant Workers Advocates (AIWA) in initiating a nationwide boycott and protest campaign against the company's garment industry. One of its subcontractors, the Lucky Sewing Company, had failed to pay roughly $15,000 in back wages to twelve garment workers when it closed down its shops. The protest was also crucial in its efforts to get university students more actively involved in hands-on direct action movements.

In 1992, KIWA found its first golden opportunity to build a reputation among progressive constituencies within Los Angeles, unite with Latino workers, and utilize its homeland connections in Korea. The dispute arose when an overseas Korean company, Koreana Hotel Co., Ltd., acquired the Wilshire Hyatt in 1991. With the transfer of ownership, the Koreana Hotel management fired 175 unionized workers and replaced most of them with a nonunionized workforce at a lower wage within months after the Hotel Employees and Restaurant Employees (HERE) Local 11 had won a major contract with the previous owners (Cho 1992). Because the workforce was primarily comprised of Latinos protesting the exploitative practices of a Korean management, HERE Local 11 wanted to prevent the dispute from becoming racialized and called on some progressive Asian American organizations, including KIWA, for assistance.

According to interviewees, KIWA played a major role in not only focusing the public attention on labor-related issues but also in utilizing different ethnic and transnational networks and resources to fight against the Korean corporation, which was known for its antiunion activities even in Korea. Through letter-writing campaigns, boycotts, and protest demonstrations all the way to the Korean Consulate, the protesters forced the management to negotiate with the leaders and rehire unionized workers. Only a few years later, KIWA would use the same strategies to help HERE Local 11 in a similar case against Hanjin International, which had fired 575 mostly Latino employees from one of the largest hotels in downtown Los Angeles. In this particular incident, KIWA's strategies included rallying political support from local liberal politicians, soliciting the services of several Korean social service and religious organizations, using the ethnic media to draw attention to the corporation's labor abuses, using ties with South Korean labor unions for support, and boycotting the corporation's major subsidiary, Korean Airlines (Saito and Park 2000).

Ethnic Confrontation and the Restaurant Campaign

Throughout this period, the organization had focused its efforts on providing case management, fellowship programs, and educational seminars to workers within the community while developing their techniques in direct action movements against specific workplaces. In terms of case management, counselors provided individual advice and assistance to workers who had not been paid minimum or overtime wages or had suffered different forms of abuse and harassment at the hands of their employers. Furthermore, case management had been made open to all workers, regardless of ascriptive trait (that is, race, gender, and so forth) or type of industry—a distinctive trait of "community unionism" and one that was not often seen in mainstream labor unions (Omatsu 1995). After some time, the members of KIWA realized that the repetitive process of assisting workers on a case-by-case basis, only to have the same clients return for assistance with another employer, did little to remedy the overall economic structure that was responsible for their exploitation. As a result, KIWA organizers began to shift toward an industry-wide reform model with which to tackle labor problems in Koreatown.

Increasing interaction and exposure to workers through case management had allowed the leadership to identify problematic areas and trends among various Koreatown businesses, which ultimately drew their attention to the restaurant industry. Due to the unusually high concentration of restaurants in Koreatown, this industry is known to be one of the most competitive, unregulated, and unstable sectors in the ethnic enclave economy. As a result, employees are forced to work up to 72 hours per week for low or subminimum wages under hazardous working conditions and are subject to abusive treatment by their employers. In April 1998, a sweep of Koreatown restaurants by the Department of Labor revealed that only forty-one out of the forty-three restaurants investigated were in compliance with basic labor law regulations, as later reported in the *Los Angeles Times* (Kang 1998). In response to these conditions, KIWA organized and won several important protest demonstrations throughout 1995 and 1996 against Korean-owned restaurants that had failed to provide their workers minimum and/or overtime wages. In late 1996, KIWA consolidated these efforts into a broader and long-term movement called the Koreatown Restaurant Workers Justice Campaign, the aim of which was to demand reform on an industry-wide level while simultaneously empowering workers to fight for their rights.

During the campaign period, some of the owners that KIWA confronted resorted to blacklisting participating workers. One of the primary agents through which such blacklisting occurred was the Korean Restaurant Owners Association (KROA), which became one of KIWA's major adversaries in the fight against poor working conditions in the industry. KROA was also backed by conservative community leaders and the ethnic media, which used "red-baiting" tactics to paint KIWA in a negative light. Workers in the study explained how they were initially reluctant to approach the organization, because they had been told that the organization was affiliated with the Communist Party in North Korea or was involved in illegal activities to extort money from business owners. The entrepreneurial elite are also able to utilize powerful social networks and collective resources to counter the demands of coethnic immigrant workers. The most extreme example of this was when a business owner targeted by KIWA for failing to pay back wages called in a favor from a Korean agent of the Federal Bureau of Investigation (FBI), who contacted allies of KIWA falsely claiming that the organization was under FBI investigation for extortion. As KIWA grew more visible and bolder in its demands, one male organizer noticed that workers became more reluctant to seek assistance until the situation became worse and were hence more likely to bring more complicated cases to KIWA than they had in the past. To address this issue, the organization hired on a full-time attorney and developed its legal department.

Realizing that they could not effectively remedy workplace conditions unless they fought such blacklisting practices, the organization responded with heightened protest demonstrations and a major lawsuit directed against KROA for $500,000 in punitive damages in August 1996, reported the *Korea*

Times (Lee 1996). Although its allies have lacked the kinds of financial re-sources that KYCC attracts from some of its own outside sources, KIWA has benefited substantially from the manpower that other non-Korean organiza-tions have provided for these types of protest demonstrations. Due to lack of political expertise and diminishing resources, the president of KROA eventu-ally conceded, signing an agreement that included the establishment of labor law seminars at individual restaurants and the creation of a $10,000 workers' defense fund financed by KROA (*Korea Times*, September 19, 1997a). How-ever, a hard-line faction organized under the new president of KROA disputed the former president's authority to agree to such a contract and nullified the agreement.

Around this time, representatives from ten major immigrant organizations gathered together for a meeting of the Southern California Korean American Coalition of Business Associations to discuss ways to counter KIWA's boycott demonstrations (*The Korea Times*, October 24, 1997b). During the meeting, the leaders characterized KIWA's tactics as "excessive" and "hurtful" to indi-vidual businesses as well as the Koreatown economy and argued that grievances should be addressed through proper legal channels, such as the Labor Admin-istration. Months later, representatives from upper-tier immigrant organiza-tions such as the Korean-American Federation (KAF), the Koreatown Asso-ciation, and the Korean Chamber of Commerce formed a labor-management dispute subcommittee to deal with similar conflicts between employers and employees in the future. In coordination with KROA, the 1.5/second genera-tion Korean American Coalition (KAC) formed another Mediation Panel for Workers Program, whose aim is to "dissolve disputes between workers and Korean restaurant owners" (KAC brochure).

KIWA found its chance to respond concretely to KROA's resistance when one of the leading proponents of KROA, who had contributed his own re-sources to these disputes, committed a labor violation of his own. In Septem-ber 1997, the owner fired his head chef when he consulted with KIWA after refusing to sign an illegal document that would have made the employee re-sponsible for part of his payroll taxes. In response, KIWA staged major pro-test demonstrations, letter-writing campaigns, and a ten-day hunger strike in front of the business establishment for roughly six months until the restau-rant owner finally conceded in 1998. These types of militant strategies again allowed the organization to publicize injustices in Koreatown with minimal financial costs. The owner eventually agreed to rehire the worker and pay him back wages as well as comply with labor laws. KIWA also spearheaded another six-month campaign in July 1998 against a major Korean-owned restaurant, this time over failure to pay minimum wage to two Latino employees. Because the owner had threatened to report the workers to the immigration authorities, KIWA brought the protest to another level by instituting a consumer boycott to assert the rights of all immigrant workers with the help of other community activists. The campaign also resulted in the successful payment of back wages for the two workers and reaffirmed relations between Korean and Latino supporters.

In March 1999, KROA finally began to acknowledge problems between employers and workers in the Koreatown restaurant industry and, in conjunction with KIWA, officially announced the formation of a mediation and arbitration panel. KIWA had also filed a second lawsuit against KROA, which was finally resolved in April 1999 when KROA gave in to another agreement that included the institution of a health fair, a hiring hall, and a standard wage scale for workers. KROA eventually dissolved, although more recent news is that both moderate and hard-line factions of the original association have each discussed resurrecting their own organizations. Since then, KIWA has engaged in a number of activities, such as town hall meetings and workers' marches through Koreatown, while continuing to assist workers with wage claims and other workplace violations through letters, negotiations, and when necessary direct-action protest campaigns.

As KIWA transitioned into an established constituency albeit on the margins of ethnic political structures, its focus grew to include more international activities and transnational support networks. Throughout 1996, KIWA actively participated in the North Korea Famine Relief movement in Koreatown and projects to support international solidarity for striking workers in South Korea. In 1997, the projects for international solidarity were extended to include workers in Mexico. Among other things, they have helped to foster support among Korean American organizations and American labor unions for workers' movements in South Korea. For instance, the current executive director, Danny Park, informs me that when key organizers from South Korea have made visits to the United States, KIWA has helped to organize seminars and presentations and has introduced them to other union activists in the country. He also told me that they have even accompanied Korean organizers to Mexico in order to educate them on the global nature of class issues and exploitative working conditions in these areas. Thus, the organization has begun to cultivate transnational organizational linkages for labor activists across race, ethnicity, and nationality, although they remain firmly committed to focusing on domestic issues.

More recently, the organization has directed its attention toward the working conditions and unionization of workers in Korean-owned supermarkets in Koreatown. KIWA's recent campaign on Korean supermarkets, many of which are national and international enterprises, represent a new stage in the organization's political development in terms of its interest in demanding "living wages" from large-scale, money-making businesses in Koreatown. "Living wages" are the wages a worker would need to get paid in order to live at subsistence level. According to activists, the minimum wage required by law is insufficient for workers to live on and that Korean supermarkets can afford to match the living wages offered by equivalent American supermarkets such as Vons and Ralph's. KIWA has framed this campaign as a united effort by business owners and workers to combat poverty in enclave economies like Koreatown. According to the current director, tackling large-scale supermarkets as opposed to small, individual restaurants is in some ways easier because of the large number of workers that can be mobilized to pressure owners. However, employers have more resources at their disposal and can employ the services of powerful professionals outside the ethnic community—pressure which KIWA has matched by using the combined power of workers, consumers, and politicians to protest unfair labor practices.

After a few months of negotiation, KIWA was able to convince the owners of Han-guk Market and the Galleria to implement a living wage for their workers. The most recent efforts of the Market Workers Justice Campaign have focused on the owners of Assi supermarket, who had allegedly harassed, discriminated against, and denied hire to Korean and Latino workers. Assi supermarket is one of the largest importers of Asian food products in North America with branches all across the United States. With the assistance of KIWA, the Immigrant Workers Union has been trying to gain recognition from the owners, an action that last ended with the suspension of over fifty workers in 2002. Negotiations were at a standstill at the time of the study until Assi agreed to rehire those workers.

An analysis on the evolution and contemporary structures of KIWA and KYCC reveals how the context for their emergence were very much shaped by the ways they were able to navigate their political agenda within traditional ethnic hierarchies. Both KYCC and KIWA lacked status and recognition in the Koreatown community, as part of a new generation dealing with issues considered inconsequential to immigrants preoccupied with economic survival. Since then, KYCC has followed a divergent path from KIWA, mainly because of its greater capacity and willingness to negotiate its political vision with their relations with the ethnic elite. For KYCC, its access to valuable information, resources, and networks with mainstream institutions made it an invaluable partner to the immigrant elite leadership, who also sought some of the same goals despite divergent, generation-based approaches and outlooks. For KIWA, gradual entrenchment within the political structures of the ethnic community was much more strategic and surreptitious, because its progressive politics and goal to empower Koreatown workers clashed with those of the ethnic elite. Over time, the leadership, ideological base, and internal structures of these organizations have been significantly shaped in turn by pre established relations with both ethnic and mainstream institutions. Those organizations intimately associated with immigrant power holders place greater emphasis on maintaining their elite networks, while those on the margins of ethnic power structures tend to be driven more by their political vision.

Regardless of strategy, both organizations have been able to build on their individual strengths in order to serve the broader community. Based on the resources of outside networks, 1.5/second generation organizations have implemented the type of services and programs that they feel will best help groups to achieve their goals of self- and collective empowerment. Having assumed different roles within ethnic politics, KIWA and KYCC have developed different internal cultures and structures that have sculpted members' concepts of "ethnicity" and "politics" in very distinct ways. The following chapter will explore in greater depth the way bridging organizations like these are able to appeal to the diverse experiences of 1.5/second generation Korean Americans and cultivate ethnic political solidarity among their membership.

7 Giving Back to the Community

ON THE SURFACE, THE NEW SECOND GENERATION seems to show all the signs of having truly "assimilated" into mainstream America. More and more Korean Americans are beginning to relinquish their parents' native tongue and homeland culture in favor of the American way of life. Many have made close friends and found romantic partners outside their ethnic circles. Whatever their socioeconomic roots, a significant number have mastered the educational system and moved on to prosperous careers as upwardly mobile, young professionals. And only a few have chosen to continue working or living in the booming enclave economy of Koreatown. In light of these different trends, some may interpret this to mean that ethnic ties and identities have little relevance in the daily lives of middle-class Korean Americans. Such shifts are said to be indicative of the declining significance of ethnicity among young generations of Korean Americans, yet in the case of ethnic nonprofits, the question arises: why do they return?

To some degree, much of what is taking place among the second generation does have to do with the inevitable effects of socioeconomic, cultural, and spatial assimilation into American society. However, these experiences are further complicated by the continuing struggles of Korean Americans with race and ethnicity in their personal and political lives. I apply the concept of *ethnic-centered experiences* to understand the variable but persistent significance of ethnicity in the diverse lives of Korean Americans who choose to work in nonprofits but live outside the Koreatown community. As opposed to perceiving ethnicity as the product of homogeneous identities and experiences centered on the enclave, ethnic-centered experiences refer to the increasingly diverse ways in which individuals and groups find ethnicity as having some relevance in shaping their lives. These experiences may include living in dual worlds as children of immigrants, negotiating ethnic consciousness with sexism as Korean American women, or struggling with racialized experiences as a Korean Asian American minority in a White-dominated neighborhood. Bridging organizations offer them the political framework and institutional structure within which to make sense of their ethnic-centered experiences and find common interests with other Korean Americans from similar backgrounds.

This chapter will first examine the diverse ethnic-centered perspectives and experiences that set the context for 1.5/second generation involvement in the Korean Immigrant Workers Advocates (KIWA), the Korean Youth and Community Center (KYCC), and other Koreatown organizations.[1] It is shown how bridging organizations create an alternative type of community for their members by providing a "place" where they can pursue their individual goals, embrace their dual identities as Korean Americans, and connect with other like-minded staff members. As the case studies of KYCC and KIWA reveal, bridging organizations tend to attract a specific subgroup of Korean Americans, depending on the roles they have assumed within the ethnic community. Related to this, an overview of KYCC's and KIWA's missions, internal structures, organizational support networks, and membership composition shows how each organization promotes and reinforces different frameworks of ethnic political solidarity to their respective membership. The last section examines how these political frameworks shape the way these two organizations approach community work in different ways.

Why They Come

Among 1.5/second generation interviewees, one of the most common responses to the question of community involvement centers on the concept of "giving back to the community." Giving back to the community generally refers to the feeling that one has benefited from some broadly defined ethnic community to which one feels obligated to contribute in return, whether in the form of time or money. The benefits received may be either specifically or vaguely defined; how the respondents define "community" may also vary widely. The concept itself is emblematic of the wide-ranging identities and experiences that have drawn Korean Americans from all spectrums to ethnic organizational work.

In the study, the community to which Korean Americans felt this deep sense of obligation was not necessarily circumscribed by the geographical boundaries of Koreatown or even by ethnic membership as Korean Americans. Some followed the traditional path of living in the enclave and working with Korean American churches and organizations as youths and then transitioning into the growing nonprofit sector as adults. However, many others explained how their commitment to Korean Americans stemmed from their sense of affinity with more broadly defined communities of interest, including immigrants, people of color, workers, or Asian Americans. For example, one program organizer for KYCC was drawn to Korean American nonprofits during the Korean-Black conflicts because of his childhood experiences growing up in a Black-dominated neighborhood where he learned to speak "street slang," intermingled mostly with African American youth, and became strongly influenced by African American mentors. Another activist explained to me how her eventual position in KIWA took shape from her life experiences growing up in a predominantly white neighborhood to working with the poor and the homeless in college to her political and student labor activities in Korea. However interviewees defined this community, it was understood that the Korean Americans they served were considered to be an integral part of it.

The people I interviewed were likely to have had at least some minimal contact with a minority community (Korean or otherwise), because they had lived in a racially diverse neighborhood, socialized and organized with other minority groups, or were exposed to organizational work at an early age. But notably, not all their experiences began in the Koreatown enclave. For instance, undergraduate student organizations create ideological passageways to nonprofit organizations like these, either by cultivating social awareness or organizing cosponsored activities with local organizations. A good number of the longer-term staff members had also participated in Korean American after-school programs as youths—an experience that allowed them to recognize the importance of community work later in life. Still others were steered into ethnic nonprofits because of their previous involvement in social work, educational institutions, or other community-based organizations (CBOs) that cater to disadvantaged groups. Considering the overwhelming influence of Christian churches in the Korean American community, it is not surprising that some Korean Americans had also been led to organizational work through their local churches.

Ethnic organizational work gave many 1.5/second generation Korean Americans the opportunity to negotiate tensions they felt living in the bicultural world of Korean America. While dual identity crisis is certainly not an uncommon phenomenon among the younger generation, these tensions were most poignantly felt among those interviewees raised in White-dominated neighborhoods or older respondents who had grown up in the earlier years of the ethnic community's formation when other Korean Americans were few and far between. Organizations play an especially critical role for those disconnected from the ethnic community, because they offer a visible and relatively open entryway into the community, as well as a chance to work alongside other 1.5/second generation members with similar experiences.

Having grown up when there were few Korean Americans with whom to relate, several older people ranging from their late forties to early sixties recounted to me their personal struggles with their own bicultural identities. One forty-seven-year-old, 1.5 generation counselor describes how her experiences as a youth inspired her to work for a Korean social service agency.

> I came here when I was in junior high school, and I had very difficult time adjusting because not only was I the only Korean in school, but also the Korean community itself was not actually there. I felt I was very lost, and I had a very difficult time trying to overcome my identity crisis, and you don't feel like you belong anywhere. After I graduated, I wanted to find out what my skills and my assets are and what I can do with it, and my conclusion was that I have the Korean background, I know how Korean immigrants are, I know the difficult times that I went through as a youth growing up as a Korean in America. So I felt that the thing I can contribute to Korean community is to really link up with Korean immigrant youth, who are going through many difficult periods. I wanted to be the kind of person who can listen to them and see if there's any way that I can narrow the gap between young people, parents, and the society as a whole.

Another twenty-six-year-old, 1.5 generation Korean American woman explains how her work as a counselor helped her to negotiate the tensions of being Korean and American. By developing new relationships with the community around her, she began to form a stronger bond with Koreatown itself beyond its superficial role as a place to shop and go to church.

> I always knew myself as a Korean American, but I was confused between being a Korean or American and this is the agency that taught me that I can

be a Korean American. I think I'm now more involved with the Koreatown community. Before I came out and shopped, but I was never really involved in Koreatown and that changed. I was very involved with Korean bible study and was very religious, and I think they opened my eyes a little more. [Churches] can be close-minded sometimes. They don't want to deal with things that are not Christian-related so they're closed minded and [this organization] just helped me to see that you can be a Christian and still help out as a social worker.

These passages remind us how even the middle-class suburban context may shape the various dimensions of ethnic identity formation and the different trajectories along which 1.5/second generation members may eventually return to the ethnic community.

One twenty-nine-year-old, 1.5 generation woman states how a sense of racial isolation at her workplace led her to become involved with KYCC. She goes on to explain how, over time, community work taught her how to interact with the first generation and also dispelled preconceived conceptions she had about other Korean Americans.

I think KYCC made me realize that I am a Korean person. I was always having this perception that if you work with Koreans too much, too many Koreans around you, it won't be too productive, you won't get anywhere [laughs]. But as I joined KYCC, I noticed that it's not like that. It's more productive, more supportive. Having to share the same language I think brings us more closer together.

Involvement in ethnic organizations provides a social context within which to develop self-pride and a sense of identity and belonging centered on ethnicity and service work. In so doing, this woman became better integrated into the community she had once disdained.

Another thirty-eight-year-old, second generation staff member who grew up in Ohio tells me how his transition into understanding his Korean American identity developed first with his connection with other Asian Americans. He states:

Until I started working here, I identified first as being Asian so what was critical in my life was my race, some of the racism I had to deal with, you know all of that, and so my ethnicity as being Korean didn't come into play a lot. And I think also during college I had some bad experiences with Koreans too. You know lot of the Koreans, I mean not all of them, but you know the

Koreans that were in like the Korean groups were international students. I felt that they looked down on me because I couldn't speak Korean. And I looked at some of the ways they acted, you know some of the faces they put on, the gossip, all of that; you know I really came to disdain Korean people for a long time. So I think after I came here, that changed somewhat so that I realized Koreans are no different than anybody else.

This particular interviewee initially identified more closely with the pan-ethnic community not only because of the racialized framework within which he felt society operated, but also because of his felt detachment from foreign-born Koreans within his local community. It was only in working with a 1.5/second generation ethnic organization as an adult that he could garner the kind of insights that would allow him to relate to other Korean Americans.

For 1.5 generation members, stereotypical notions about Korean Americans seem to come from community gossip and the countless stories they read about scandals, briberies, and political infighting among Korean leaders in the ethnic media. For second generation members, limited interaction with the Korean American community, mainstream stereotypes about Asians, and negative images from their parents and peers about the "typical Korean" also serve to perpetuate these preconceptions, especially among those who do not live in Koreatown. Exposing members to other Korean Americans from diverse backgrounds and similar experiences helped many of them to deal with their personal ethnic-based struggles. This is not to say that all their experiences with Korean Americans have been positive, but that being exposed to so many different types of Koreans made them realize that the community was more diverse than they had imagined and that somewhere within the large ethnic community, they could find people with values and experiences similar to theirs.

Young Korean Americans made observations about the more positive sense of community that these organizations create as an alternative to the nightclubs, pool halls, and karaoke bars that Koreatown is most known for. The following quote is from a twenty-year-old ex-gang member, who interned for KYCC's Gang Awareness Program (GAP):

I think GAP and gangs are similar. GAP gives you a sense of family and a sense of belonging as well as a sense of responsibility. It's just that gangs, what they do as gangs, are wrong. They break the law and whatnot. The good thing [about GAP] is that it also helped me to get my life on track. When I was doing data entry at my last job, it was a one-track job; you don't do nothing but data entry, you know. You don't just get nowhere from that. From here, you could learn and could get experience, and you know, do a lot of good things I could put on my resume. And that's one big reason I enjoy this job: 'cause it's gonna help me in the future. I know that for sure.

The interviewee draws interesting parallels between the social networks of Koreatown gangs and those of GAP, distinguishing them only by the positive or negative nature of the values and activities they encourage. Ethnic solidarity becomes an integral aspect of his experience at GAP. As suggested, the values and activities of GAP help to foster higher career aspirations and equip youth with the tools to achieve these goals within a supportive coethnic environment. In the process, the intern picked up distinct skills and experience from working at the organization, which offered him a way out of dead-end jobs he had held in the past.

This realization however can take the form of a more nuanced and layered interpretation of ethnicity that seems to contradict itself at times. In general, many community members with whom I spoke tended to make clear distinctions between the way they themselves view and practice being "Korean" and the cultural behaviors of "typical" Koreatown Koreans, who flaunt expensive brand-name clothes, smoke and drink excessively, and hang out at local pool halls and karaoke clubs. For some, this is a way for them to separate themselves from the materialistic or exploitative practices of Koreatown Korean Americans; for others, it is a means to elevate themselves above a "lower class" of Korean FOBs ("fresh off the boat"); and for still others, it is a way to articulate their individuality against the negative stereotypical representations people may hold about Korean Americans.

For instance, one intern of a gang awareness program expressed distaste for Koreans who tended to hang around in packs in the typical Koreatown places—something that he felt he could not relate to. Almost in the same breath, he said that he now hung out mainly with Korean ex-gang members in his program, because they could best relate to his experiences. In a similar manner, an eighteen-year-old female youth program leader from the suburbs stated her aversion to "the stereotypical Korean girl or like stereotypical guy. I hate the fact that a lot of people associate Koreans with that image. I think that's generally true of a lot of Koreans in Koreatown, but if you go outside of Koreatown, it's so not like that." Despite her desire to disassociate from this

stereotypical image, she admits that she herself hangs out in Koreatown frequently for KYCC business or social reasons. Interestingly, both interviewees
were able to explain these contradictions by differentiating their own unique
"ethnic" behaviors from those of "typical" Korean Americans.

Community workers also maintain a hazy distinction between their personal identities and practices at home and the broader political persona they
adopt within the organizational setting. Such boundary-affirming practices
allow them to preserve a sense of their individuality within the social structures of a rapidly diversifying, internally divided, and politically charged
community. Interviewees oftentimes will articulate their need to hold onto
their personalized interpretation of "Korean Americanness" even as they recognize their political identification and solidarity with other racial and ethnic
groups.

Take, for instance, the example of one second generation Korean American staff member whom both Koreans and Latinos within the organization
jokingly refer to as "Latino," because he seemed to live, eat, and breathe anything Mexican at work. Nevertheless, when I ask him if he feels the "Korean"
part of the organization means anything to him personally, he responds:

> I identify with the name Korean in just my personal sense of identity. And
> so from that, I think there is kind of a personal and now a political kind of
> "affinity" or a sense of closeness with what happens in Korea and with also
> what happens I guess to Koreans here too. Then you start to cross into more
> of a political landscape where it's not just Korean, it's actually Latino as well. I
> guess I have a strong sort of Korean identity, but at the same time, in terms of
> my work or externally from outside of myself, I would say it's more immigrant
> and obviously being here for ten years with immigrant workers, low-wage
> workers, and things like that. And in many ways, I would feel a more closeness
> with more immigrant workers than say just Koreans in Koreatown, because
> quite frankly for me a lot of Koreans in Koreatown kind of disgust me.

Again, this interviewee expressed particular aversion to the exploitative
practices of dominant Korean groups upon which the Koreatown enclave
economy was founded, yet he still felt a sense of connection to his ethnic roots.
He goes on to say that this identity stems from some inexplicable connection
he feels with those who share similar cultural values. This type of relationship
does not necessarily preclude all non-Koreans nor does it necessarily include
all Koreans but is best articulated through his ethnic identity. It is also inter-

esting the way the interviewee also constructs his own sense of ethnic identity in juxtaposition to the predominant framework of "Koreanness" that he feels characterizes Koreatown Korean Americans.

Another second generation activist who is active with the Korean and Asian American lesbian, gay, bisexual, and transgender (LGBT) community also expresses similar interests in practicing "Korean Americanness" her own way.

> *Is there any reason you don't work with some of the other major Korean American organizations?* Almost everything I do has to do with Korean Americans so it's not like I don't work with the Koreans or somehow distance myself, but it's kind of hard to find the terms in which to engage in with the Korean American community. Like I really wouldn't feel comfortable working with the Korean American social service agencies if I know that some of the staff and board members are blatantly homophobic. It's not just a political difference you know, but it affects me very personally. Something like that happened throughout my college years too, because I'm 1.5, speak English, and queer people just assume that I don't have anything to do with Koreans and that I don't know anything about Korean issues. Like if I walk into a Korean bookstore people are like we don't have anything in English, or on campus if I walk up to a Korean student group and they think I'm reading something in Korean they would try to take it away from me telling me it's in Korean while I'm reading it. So there's a lot of these questions of authenticity and credibility that I personally don't feel very comfortable with. *So you find the Korean to be part of your identity?* Oh yeah, absolutely. But Korean American my way, not their way kind of thing. [Interviewer's questions in *italics*]

This particular passage gives us insight into the narrow and hegemonic ways Korean Americanness may be constructed within the broader community. This feeling of distance does not so much alienate this interviewee from her Korean American roots but pushes her to re-conceptualize her ethnic identity in her own individualistic way.

Many interviewees chose to get involved with their ethnic community not only because of personal struggles they may have directly experienced, but also, because of people and events that strengthened their felt symbolic ties with other Korean Americans. As described in Chapter 4, some interviewees in the study were driven by strong political ideologies about the situation of Koreans in America and their role as community organizers in both homeland Korea and American society. The 1992 Los Angeles civil unrest best exemplifies how this abstract sense of empathy can heighten the younger generation's desire to return to the community. By bringing to light the victimization of parents, relatives, family friends, and other familiar acquaintances, many second generation members were able to overcome their personal struggles with intergenerational tensions both within the family and the community at large and develop a strong sense of coethnic empathy for the Korean American community.

A twenty-nine-year-old, 1.5 generation female interviewee explains how the 1992 Los Angeles civil unrest pushed her to become active with KIWA.

> I have never been exposed to the Korean community before KIWA or never thought of certain issues that the Korean American community faced. I grew up in a predominantly White neighborhood in San Fernando Valley, and you never think about your ethnic identity or what it means. I think the '92 riots kind of made me start thinking about things like that, about my community and the kind of issues our community faces in terms of racism or classism. And then I met KIWA. KIWA has this perspective that the Korean community is very much represented by middle-class elite conservative businessmen, and they represent Korean community to the mainstream society. And KIWA has looked [at] the lowest of the ladder, focusing on low-income workers in Koreatown who aren't being represented by the conservative elite Korean businessmen. I thought KIWA was a good organization to learn about the Korean community and to think about how to address some of our issues.

The preceding excerpt shows how organizational work allowed the interviewee to expand her understanding of ethnicity beyond her experiences in a predominantly White neighborhood.

Some interviewees emphasized the symbolic connection they felt with the Korean American community as a result of their own experiences with discrimination and racial and ethnic profiling in different stages of their lives. One twenty-five-year-old, second generation woman described her experiences with discrimination in Minnesota where she encountered "a different stereotype of Asians as being poor or part of Asian gangs." She recalled hearing people make racist comments about Korean storeowners and being followed around in stores because of her punk look. She later remarks:

> It's really important to know where you come from and where your parents came from, the whole immigrant thing like how you ended up here. *It's the*

knowledge value then? The knowledge value and the associational value 'cause you've always been Korean, you'll be identified as Korean, and I think you have to maintain those ties. You can't forget it, 'cause you're always gonna be marked as such. It's not something that you can walk away from. [Interviewer's question in *italics*].

Discrimination also had a flip side in that this woman felt that she was treated better than other racial minority groups in other contexts because of the model minority stereotype. Nevertheless, this experience of being made to feel "different" in either way had the effect of strengthening her sense of solidarity with other Korean Americans, although she expressed disdain for prejudices that Koreans often harbored against Blacks and Latinos.

In other instances, the interviewees' identification with the ethnic community was based on more abstract and indirect feelings of empathy for important people in their lives. For example, some interviewees said that they had become connected to the Korean American community because of the formative experiences of close friends or family members. The sacrifices and hardships of parents were particularly crucial in enhancing their felt obligation to return to the community. One of KIWA's cofounders relates how such parental connections motivated him to get involved in community work.

Ever since we immigrated to U.S., I was only in junior high, but I saw my parents, especially my mother, having to work in a hotel as a maid, having to work as a seamstress. And I knew that indirectly such exploitation and suffering exists. I knew even after so many years that it's still going on in the immigrant community. Through my parents' suffering, I did get an education and I was offered a chance to do something that I would like to do, anything that I would like to do. So I chose to be in community organization where we could assist my parents' generation or the newer recent immigrant workforce from repeating the same suffering and exploitation.

For this respondent, the experiences of his parents represented the suffering of Korean immigrant workers everywhere, and it was important for him to find that organizational niche that could recognize the distinctive experiences of immigrant workers.

Above all, interviewees regardless of age, gender, class, generation, or political partisanship expressed a deep commitment to giving back to the community. Oftentimes, this meant facing the doubts, criticisms, and general discouragement of parents and fellow community members, whose idea of success centered on studying hard and making money. For many first generation immigrants, community service was a way to help the less fortunate or to show their graciousness to their new homeland, but for second generation members, it was more a way to deal with the tensions of being a Korean American and to expand their social horizons and those of the communities around them beyond their immigrant parents' single-minded focus on economic survival. As the following second generation male community organizer explains:

> I think it's important to get in an academic sense a good education. I think it's, I would say it's 50-50. That's important but it's important to have a good social experience. And social experience meaning that you participate as a student in things that are not academic oriented. You know if you're in high school, being part of a club or something, or it could be even playing sports, it could be being active on campus or in some capacity, or even having a good diversity of friends. You know, not just Korean friends but just a diversity of friends. And having a real kind of balanced experience along with you know learning how to add and subtract.

Many high school and college interns complain that they have trouble justifying the time they devote to volunteering or interning at the organization to parents who feel as if it is taking away from their studies. In response, they argue that volunteer work not only teaches them skills and provides non-academic experiences that will help them in the future, but also assists them with resolving identity conflicts, self-esteem problems, and the need for social support systems that are otherwise lacking in their home environment and school life.

For some, this means negotiating the weight of their parents' immigrant dreams with their dedication to give back to the ethnic community. Some second generation female interviewees were particularly aware of the sacrifices their parents had made to give their children a better life and could not always reconcile this with their decision to enter a nonprofit career.

> My parents come from very poor backgrounds but they have a very upwardly mobile mentality. I guess they're very typical Koreans in some ways but very atypical in other ways. They're typical in the sense that they place a lot of value on education. Like I have friends whose families own small businesses and they ask their kids to help out at the stores and stuff. And my parents were

very clear about that: they were like "no, your role is to study." I mean we might help out in the weekends a little bit, but basically, they just did not want us to be involved in the business. They just wanted us to study, and you know they're basically trying to push us up into the upper class [short laugh], right? You know, you need to go and study and become someone better, right? So they really are strong in that mentality. And that's 'cause they struggled a lot when they were younger. Like my mother did very well in school but because she was a woman, her parents didn't send her to school and they were sort of poor and stuff. So she kind of worked her way through school and became a teacher. And she was very hard working. And then the whole sense of like I went to Harvard and now I'm working in the first generation community. And I get this from a lot of the workers or community members too: "You went to Harvard, what are you doing here?" You know, they're saying you couldn't make it you know in mainstream society so that's why you're here kind of thing. And it's totally seen as looked down upon, you know. And that's hard for me, just cause I think I have a lot of that baggage. Of course I want to be competent, I want to be good at what I do, I want to be respected for being a good lawyer, whatever. You know, that's what a lot of people want, right, and it's hard when sometimes I feel disrespected like that.

In this particular case, the interviewee's personal dilemma partly stems from having been unable to garner the kind of respect that her mother had fought so hard to attain despite her marginal status as a woman. In other words, by opting to work for the Korean American community, she feels like she is not only shattering her parents' middle-class immigrant dreams, but also undoing the gains her mother had made as a woman. Moreover, the pressure the interviewee feels at home continually resonates in the words of other Korean immigrants with whom she interacts within the community.

Constructing Ethnicity, Building Community

As seen, community-based organizations like KYCC and KIWA bridge the ethnic community and mainstream society by exposing members to a diversity of networks and experiences beyond the isolating haven of Koreatown and beyond the homogeneity of corporate America. Members who had not had previous contact with a large Korean American population in the past found an entryway into the community on terms with which they could relate. Conversely, those who had experienced very little beyond their ethnic-bounded worlds discovered new opportunities and relationships by interacting with mainstream institutions. Over time, their active community involvement and close interactions with other coethnics added texture to their political understandings about the Korean American experience and altered previous misconceptions about their own ethnic community. The question then is, how are KYCC and KIWA uniquely structured to offer these kinds of opportunities for 1.5/second generation Korean Americans?

The Institutional Context of KYCC

One of the most defining characteristics of KYCC today is its rigid, hierarchical, and bureaucratic structure, which shapes the decision-making processes, ideological base, and political culture of the organization. As the recipient of substantial funding from both the ethnic community and mainstream institutions, the organization is structured in a way that best allows it to coordinate all its resources. The internal decision-making structure is organized top-down, from the board of directors to the executive director to the management team to part-time/full-time staff and finally to interns and volunteers. This hierarchical ranking system allows it to effectively manage the large bureaucratic framework of the organization and upkeep its positive image within the ethnic community. Because of its dependency on financial resources and general support from outside groups, the primary interest of the agency centers on maintaining its relations with established allies—an arrangement that is best managed within such a well-regulated setting.

First and foremost, the organization is supervised by a broad base of affiliated community members who are able to draw on their own extensive networks of supporters within the ethnic community and mainstream institutions. As the so-called "proprietors" of the organization, the board sets the policies of the organizations and makes final approval decisions on internal matters. More importantly, the board members function as fund-raisers, vision makers, and managers of KYCC's public image since they are deemed to be accountable for whatever happens to the organization. In this sense, they are instrumental in supplying and maintaining social networks with outside communities. They are less in contact with the staff and also less involved with the day-to-day operations of the organization, for which they rely on the director to provide guidance. Revealing the organization's strong roots among the ethnic elite and corporate America, the board includes representatives from various corporations, including Nara Bank, the Los Angeles Times, and Southern California Edison Gas and Electric Company, as well as a good mix of young professionals. At the time of the study, about three-quarters of the board members were Korean Americans, predominately second generation, with a good balance of male and female representation.

Organizations that depend on strong bases of elite support also need one top official to act as the representative of the organization and as the liaison between board members and staff. While playing a similar role as board members with somewhat less power, the executive director is essentially the organization's visible "face" to both the staff and the community they serve. To this end, the executive director is primarily responsible for directly interfacing with the organization's supporters—for example, by going to dinners with potential funders and acting as the main spokesperson for the ethnic and mainstream media. Because they are like the physical embodiment of the organization, directors are generally less transient than most staff members and are oftentimes associated with specific organizations long after their departure. Based on his or her dual interaction with the staff and the board, the director also acts as an intermediary decision maker on internal matters. The director processes the information and advice given by managers and comes up with specific recommendations to be approved by board members while also developing the organization's broader vision and running personnel operations. In this sense, the director's primary role lies in developing and strengthening networks, overseeing internal operations, soliciting community resources, and "selling" the organization to the staff and the community. At KYCC, the executive director position has been occupied primarily by 1.5/second generation male leaders, with the crucial exception of the first formal director, who was a 1.5 generation female.

Once an organization garners its resources from outside, it needs a workforce to consolidate and convert what it has into services and programs that community members can use. Although less directly involved with cultivating or maintaining the organization's networks, the general staff, which is comprised of managers, program coordinators, and volunteer interns, both directly and indirectly constitutes the operational machinery of the organization by writing up grant proposals, providing services to community members, and collaborating with other organizations both within and outside the Korean American community. The full-time staff has much less organizational authority but does exert some control over individual program decisions and how services are implemented. Because they are more involved with day-to-day operations, they are most likely to be in contact with the people they service. The manager is responsible for coordinating and overseeing all these programs.

Table 7.1 shows the results of a 2000 survey conducted on Korean American members of KYCC and KIWA, including staff, volunteers, executive directors, and board members. As shown, there is a good balance of male and female staff members in KYCC. The composition of the managerial staff is also relatively well balanced in terms of gender, although men slightly outnumber women. The age range of members varies, indicating that Korean Americans at all stages of life may benefit from community work at KYCC, but there is a stronger representation of members in their twenties and thirties. Over half of KYCC's general staff is second generation, while the remaining half is equally divided among the 1.5 and first generations. In addition, half of the staff have a college degree, and a good proportion of them also have a master's or a higher postgraduate degree. Almost a third of staff members live in or near the Koreatown area, but the survey indicates that the majority live in other areas of Los Angeles and Orange Counties, particularly in the valley, the west side, and new ethnic suburbs around Torrance and Gardena. In terms of language proficiency, the organizational staff is mostly English speaking or bilingual Korean-English speakers. Although Table 7.1 shows a greater number of members who have been with KYCC for more than three years, the results indicate that omitting executive directors and board members, the majority of general staff have been at the organization for a short period, with the exception of a small core group of old-timers.

A more updated informal survey conducted in 2005 shows that the composition of KYCC staff has not changed much in terms of generation, gender, age, city of residence, and educational background. However, the staff is more racially diverse in all of its administrative units, with almost half of the members non–Korean Americans. The board membership and management staff is still dominated by Korean Americans, although the executive director claims it is only a matter of time before non–Korean American staff take root and begin "growing into the organization." As a result of these internal changes, the language proficiency of the membership has also shifted somewhat, with more claiming Spanish-speaking proficiency, but the majority still speak some combination of English and/or Korean. A core group of staff members has stayed with KYCC, but the majority of members have moved on and been replaced by new employees. Still, the organization may be reaching its goal of attracting more long-term members. It is too soon to tell, but slightly more of

Table 7.1 Profile of past and present Korean members at KIWA and KYCC, 2000

	KYCC		KIWA	
	No.	%	No.	%
Gender				
Male	14	46.7	5	35.7
Female	16	53.3	9	64.3
Age				
Under 22	5	16.7	0	0.0
22–29	10	33.3	7	50.0
30–39	8	26.7	5	35.7
40 +	6	20.0	2	14.3
Not available	1	3.3	0	0.0
Generation				
First generation	7	23.3	4	28.6
1.5 generation	7	23.3	5	35.7
Second generation	15	50.0	5	35.7
Not available	1	3.3	0	0.0
Education				
No/some high school	2	6.7	1	7.1
High school graduate	4	13.3	3	21.4
B.A. degree	15	50.0	6	42.9
M.A. degree	3	10.0	0	0.0
Postgraduate degree	3	10.0	2	14.3
Not available	3	10.0	2	14.3
City of Residence				
In/near Koreatown[1]	9	30.0	5	35.7
Outside Koreatown	20	66.7	9	64.3
Not available	1	3.3	0	0.0
Language[2]				
Mostly English	13	43.3	3	21.4
Mostly Korean	3	10.0	4	28.6
Korean-English	12	40.0	2	14.3
Korean-Spanish	0	0.0	1	7.1
Korean-English-Spanish	2	6.7	4	28.6
Years with organization				
Less than a year	8	26.7	4	28.6
1–3 years	9	30.0	5	35.7
More than 3 years	11	36.7	5	35.7
Not available	2	6.7	0	0.0
Total	30	100.0	14	100.0

SOURCE: Courtesy of author

NOTES:
1. Indicates those who reported living in an area within a mile radius of Koreatown as defined in Chapter 3.
2. Respondents were asked to indicate all languages spoken and their level of proficiency on a scale of 1 to 5, with 5 being fluent. Those who indicated a score of 4–5 were considered to be proficient in that language. The languages indicated are based on proficiency in the language, with the exception of Spanish where scores of 3–5 were accepted as a sign of proficiency.

those surveyed state that they have been with the organization between one to three years, while fewer report being new hires.

Most of the clients at KYCC and KIWA are socioeconomically disadvantaged groups who face a range of social problems including poverty, language/cultural difficulties, atypical family structures, and minimal access to quality schools and mainstream institutions. However, KYCC also includes a significant proportion of business owners, suburban youth, and more well-off clients who face other disadvantages that require the organization's services. For example, business owners who do not speak English and are not familiar with American financial institutions seek counseling and advice on how to acquire loans to finance their enterprises. Although KYCC concentrates its services on low-income youth within the Koreatown community, youth from middle-class suburban communities are still able to take advantage of some of the programs, such as counseling services, leadership programs, and privately funded Student Activist Training (SAT) classes. Because of its extensive financial base and range of services, KYCC targets Latinos from a wider age and income range, than does KIWA, through its juvenile delinquency, inschool counseling, and water-conservation programs, with focus on Latino youth and their families.

The Eth-Class Framework of Solidarity

As high rollers in the upper tiers of ethnic organizational structures, the KYCC provides a strong resource base from which staff members can transition into established institutions within mainstream society, including large nonprofits, government agencies, corporations, and political office. The organization gets the information, funding, and political influence it needs to achieve its ambitious political agenda through resource-rich, established networks within the ethnic community and mainstream society. Based on organizational records, interviews, and general observation of KYCC events, I compiled the following categories of individuals and institutions as being the primary donors or supporters of the organization.

1. Governmental agencies and politicians on a city, county, state, and federal level
2. Private foundations
3. Large mainstream corporations (for example, Southern California Edison)

4. Large Korean banks and corporations (for example, The Korea Times, Korean Air, Korean Television Enterprise, Hanmi Bank, University of Southern California)
5. Established first generation immigrant organizations (for example, Korean Consulate General, Korean Chamber of Commerce, Korean-American Federation [KAF])
6. Small businesses
7. Churches and religious organizations
8. Other Korean CBOs (for example, Korean Health, Education, Information and Research Center [KHEIR], Koreatown Plaza, Korean Garment Wholesalers Association)
9. Non-Korean ethnic organizations, coalitions, and social service agencies (for example, Little Tokyo Service Center, El Centro del Pueblo, Salvation Army)
10. Individual sponsors, especially young professionals such as certified public accountants and lawyers

As shown, the organization's main bases of support come from the elite sectors of the ethnic community such as businesses and churches and larger mainstream institutions and corporations. According to the executive director, government agencies provide about 65 percent of the organization's financial resources, while corporations and private foundations provide about 25 percent. Many of these supporters are well-positioned to offer KYCC considerable financial support in the form of program endowments or donations during the organization's annual fund-raising dinners. Although donations from individuals and community organizations comprise only a small amount of KYCC's budget, they nevertheless provide the support network and community base which most organizations need for legitimacy, publicity, manpower, advice, and clientele. These different bases of support offer ideal sources from which to develop the corporate agency and the career aspirations of its membership.

Other than financial support, KYCC has been shown to depend on the ethnic elite to maintain political legitimacy within the ethnic community. Although a few interviewees have complained about the organization's preoccupation with its image over the needs of the clientele, others contend that KYCC's reputation and backdoor networking is what allows them to draw and effectively serve clients in the first place. The current executive director firmly states that KYCC is concerned with one value alone: "You have to respect the clients you serve and the people you work with in order to be part of this family." Political stature is a key factor in the organization's ability to bring in clients, provide the resources to serve the clients, and also gain the kind of recognition within the ethnic community it needs to justify funding from outside mainstream agencies. KYCC has collaborated with the immigrant elite on various levels, from individual consultation exchanges to interorganizational collaborative projects.

The agency's political agenda is predicated on a combination of ethnic and class interests that perceive the success of the community as depending on the ability to both unite on an ethnic level and integrate into mainstream society through traditional routes of acculturation and upward mobility. One third generation Korean American board member describes the political mission of KYCC as follows:

> Many Korean Americans [in KYCC] generally promote the idea of trying to integrate this agency into the fabric of the city. Integrate not in the sense of you know becoming a Red Cross or United, or a YMCA that is wholly homogenized. The second and third generation[s] still see the very significant importance of keeping a Korean orientation. But as part of that Korean orientation, the role of making sure that the Korean community is a part of the L. A. community. And that's both about putting KYCC out into the community as well as bringing members of the community into KYCC.

The organization's political mission reflects values that are in some ways compatible with those of the immigrant elite. Among other things, its programs and services are aimed at promoting education and career mobility, the healthy functioning of the traditional family unit, the growth of elite political leadership, and greater ties with the ethnic community.

Within this context, staff members generally see the role of the organization as helping underprivileged Korean American youth and their families to nurture the knowledge and skills to succeed on an individual level while also empowering and uniting the ethnic community on a collective level. The organization cultivates a positive type of institutional community for children, who are otherwise vulnerable to the negative effects of attending poor schools, socializing at delinquent hangouts, and joining local youth gangs in Koreatown.

A twenty-four-year-old second generation male youth coordinator explains:

I was raised in the suburbs, Cerritos, and it's kind of well known for a lot of Asians there. It's a very affluent suburb. Kids tend to be pressured more to do well in school, because kids around them, the peers and their environment, they're focused a lot on education so college is not an option. It's another step for kids in the suburbs and they are very career-driven and have a lot of other activities like involving themselves in church or other organizations. In Koreatown, the resources are very limited and the environment itself is not geared towards academic issues. Just remembering how it was in middle school and how I was studying all the time versus these kids are missing a lot of things in their lives, and I feel really bad for them. So it motivates me to do more for them.

The respondent makes a clear distinction between the marginalized Koreatown community they service and the suburban middle-class ideals of the ethnic community they aspire to cultivate.

Another twenty-four-year-old, second generation youth program coordinator states how the inspiration to pass on these aspirations led him to his position at KYCC.

I wanted to do great things in my life, but I realize I have my limitations, lack of knowledge and skills. One of the great things about education is I can't be a lawyer, but I could inspire another person to become a lawyer. So I could contribute to society and his life by making him what he wants to be. So education, even though it's very difficult, I recognize the financial rewards are lower, but I think more personal rewards are higher than some other occupations.

This collective consciousness also pervades the accounts of KYCC's clientele. For instance, one ex-gang member I interviewed, who told me that he did not have high aspirations before coming to KYCC, excitedly relayed to me his plans to start a juice bar business—an idea he got from his supervisor. He would use part of the profits to employ other ex-gang members like himself. Thus, he could start up a successful business while also contributing to the betterment of the community. Another eighteen-year-old female intern explained how the organization taught her to be more assertive and motivated in her academic pursuits. For instance, she told me that she was now in the process of contesting a college decision that was made based on a technical error in her application; she went onto explain how this was a bold move she would have never made before she joined the organization.

Although the staff members come from relatively diverse backgrounds and, as we shall see, hold on to different political beliefs, the one common strand that ties them together is their desire to work in a formal setting where they can develop their individual job or career goals. Most employees I interviewed told me that they had come to KYCC, because they needed a job, a different type of work experience, a chance to hone their knowledge and skills with a nonprofit, or the chance to learn from more experienced mentors. The majority of the line staff are either beginning career trajectories or have had some experience working with service-oriented organizations in the past. Some members are also actively involved with churches, which reaffirms their roots with the ethnic elite and their ideologies about ethnic solidarity, social service, and humanitarianism. Ultimately, they hope to either continue working with social service agencies or the general nonprofit sector or pursue middle-class professional careers within government, medicine, law, or education, among other things.

According to an informal survey of staff members at KYCC, the organization's greatest assets include the sincere dedication of staff members to community work, the quality and diversity of services offered, and the organization's reputation within the broader community. A few other respondents commended the organization's ability to mediate between different cultures and generations of Korean Americans. Most of the weaknesses reported focused on the organization's integration into the community, its inability to communicate effectively with the immigrant generation, and program development as it relates to funding. Confirming their interest in the agency as a route to individual mobility, a few referred to KYCC's ability to contribute to their current economic situation or their long-term careers. Staff members have complained that although analogous to the traditional structure of corporations, KYCC lacks the opportunity for vertical mobility available in most business professions. For instance, most members cannot progress beyond the management level and have only the option of moving into other programs horizontally. Furthermore, people have expressed their dissatisfaction with the salary level, which is not commensurate with the amount of time and effort required by their positions and which they argue is a major obstacle in seeing their jobs as a permanent career.

Thus, the benefits that KYCC endows on its members mainly have to do with its formal, bureaucratic structure, which provides significant training for upwardly mobile staff and relatively stable wages and benefits for a nonprofit organization. KYCC is able to provide these types of opportunities because they have the financial resources and support networks to build a large, bureaucratic organization with the capacity to train, develop, and promote individual staff members. Because of its interconnectedness with elite leadership in the ethnic community and mainstream society, KYCC can help members to promote their career aspirations by exposing them to new experiences and critical social networks for future occupational mobility. One former male staff member points out that herein lies the advantage of working at an organization like KYCC over smaller organizations like KIWA.

> If you look at a large organization like KYCC, you know the salary has to be better, the benefits tend to be better. You know KYCC pays for the health benefits for all of its staff as well as all the dependents as well. So even if you had like five children, you know, you get healthcare for yourself, you get healthcare for all five of your children. So that's something that you know small organizations, although I'm sure they'd like to offer it, they just can't offer it if they don't have the capacity. And then the potential for getting funding is much better at a credible organization like KYCC so it means it's easier to start programs.

However, the wages and benefits are often not high enough to build a career upon for many of its highly educated members who perceive the organization as a "stepping-stone" for other professions or workplaces.

The political base of the agency is not as strong and well developed as that of other organizations such as KIWA, so that the primary attractions of organizations like this seem to be personal, social, and employment reasons. So a good number of staff members who once participated in KYCC programs as children return as employees, because they know the agency to be the best way to "give back to the community" and gain employment experience at the same time. Others came to recognize the benefits of organizational participation only incidentally, so that over time what was once a job became a career, what was once a career became a supportive network, and what was once an emotional self-exploration became a new way to look at community. For them, therein lay one of the magical effects of "giving back": inadvertently finding once again something for themselves in return.

Those pursuing political careers also recognized the practical uses of connecting with their ethnic roots, particularly in a city that was shaped by its ethnic fault lines. As one board member relates to me:

One of my first jobs in Los Angeles was I worked for Mayor Tom Bradley in his early years and in a political office, and any given person has a number of different responsibilities, and I had a number of different responsibilities, one of which was liaison to the Korean community. So I did get to meet a lot of the Korean organizations and Korean individuals and, uh, I rode in the Koreatown parade [short laugh], representing the mayor, waved at everybody. So then, you know the idea then of wanting to be a part of the community, also realizing at that point that I wasn't this comfortable in a fully Korean milieu; you know I gravitated towards this organization because I really saw kind of the idea that they wanted to do something in kind of a crossover area where they're dealing with Koreans who are dealing with America and there were issues there, and they weren't dealing simply with organizing within the Korean community or you know they're doing things kind of in that crossover area. And that was an area I was interested in.

One second generation female staff member with experience working in political offices informed me that Korean Americans interested in going into mainstream politics oftentimes start out by working in ethnic nonprofits such as KYCC, because it provides them with critical networks and legitimacy within the ethnic community. She said that before coming to KYCC, she had worked at a congressional office but came to realize how people acted a bit "standoffish" because she did not have any connections within Koreatown.

Nevertheless, the organization's greatest strength, its embeddedness within resource-rich networks, may also be considered the source of its weakness, according to a few staff members. Several interviewees expressed concern that the organization's image is occasionally prioritized over the needs of their clients, as captured in the following statement by one former female staffer: "*This organization exists for this organization.* How much a student progressed in his grades or how much English a non-English-speaking student learned within a short time—rather than KYCC being known for these accomplishments outside, it is known by its events [and] activities. They seem to try to appeal through these tactics" [Korean statements in *italics*]. For professional nonprofits like KYCC, this careful attention to organizational image is a key to maintaining strong networks with ethnic elite bases. Having built their organization around these networks, Korean American board members generally believe that maintaining status within the ethnic community is vital to its survival.

Among other things, these passages reflect underlying tensions that occasionally emerge between members' aspirations to serve the community and the significance of organizational status in elite structures. As the current director explains:

> One thing that I really hope was that the Korean American community would have a better understanding as to what nonprofits do in the community. First of all, Korean Americans tend to think that nonprofits are where all the volunteers and staff come and hang out and provide services to kids, you know. They think that we're more like the YMCA type of service. They don't necessarily see this as a career for their kids, you know. They don't understand that we run and operate with millions of dollars of budget. You know you plan, you run [it] like a business.

Backed by the firm support of fellow board members, the executive director has repeatedly expressed his long-term vision of making the nonprofit profession a legitimate career for young Korean Americans, as worthy as becoming a lawyer or a doctor. The irony is that by encouraging members to pursue traditional paths of upward mobility, KYCC unwittingly undermines the foundations for retaining highly skilled and ambitious members of their staff. As a result, high turnover rates have been a major problem that the organization faces among its staff, and the current executive director has been trying to resolve this by offering better benefit packages.

Underlying congruities between the organization's eth-class approach to community work and the value systems of the ethnic elite have allowed it to adopt a strategy of measured accommodation with the traditional immigrant leadership. Through its emphasis on education, hard work, and achievement, KYCC reaffirms the same broader values of socioeconomic mobility and ethnic solidarity that the immigrant leadership tends to embrace, even as the strategy for achieving this goal may diverge. Several of the most important youth-related institutions within Koreatown, such as churches and tutoring schools, are the protected spaces of the ethnic elite. As such, it would not work to the interest of KYCC to alienate itself from these important systems of youth support.

At the same time, the organization does draw clear limits on the extent to which it is willing to compromise its political agenda in order to maintain its position within the existing power structure. KYCC continues to grapple with the same cultural tensions and ideological differences that KIWA faces

in its interactions with the ethnic elite. Like most 1.5/second generation organizations, KYCC must deal with the immigrant leadership's hierarchical
norms of respect, differences in organizational style, its prioritization of entrepreneurial interests over youth and family development, and its isolationist
approaches to other racial and ethnic groups. Business owners have built a
very profitable industry from youth hangouts that sell alcohol and encourage delinquent activities to the extent that their interests would seem to clash
with those of a youth and family organization. Interestingly, some of these
types of complaints come from the lower end of the staff in their day-to-day
interactions with immigrants; in this sense, the current director and board
members are instrumental in managing the generational divide on a broader
organizational level. Nevertheless, the argument here is that mutual interest
in sustaining this relationship and overlapping interests in eth-class mobility
make it much easier for the leadership to negotiate its agenda within traditional hierarchies.

The Institutional Context of KIWA

KIWA may be characterized as small, informal and quasihierarchical in structure. Although the levels of association are not too much different from KYCC,
the numbers are fewer and power is distributed in a more equitable way. The
levels of association include the board of directors, the executive director, the
organizing staff, the worker staff, and the volunteer and paid interns. As one
male staff member describes it, the structure of KIWA falls in between the
strict hierarchical structure found in social service agencies like KYCC and a
democratic organization where the membership determines leadership.

Compared to most Korean and Korean American organizations, the board
of directors has played a much lesser role in the decision-making process and
has relied more heavily on the insights of the executive director and staff.
In fact, the director is considered one of the official members of the board.
In alignment with its commitment to greater worker representation, the organization elects mostly working-class immigrant members to its executive
board, with only a few exceptions. At the time of the study, there was only
one female board member, but the organization is now in the processes of ap-
pointing its first two Latino workers and one additional female representative
to the board. One of the members explains that the board plays a different
function than most other organizational boards because of the working-class
character of the organization and the lack of high-income, educated members

among its ranks. Whereas most organizations rely on board members to provide funding and ties to resource-wealthy individuals and institutions within
the community or mainstream institutions, KIWA's executive board has been
characterized by its relative exclusion from ethnic elite networks and lack of
financial resources. Drawing on their experience as workers, the board mainly
functions to provide advice to the staff, who remain at least on a theoretical
level accountable to the board. In addition, the board meets with the director
on a quarterly basis to get updates on organizational activities, set policies,
and pass a budget.

The executive director, as suggested, holds the highest position within the
organization, but not so much that it has taken too much away from KIWA's
"democratic" and staff-driven structure. The executive director is the organization's main linkage to outside supporters and has taken on some functions
that board members would normally assume within other organizations. Several staff members informed me that proposals were only the first step in ac-
quiring financial resources and that intimate relations with funders such as
the ones Roy Hong developed were vital assets in terms of securing support
from private foundations. As one of the cofounders of the organization, Hong
took the lead role in building the organization around his vision, although he
drew heavily on staff input to shape this vision along the way. Still, the director continues to be recognized as the "face" of the organization to the ethnic
community and to some groups outside the community—a role comparable
to that of KYCC's directorship. Having established the organization within
the community, however, Hong felt that it was time to move on to other projects and, in 2001, officially passed the reigns over to the other cofounder of the
organization, Danny Park. KIWA has had only two executive directors in its
lifetime—namely, the two 1.5 generation male founders of the organization.

In many ways, the role that the regular staff plays in KIWA overlaps with
that of the executive director, although emphasis is placed on the staff's ability to directly work with other community-based organizations and labor
unions and coordinate the programs, protests, and events that constitute the
core of KIWA. As a peripheral organization in the ethnic enclave, KIWA must
invest time and energy into building the organization and spearheading its
campaigns without major funding. In this way, the day-to-day work that staff
members do is almost more important than getting the money they need to do
them since they have developed alternative strategies for achieving their goals
with minimal resources. Although staff members are assigned to specific du-

ties within the organization such as community relations, legal clinic, and case management, the division of labor is not quite strictly defined, and many times staff members are seen doing multiple tasks above and beyond the call of duty. In addition, language is an important factor in determining the type of responsibilities a staff member is given, particularly those who interact with non-English-speaking Korean and Latino workers.

As part of its philosophy to help workers empower themselves, KIWA has helped Korean and Latino workers to start up an independent organization called the Restaurant Workers Association of Koreatown (RWAK). Reflecting the composition of workers in the local restaurant industry, RWAK is mostly comprised of young Latino male workers and middle-aged Korean immigrant female workers. Although the association has since assumed a semi-independent identity from KIWA, worker staff members originally occupied a position a step below that of regular staff organizers. Functioning as intermediary representatives of KIWA and RWAK, one Latino and one Korean representative from RWAK assumed the dual duty of staff and intern as they learned the skills they would need to eventually create their own association. Although RWAK is now officially an independent entity with a small office space in the same building, the organization still relies on the secondary assistance of KIWA until it will be able to operate completely on its own.

The organization maintains a balance between a democratic-style structure built on ideologies of social equality and the leadership of the executive director, who for practical purposes is accountable for the fate of the organization. The environment of KIWA is extremely casual and informally run, lacking the rigid hierarchical supervision or labor division of more micromanaged CBOs. Yet due to the marginal status of the organization within the general ethnic community and as some call it, the "martyr"-like commitment of those willing to work in such organizations, the staff members often toil for long hours, battling the obstacles thrown in their way by both ethnic and mainstream power holders. Some complain that this has made the organization more reactive than proactive or long-term in strategy. Preoccupation with outside parties and events also prevents the organization from being able to strengthen its own internal structure and staff development. However, it should be noted that many current and former staff members seem to maintain strong ties with the organization because of their ideological commitment to what the organization represents.

Returning to Table 7.1 on the composition of Korean American staff members, we can observe that women are better represented in KIWA than we saw in KYCC, with the exception of the executive director. In part, this slight gender difference can be attributed to the greater amount of grassroots work involved and the organization's current focus on Korean restaurant workers, most of whom are female. Like KYCC, staff members are mostly in their twenties and thirties but show a greater balance of first, 1.5, and second generation members than its counterpart. While the majority of organizers and interns have at least a bachelor's degree, the only two members of the organization with a higher degree than this are from the legal department. A similar proportion of the staff live within the vicinity of Koreatown, but the majority of the remaining staff live in both urban and suburban neighborhoods throughout Los Angeles County. Furthermore, the membership of KIWA is much more diverse in terms of language proficiency, with only three members speaking English only and about half speaking two or more languages including different combinations of Korean, English, and Spanish. In stark contrast to KYCC, half of the organizers (minus volunteer interns and workers) have been with the organization for at least three years or more. The numbers take on added significance considering the small size of the organization.

When surveyed five years later, KIWA had lost a few staff positions as a result of the declining economy and social service cutbacks under the Bush administration. The organization had experienced some turnover among its staff; a few of them were replaced by other non–Korean Asian American organizers, but the organization also retained a good number of its core Korean American organizers. As a result, fewer staff members reported being with the organization for less than a year and more had been around for at least a few years. Give or take a few members, the bilingual/multilingual capacity of the staff, their educational background, city of residence, and age and generational distribution remained the same.

Although there may be some overlap in clientele, KIWA is more likely to reach out to more marginalized segments of the Korean and Latino populations. The majority of KIWA's target population includes Korean immigrants who are disadvantaged not only because of their income, but also because of their status as low-income workers both before and after migration. Because of its focus on workplace-related problems in the restaurant industry, KIWA also services young male Latino immigrants who are either single or whose families are back in their native country. In this sense, the workers that KIWA services constitute the "marginalized within the marginalized" in that they have very few resources, networks, or status upon which to alleviate their daily burdens and overcome their situation of disempowerment. Because of their status as workers in Koreatown, they are also positioned in opposition to one of the most powerful groups in the community, Korean entrepreneurs—a status that puts them at a further disadvantage in terms of exploitation. They are also more likely to be lower on the rungs of the socioeconomic ladder than the low-income youth and families at KYCC.

The Border-Crossing Framework of Solidarity

KIWA, in contrast to KYCC, acts more as an ideological channel through which members can articulate and act on their political beliefs, whether it be in terms of organizing labor, fighting racial and ethnic discrimination, working on behalf of immigrants, or creating bridges among leftist constituencies. In so doing, the organization may also act as an organizational feeder into nonprofit work and social justice movements, although this is only secondary to its political significance in members' lives.

With interests that conflict with those of the ethnic elite, KIWA has found its greatest supporters and funders among other marginalized, progressive Korean organizations or ethnic, labor, and other liberal organizations outside the community. These include:

1. Labor unions (such as Hotel Employees and Restaurant Employees [HERE] Local 11, Bus Riders Union)
2. Other labor and leftist organizations (including Sweatshop Watch, Association of Community Organizations for Reform Now [ACORN])
3. Private progressive foundations (for example, Liberty Hill Foundation)
4. Marginal, progressive Korean organizations (for example, Korean Resource Center [KRC], Korean Youth and Student Union [KYSU])
5. Non–Korean Asian American organizations (such as Thai Community Development Center [Thai CDC], Pilipino Workers Center [PWC])
6. Latino organizations (including Coalition for Human Immigrant Rights L.A. [CHIRLA])
7. Other outside liberal organizations
8. Individual supporters, especially workers

KIWA's organizational budget is much smaller than that of KYCC, because it solicits fewer federal contracts and relies on the support of less financially endowed community-based organizations.

Because KIWA wants to avoid the restrictions of government contracts and the conflict of interests that would arise from corporate funding, the organization draws on the financial support of private progressive foundations, which support about 60 percent of their budget. A grantwriter for the organization explains:

> You know, government funding, or a lot of mainstream funders, don't want our type of work 'cause they probably think it's controversial. On the other hand, because we don't receive those fundings, we're not restricted. I think the granters that give us money, they don't really tell us what to do. We still do the kind of work we want to do and the way we want to do it.

The organization gets the remainder of its funding from the donations of other community organizations and individuals, such as clients who voluntarily contribute a portion of their settlement to KIWA when they win cases.

KIWA's progressive mission and strong stance against the exploitative labor practices of Korean business owners have raised major opposition from the Korean entrepreneurial elite and, hence, ignited tensions with other members of the traditional ethnic elite. The organization has worked with immigrant powerholders on an issue-to-issue basis, but they have been most well known for their boycotts of Korean-owned businesses and militant protests against injustices within the Korean American community and have thus relied on a stronger base of support outside the ethnic community. If we look at the list, we will notice that KIWA's main networks include other similar leftist organizations outside the ethnic elite circle as well as many organizations outside the ethnic community itself. Interestingly, their noncoethnic bases of support include a diversity of constituencies including labor unions, Asian American and Latino organizations, and South Korean activist groups.

Although they may not be able to solicit substantial financial contributions from their allies, ties with other progressive organizations provide a crucial source of support in the form of manpower, organizing experience, and outside publicity. As one interviewee related to me, being a relatively new organization in a largely conservative community, KIWA tends to find role models with longer histories of organizing experience from outside the Korean American community. For instance, the executive director has been known to visit other organizations to gain insights on how to fight more powerful groups, with limited resources.

KIWA challenges the ideology of meritocracy, capitalist wealth, and "family values" that underlies entrepreneurial success and instead argues that the success of the community must draw on broader visions than that of individual achievement and hard work for middle-class aspirations. Although KIWA staff understand the role of these ethnic resources in empowering the Korean American community within mainstream society, they claim that they are also used to reaffirm the dominance of conservative immigrant leaders and to exploit indigenously marginalized groups, such as immigrant workers. The current executive director argues:

> A lot of people still think immigration to U.S. is an opportunity to prosper economically and a lot of their excuse is to provide education to their children. So they're still really, really working hard and trying to improve their economic conditions. I think KIWA is saying that it's true that community's working hard to improve their lives and community as a whole. But if all these different issues, such as workers' issue, and other political issue are not addressed, the Korean community's not developing with balance.

The activities of the traditional ethnic elite are seen as supporting American hierarchies of race/ethnicity, class, and gender by aspiring to work within the system and promoting hierarchical ideologies.

As opposed to treating workers as mere victims of Korean merchant exploitation, the ideological framework for the organization perceives labor exploitation within the broader context of power and oppression in mainstream American society. It is understood that Korean immigrant entrepreneurs occupy an intermediary position within an economic structure that primarily benefits capitalists while small business owners continue to face disadvantages related to their status and culture. However, KIWA represents those at the lowest end of the economic spectrum: immigrant minority workers. Business owners are seen as having access to substantial ethnic resources with which to protect their interests, whereas workers have close to none.

KIWA attracts primarily liberal, college-educated Korean Americans in their twenties and thirties, whose political consciousness was shaped earlier by formative life experiences and political involvement with other progressive organizations and social movements in the United States and Korea, including labor organizations, Korean American organizations, progressive movements in Korea, and other Asian American/racial minority alliances. Staff and volunteers are less career oriented in their motivations and more drawn to the organization by its broader vision of social justice, coalition building, and progressive politics within the Korean American community. Most members are drawn to ethnic community work because of ideological linkages they make between KIWA's border-crossing framework of social justice and their personal ethnic-centered experiences as Korean Americans.

The ideological evolution of members prior to their organizational involvement reflects a long and convoluted journey within and across ethnic and geographical boundaries—a path that eventually led them to KIWA. Membership within the organization represents the culmination of years of border-crossing practices that ultimately gave meaning to the value of ethnic identity for its constituents but in a flexible and permeable manner. Some were raised in predominantly White suburbs and became involved with Korean/Korean American, Asian American, or other race-based organizations in order to find a sense of connectedness with their ethnic community. With the exception of the Latino members, a minority of members is marginally associated with churches, much less Korean churches. Only a few of them hope to pursue upper white-collar professional careers, and even those who do are committed to careers that help the community (for example, public interest law). Instead, the majority of them have expressed the desire to continue struggling for the larger goal of social justice through less profitable but community-oriented jobs like teaching and participation in liberal organizations like KIWA and the nonprofit sector.

According to the organizational survey, KIWA members find that the general vision of KIWA—to develop a progressive base within the Korean American community, to help indigenously marginalized groups, and to work intimately with other racial groups—to be its greatest contribution to the development of the community and their own political consciousness. As one second generation female staff member explains, "Our organizing base is among low-wage workers, but we also want to be a progressive voice in the Korean community that brings the community's attention to broader issues in American society and to promote civil rights for minorities and issues that involve marginalized groups whether that be people of color or women or other groups that are not respected equally in society." Most of the staff who were surveyed emphasized the ideological and strategic base of the organization as its greatest strengths. Among these were its "progressiveness/militancy," its ties to other mainstream and ethnic organizations, and its assistance to low-wage workers and other marginalized subpopulations of Koreatown. Staff perceptions on organizational weaknesses focused mainly on lack of funding and its relations with the Korean community. The ways members perceive organizational strengths and weaknesses are primarily related to issues concerning the vision and ideological orientation of the organization, its internal political culture, and its relationship to others within the Korean American community. All aspects are in some way linked to the ideological motivation and marginal status of the organization within the larger ethnic community.

Members have continually related to me their admiration of KIWA organizers for taking a stand against issues of social justice that most other Korean American organizations are unwilling to touch. Although she had heard negative things about KIWA, one college-age female intern explains her interest in KIWA as follows:

> I worked in social service organizations [such as] KYCC and KHEIR. Even though they're good and they do good work, they're always treading that line like they're scared what to say and had to watch what they do. So I wanted to see what KIWA was like 'cause they were passionate about what they were fighting for, and they didn't censor themselves and say things that the Korean community needed to hear—you know, willing to be the devil's advocate.

Thus, aside from the content of organizational work, staff members are attracted to KIWA for its willingness to challenge powerful constituencies within the ethnic community to protect what they believe in. In this way, KIWA offers progressive Korean Americans an ideological passageway and training ground to take part in larger organizations and movements for social justice, as well as developing the organizing skills to help workers to empower themselves.

Staff members also see the personal benefits of working in an organization like KIWA, because it promotes an alternative space within which to practice their own version of ethnicity. Because the Korean American community is predominantly immigrant as well as conservative, current members initially sought sanctuary in other racial and ethnic communities. While they consider their personal identities as being formatively shaped by their experiences as Korean Americans, the dominance of traditional ethnic elite interests in the new immigrant community shapes politics in such a way that more progressive Korean Americans, from students to workers to leftist and coalitional activists, have had a difficult time finding an established channel through which to articulate and act upon their distinctive experiences.

A twenty-three-year-old second generation activist states that she feels the contradiction between who she is as a Korean American and how the Koreatown power structure conceptualizes Korean Americanness.

I don't really feel connected to the Korean American community, but I feel like it is diverse and that diversity isn't often represented. But then I'm still part of the Korean American community. But sometimes I feel like there's no one that I can relate to in the Korean American community as opposed to the Filipino community or Japanese or Chinese. It's just different, because Korean Americans are still very traditional and more conservative and stuff, even in areas like homosexuality and religion. I guess in other communities, it seems like they're a little bit more accepting, because they've been here longer. I kind of see Korean Americans going in that direction. But I still feel like I'm a Korean American and I need to work toward my immediate community.

The passage underscores the centrality of the respondent's ethnic identity in her sense of political consciousness but suggests how this creates tensions with the conservative nature of ethnic power structures. KIWA allows such individuals to feel free to express their own version of Korean Americanness that may not agree with the dominant framework, even as they are taught how to articulate their political concerns through non-Korean forums.

Although staff members had prior exposure to organizational and activist work in the past, working at KIWA refined their political consciousnesses by helping them to understand the world around them in more complex ways. Before coming to KIWA, some of the members tell me that they simply saw Korean businesses as one of the most positive and empowering aspects of their community, with little thought to how this success often involved the exploitation of workers. However, as they began to learn more about business practices through KIWA, they developed a more intricate understanding about the dynamics of Korean enterprise so that their views became more "balanced." As one second generation female organizer remarks, "[KIWA] helped me to have more of a balanced view. I came into it thinking that it's about bad or good, but I think that most of the members try to strike that balance, like they understand the immigrant perspective, but they also understand that you can't exploit people either." Other staff members who came from more class-oriented perspectives and experiences state that KIWA helped them to see that the struggles of working-class immigrants of color were more complex than that of class and was closely intertwined with other inequalities, such as race, ethnicity, and gender.

In this sense, the organization promotes a border-crossing framework of ethnic political solidarity that anchors itself on ethnicity as the platform for political mobilization but infuses its internal culture with ideologies and support networks that transcend those boundaries. The organization's rootedness within local community politics does not obviate its ability to cultivate ethnic political cultures that encourage transnational networks or worldviews among their membership. Indeed, its political culture promotes a global perspective on inequality that pushes them to consider how homeland affairs are intertwined with their experiences in the United States. By linking together the fates of the Korean diaspora, the organization gives members the opportunity to translate ethnic solidarity into more substantive transnational networks and border-crossing practices. In many ways, this global focus is inevitable considering the way that worker exploitation in America is inextricably tied to the capitalist excesses of the corporate-driven global economy. Yet this transnational linkage also stems from the lack of progressive models within the Korean American community that has helped to spiritually link the organization to prodemocratic labor and student movements in Korea.

Without losing sight of its mission in the United States, the organization gives full support to leftist prodemocratic organizations from Koreatown to the Korean peninsula by cosponsoring guest lectures from the Korean Confederation of Trade Unions (KCTU), a militant, prodemocratic trade union in Korea,[2] and working together with homeland-focused advocacy groups such as Mindullae for Korean Community Empowerment and KYSU. More recently, they have joined Korean organizations, labor groups, and other leftist activists across the nation to protest free trade negotiations between the United States and Korea. KIWA's staff members, including the current and former executive directors, have backgrounds in student activism and protests in Korea or have been exposed to progressive labor organizations in Korea through programs like the Korean Exposure and Education Program (KEEP). Indeed, KIWA models itself on a revised version of the student prodemocratic movements in Korea and to some extent on minority student activism during the civil rights era. Even beyond linkages with Korea, KIWA is also a member of transnational coalitions like Enlace, an umbrella organization of forty labor and workers' groups in Mexico and the United States whose mission is to build a strong foundation for achieving economic justice for low-wage workers. Now of course not all members necessarily engage in transnational activities nor is the organization "transnational" in the traditional sense. However, KIWA provides an ideological passageway for different manifestations of transnationalism among its members.

The organizational structure of KIWA is viewed in both a positive and negative light. As previously mentioned, KIWA's informal structure has been praised as one of its greatest assets in that it allows the organization to learn from its mistakes and adjust to shifts within the community. Its relative emphasis on democratic decision making, open honesty on different issues, and small casual atmosphere engenders intimate relations among its staff members, several of whom socialize together outside the workplace. The strong ideological foundations of their work provide the incentive for working long hours on different campaigns and projects and attending workers' meetings, which must often take place during odd hours or on weekends to fit with the workers' schedules.

One of the downsides of KIWA's ethnic network structure is that it is mainly based on other lower-tier organizations whose financial base is already spread thin. Although few actually question the mission of the organization, members constantly struggle between what they are trying to achieve and how the people outside the organization perceive them. As one second generation staff member complained, "People have this view that KIWA only survives to be like in opposition. You know, they see us as the rioters and the picketers, not a friend to the Korean immigrant." The inability of the organization to provide higher wages or other work benefits itself elicits few concerns from most members, but a combination of the "martyr" syndrome, preoccupation with day-to-day operations, and continuously reactive activities against others within the community has stripped the organization of its ability to focus on its own internal development. While respected on one level, a couple of members have expressed concerns that this proclivity toward sacrifice at the expense of self has also had the ironic effect of compromising the underlying mission by affecting the personal well-being and lives of staff members. Thus, the strong ideological base of the organization plays a critical role in creating this "martyr"-like organizational culture that simultaneously holds up the organization against external threats as it inflicts undue pressure on its staff.

It is simply not the case that young generations of Korean Americans embrace and express their ethnic political identities through organizational work in any uniform way. Indeed, interviews with staff members of KYCC and KIWA reveal that each has traversed different paths throughout his or her life in order to find a way back to the Korean American community. Nevertheless, these different life experiences ultimately pushed them all to explore the relevance of ethnicity in relation to themselves as well as the people and communities around them. For some, community work was merely the stepping-stone to bigger and better opportunities in the future, while for others it was the much-needed answer to ideological struggles in their personal lives. However, ethnic-centered experiences provide the framework through which most community organizers have viewed their organizational roles. It is at the intersection of these heterogeneous perspectives and experiences that new generations of Korean American leadership have come together to give back to their respective communities of interest.

This evolution from the personal to the political may also help to explain the different ways staff members have come to value the distinctive positions they have carved out for themselves in their respective organizations. Because of the wide range of bridging organizations in Koreatown, it is easier for 1.5/second generation Korean Americans to find a political niche where they can reconstruct and expand the social meaning of community in a way that challenges predominant notions of ethnicity. In the process, both organizations foster a unique sense of community that helps bridge the divide between being Korean and being American. This in turn affects the type of membership they will attract and the political identities they will engender. Building on these individual understandings, each organization has had to cultivate a broader political culture within which to bring together their diverse constituencies, particularly in light of issues introduced by the events of the 1992 civil unrest. Because of their embeddedness within both ethnic and mainstream networks, the process of politicizing the membership also relies heavily on their ability to conform to the rules and regulations of mainstream institutions.

8 Doing Politics Without the Politics

IN THE AFTERMATH of the 1992 civil unrest, 1.5/second generation ethnic nonprofit organizations have come to play a leading role both as key service providers to the general Koreatown population and as political intermediaries between the ethnic community and mainstream society. As shown, these organizations have been best positioned to respond to the general plight of the Korean American community throughout the recovery process, because they have the financial capital, outside networks, and cultural/linguistic tools not only to address social problems, but also to demand greater political representation and empowerment within mainstream social structures.

However, these organizations face a number of bureaucratic and political obstacles that could potentially hinder their underlying interest in organizing and mobilizing the disempowered immigrant communities around them. Although this dual service-advocacy function has expanded the realm of possibilities in terms of fostering community empowerment, it has also ironically created more constraints for such organizations partly because outside funding has subjected them to federal regulations. Nonprofit organizations must meet the conflicting demands of fulfilling new political obligations within the Koreatown community without flying in the face of nonprofit statutes, federal contracts, and elite supporters that directly or indirectly disfavor certain types of political activities.

The Korean Youth and Community Center (KYCC) and the Korean Immigrant Workers Advocates (KIWA) represent some of the diverse ways that nonprofit organizations can achieve their political goals while accommodating federal regulations and outside parties that may call for more restrained involvement in the political sphere. Depending on the organization's individual vision, the governing body may even choose to forego the kind of support that may on one hand offer them a wide range of resources but on the other hand impose considerable restrictions on the organization's political activities. Within this context, this chapter takes a closer look at how this strategy materializes in the organization's "political culture," or the type of political ideologies, networks, and practices fostered by the formal and informal regulations, philosophies, and governing structure of the organization.

In general, the chapter begins by describing the strategies these organizations use to navigate their political activities within the constraint of nonprofit statutes and the way these strategies help to preserve the integrity of the organization's political agenda, staff members, and networks of support. [1] Youth leadership programs have been another important way for organizations to cultivate political leadership in the postriot era without infringing on governmental regulations. Because of their dependency on the institutional base of the enclave community, it is shown how KYCC and KIWA have extended their political agenda to include Latinos by redefining the concept of "community"; this move has in turn enabled them to gain political legitimacy and potential allies in city politics. In the end, 1.5/second generation ethnic organizations have come up with competing models of political participation, depending on how they negotiate their political agendas and nonprofit status within the constraints of bureaucratic policies.

Political Activity Among Ethnic Nonprofits

One of the underlying paradoxes of the nonprofit sector in the United States centers on the role of politics and political activities in ethnic organizational work. On the one hand, federal statutes that govern the development of nonprofit organizations with tax-exempt status curtail the extent to which such organizations may support or engage in certain delineated political activities, including visible partisanship in electoral matters. With the influx of resources in the postriot era, many community-based organizations (CBOs) within the Korean American community have also come to rely on the financial backing of federal contracts, organizations, and agencies that impose similar limitations on subsidized programs. As recipients of governmental support, nonprofit organizations are supposed to be "apolitical" institutions by nature that merely provide programs and services to the surrounding population while turning a blind eye to the politics around them.

On the other hand, the paradox lies in the inherently political nature of such organizational missions without which there is little motivation or guiding framework for facilitating community development. The cultivation of ethnic political solidarity can be an integral aspect of service provision, because it provides one compelling ideological impetus for such services (namely, giving back to the community), a means to attract and retain membership, a critical tool for community empowerment, and a training ground for future community leaders. More importantly, Korean American organizations in the aftermath of the 1992 civil unrest awoke to the realization that the communities around them could be best served only by involving themselves in civic matters and playing a central role in the political empowerment of their respective constituencies.

This study has specifically focused on those ethnic CBOs that are classified as 501(c)(3) nonprofit organizations and thereby subject to rules pertaining to tax exemption status. In general, "public charities," which generally include charitable, religious, scientific, educational, and literary entities that qualify for 501(c)(3) status, are free from paying federal income taxes—a major financial boost for such organizations that often operate on a limited budget. Because of the privileges associated with this status, these tax-exempt nonprofits must operate within certain boundaries when engaging in particular types of political activities.

In this sense, it is useful to distinguish the three ways of defining "politics": (1) first, as it relates to mainstream government, such as electoral politics and political officials; (2) second, as the act of voicing political viewpoints or mobilizing collectively on different issues in order to address some perceived injustice in mainstream society; (3) third, as a general reference to the strategic maneuvering of personal relations and social networks in order to gain power, control, or status within a given group. Nonprofit statutes generally prohibit organizational beneficiaries from investing more than a minimal percentage of their time and money toward the first type of political activity. Inevitably, such restrictions also have an indirect impact on the second type of political activity.

Affiliated organizations are strictly prohibited from endorsing, financing, or otherwise participating in any political activity on behalf of or against any political candidate, political party, or political action committee. Because nonprofits may want to pursue legislation that furthers their group's cause, the statute does allow for political lobbying efforts that seek to influence legislation but only within a certain percentage of the organization's total yearly expenditures. In addition, federally subsidized grants and contracts cannot be used toward political lobbying. Any violation of these codes can result in the loss of tax-exemption status and its associated privileges. These stipulations are obviously designed to prevent federal resources or benefits being unfairly used toward influencing the outcome of political campaigns.

Despite these restrictions, politics can be a central feature of ethnic organizations. More scholarly works in this field indicate that federal regulations do not severely curtail political activities and advocacy work among nonprofits partly because of indirect incentives that result from nonprofit status and federal funding, the ambiguity of such restrictions, and the haphazard way such statutes are applied and enforced (Chaves, Stephens, and Galaskiewicz 2004; Reid 1999). The nonprofit codes implicitly allow for certain types of campaign-related activities, including the private participation of staff members in political campaigns, efforts to inform candidates of the organization's political stance on specific issues, or assistance with nonpartisan voter registration activities. Thus, federal codes allow for a certain amount of political activity that does not conflict with the letter of the law.

Even beyond politicians, laws, and campaigns, community-based nonprofits can engage in nonelectoral activities that help to politicize and ultimately empower the Korean American community. This includes providing future leaders with the knowledge, skills, and networks to participate in social movements and voicing political viewpoints or mobilizing collectively on different issues in order to address some perceived injustice in mainstream society. Interestingly, some of the staff members interviewed denied engaging in anything "political" as a result of their nonprofit status but then described to me activities that were meant to raise the awareness and involvement of Korean Americans in mainstream politics. Based on this more broadly defined interpretation of politics, the following sections will discuss the creative ways that nonprofits have been able to negotiate their political agenda within the confines of nonprofit statutes in order to fulfill their felt political obligation to the ethnic community in the aftermath of the 1992 Los Angeles civil unrest.

KYCC Strategies of Mainstream Liberalism

As stated in the previous chapter, KYCC provides linkages from the ethnic community to mainstream corporate and governmental politics and thus traverses these traditional routes as the most effective means to political empowerment. Although generally considered a liberal organization, KYCC has structured its organization around mainstream American values that place emphasis on the significance of education and upward mobility along with ties with the Korean American community. Thus, for ideological and practical reasons, KYCC has adopted a philosophy centered on principles embedded in "mainstream liberalism." Mainstream liberalism generally refers to the organization's ideological support of middle-of-the-line liberal issues generally accepted by the dominant majority of Americans, such as multiculturalism. Although KYCC is not necessarily "apolitical" as we shall see, the organizational publicly circumvents those controversial political issues that may put them in an uneasy position with their constituents.

One of KYCC's striking features has to do with the wide representation of political perspectives among its general staff—from the conservative-liberal humanitarian views of traditional Christians to the more leftist approach of political activists. Several second generation members who had worked for labor groups and leftist Asian American organizations in the past felt that KYCC needed to take on a more politically active role within the community, while other members endorsed a more traditional approach to community work based on Christian values of family, religiosity, and social service. A few members of KYCC would go on to work with political advocacy groups while others would affiliate with more conservative institutions within the Korean American community. By taking few political stances as an organization, KYCC is able to avoid ideological rifts and conflict among its sizable staff membership. Political stability is particularly important for large bureaucratic agencies like KYCC that cannot function smoothly when its members are divided.

Aside from providing internal stability, this image allows the organization to maintain its bases of support within both the ethnic and mainstream communities. From the Korean side, KYCC's supporters include conservative factions of the traditional first generation leadership and from the mainstream side, nonpolitically affiliated government agencies and large-scale corporations that generally steer clear of groups that stray too far from middle-of-the-line politics. Although the majority of KYCC staff may be considered liberal ideologically, the organization generally avoids public stances on political issues, because they are likely to alienate one or more of their conservative, mainstream liberal, or nonpartisan constituencies. An American-born former program manager explains:

What KYCC has to do is build relationships with different kinds of people—politicians, big funders, corporations. So, for example, if a politician does something bad, you can't speak out against them because the next time you go for city funding, state funding, county funding, you know that politician's gonna be there to block your move. So those are the kind of relationships that KYCC's had to develop in order to be able to grow and prosper.

These networks of association help to cultivate a culture of mainstream liberalism within the organization and an image of political neutrality to outside observers. By antagonizing few, the leadership of KYCC is able to foster relations with certain traditional ethnic leadership and avoid major political conflicts among its diverse membership base.

Under its current board and executive leadership, KYCC promotes the idea that political issues must be addressed through traditional forums like electoral politics and political organizations and not through social service agencies. While politicians may contact them in order to understand the needs of the community, many of the staff and board members claim that their status as a 501(c)(3) organization prevents them from mobilizing on political issues and that such issues should be left to political advocacy groups, such as the Korean American Coalition (KAC). Thus, while liberal from an ideological perspective, the organization is said to be "politically neutral" in its actions. One twenty-four-year-old male staff member distinguishes KYCC from organizations like KIWA in that the latter is "fighting for political ideas. Versus us: politics is important, it affects the things that we do, but we are more focused on service so I think we want to focus not on the political aspect per se but work with what we have." Another immigrant board member states, "Although we have leverage, I don't want KYCC do that kind of political activity. Being the largest, oldest Korean American social service organization in the nation here, we served more than a thousand youngsters a year. That's leverage."

Most interviewees from KYCC say that when politics is discussed, it is discussed on an individual and personal level. At times, various social spaces within KYCC, such as the kitchen and the computer rooms, and lunch outings at local restaurants, have been sites for informal conversations and debates on different political issues, including events in the Korean American community, American politics, and even abroad. For instance, sometimes the Korean immigrant members of KYCC will briefly explain to non-Korean-speaking members what was said in that morning's Korean newspaper and occasionally engage in discourse on the topic. Young interns will explore the pros and cons of controversial political issues like Proposition 22 over dinner. Staff members will convey to others work-related anxieties, such as problems with immigrant clients who refuse to play by the rules or make derogatory comments about their age, nativity, or gender. Yet several interviewees have argued that the most that organizations like KYCC can do in terms of their public actions on political issues is educate clients and community members on the pros and cons of political issues, the various ramifications of specific legislation, and how they would go about voting.

In one instance, a couple of KYCC members came across a KIWA petition that protested the exploitative workplace practices of a local Korean restaurant owner who had allegedly recruited the services of an immigration official to suppress worker opposition. A couple of the progressive KYCC members signed the petition as individuals, but I also happened to notice an immigrant member explaining to another staff member how he could not support the campaign. I approached him to inquire about this, and he explained to me that KYCC had officially supported this business because of its compliance with the organization's smoke-free campaign and that signing this petition would be a conflict of interest. In addition, he stated that they could not behave in the same manner as KIWA, because the organization needed to develop positive relations with Korean businesses. One of the higher-ranking organizational members told me that businesses were asking him to intervene and stop KIWA from ruining their businesses, and he exclaimed, "I'm not getting involved with that!"

KYCC's response to the Proposition 22 controversy is a particularly telling example of the organization's approach to political issues arising within the Korean American community. The community-wide controversy first erupted when a congregation of Korean church leaders, including ministers from the two largest churches in Koreatown, formed a partnership with the conservative Religious Right on a series of proposed initiatives that would prevent the legalization of gay and lesbian marriages, among other things.[2] Notably, the leaders of KYCC did not take part in the Los Angeles-based alliance, Korean Americans for Civil Rights (KACR), in denouncing the initiatives. Most members with several exceptions agree that the organization should avoid political issues that test the limits of traditional Korean immigrant values and have the potential of straining relations with key supporters within and outside the Korean community. A few leftist members at KYCC were actively involved with the struggle against Proposition 22 on their personal time and pushed strongly for organizational support against what they felt were "anti-gay" propositions. Yet others, many of whom were practicing Christians, firmly opposed KYCC intervening in any visible way, whether this involved simply signing the petition or sending members to participate in one of the two coalitions.

The following is an abridged excerpt taken from my fieldnotes documenting one informal discussion that took place over KYCC's role in the controversy.

> The male staff member argued that it was KYCC's obligation to the community to take a stand against unequal treatment of any disempowered groups in the U.S. As an example of how such issues may impact the organization on a practical level, he asked how KYCC as an organization could remain silent and neutral on homophobic behaviors when youth within the organization may themselves be struggling with their own sexuality. The female staff responded that in such situations the best they could do was to provide individual advice to the youth and refer him or her to the proper organizations. From her perspective, taking a stand on such an issue would do more harm than good, since the organization would be perceived as not only approving of homosexuality, but also, fighting against church leaders who had published the pro-Prop 22 letter in the papers. She said this would result in parents withdrawing their children from KYCC and the agency losing potential clients as well. The male staff member replied back that this issue was not necessarily one of "approving" homosexuality, but rather, protecting the civil rights of gays and lesbians to live out their lives the way they wanted.

The debate interestingly juxtaposes the needs of internally marginalized clients such as gay and lesbian youth against those of the general community backed by elite institutions such as churches. Although someone later related to me that the issue would be brought up during a manager's meeting, I heard nothing more of KYCC's participation on this issue. The executive director informed me that no one approached him about the issue and that, as the face of KYCC, he could not risk antagonizing staff members and financial supporters by taking a public position on the matter.

Partly because of the expansive size of KYCC and the diversity of its programs, there seems to be more room to initiate political actions and raise awareness *within* specific programs, depending on the visions of individual

individual, influencing other community members in the community to get involved with the campaign to do fund-raising for them but not as part of the organization but a separate community.

The above passage shows how organizations like KYCC also rely on their support networks for engaging in political work. That is, while the organization does not see itself as directly campaigning for politicians or issues important to them, they must establish strong linkages to political individuals and groups that can advocate for interests that coincide with theirs.

A second generation female program director, who had been formerly affiliated with another 1.5 generation agency, argues that everything KYCC does is political because they must utilize political avenues to enact reforms that will better the services available to Koreatown residents.

It's more negotiating sitting around the table I guess than the kind of political activism that I was doing before, which was more door-to-door organizing and demonstrating and that kind of stuff. So I appreciate the power of direct action which I love to do, but I realize that sometimes I can make a better impact in a meeting room with a bunch of bureaucrats. So there's different ways in way we engage in political action I think. For example we're trying to right now negotiate with the Department of Children and Family Services to create a county API [Asian Pacific Islander] service network. The way it works now is that APIs are either subcontractors to a lead agency who doesn't care about API needs and so the services will be fragmented and not adequate for API families. And so what we're saying is we would like our own network that is funded by them in order then we can provide the most culturally appropriate and linguistically acceptable services to API families. So I think that is a political agenda because we're saying this group of body of people need a different kind of treatment from the way county conducts its normal course. We're trying to change something that they've already established, but it is political because you're trying to wrest certain resources and power from an existing authority so that certain group of people are better served and certain needs are met.

The interviewee employs a more liberal definition of political action that involves pushing for change through mainstream channels of negotiation.

In general, the political issues that the majority of organizational members tend to support do not usually conflict with the interests of the ethnic elite, partly because they do not challenge the moral base of traditional Korean culture. KYCC may sometimes win over the interests of the elite by appealing to the importance of youth and family stability or traditional family values. Political issues that are perceived to have negative ramifications on youth and family development, such as Proposition 21, have garnered more visible public support from organizational staff members because of its relevance to the broader mission of the organization. Proposition 21 would have required more juvenile delinquents to be tried as adult offenders and enacted more stringent penalties against youths and adults convicted of a gang-related or otherwise serious and violent crime.

More activist members of the organization have also been known to attend rallies, ad-hoc coalitions, and issue-based meetings on their own time when the organization's leadership refuses to respond to emergent political crises. These members must often venture out on their own without the kind of broad, informal organizational support that the members of KIWA can count on. However, on occasion, staff members who are willing to take the initiative have been successful in persuading KYCC leaders to endorse collective movements that are not perceived as being "divisive" within the Korean American community. One thirty-eight-year-old Korean American staff member explained how he was able to get KYCC's public support for various issues, such as protests against racist caricatures of Asian Americans on Abercrombie & Fitch T-shirts or petitions against animal rights activists who were depicting Koreans and other Asians as vicious dog and cat eaters.

KIWA Strategies of Social Justice

Although it is most well known for advocacy work, KIWA does consider service provision an essential component of its overall program, because members work with a stratum of people who struggle daily to make ends meet. In the past, the organization has offered private consultation, legal representation, and referrals to workers who are faced with various work-related problems; identification cards and bank accounts for workers who are without documentation; and a healthcare clinic to cater to the health and psychological needs of their clients. Without providing the kinds of social services and assistance their clientele needs, the organization would be hard-pressed to find a strong base of workers well equipped and willing to advocate for their workplace rights. Nevertheless, members strongly believe that the organization cannot achieve its central mission of assisting workers through mere service provision but must be accompanied by the politicization and collective empowerment of all marginalized groups.

As stated, one of KIWA's most important contributions has been to provide a progressive political voice within a community dominated by the conservative interests of the immigrant elite. In particular, the political culture of the organization is firmly rooted in the leftist tradition of "social justice politics." Social justice politics conceptualizes social problems within the context of both ethnic and mainstream power structures based on a complex understanding of the multiple bases of oppression, including race/ethnicity, nativity, class, gender, and sexual orientation. As the former executive director states:

> We see hyperexploitation happening in our community, predominantly among recent immigrant workers both Korean and Latino and the vision is to try and address that problem from the vantage point of the workers themselves. Our community is dominated by views that are very narrow, and we feel that there needs to be leaders of our community to be more diverse and healthy, to have progressive views injected into our community debate, especially on social issues that our community confronts as part of the society. So we think we would be one of the organizations that would play that role.

As he suggests, the organization sees itself as something more than an issue-based advocacy group and as a vehicle for broadening the political visions of the ethnic community.

Because of its strong ideological focus, KIWA brings in members who come from diverse organizational backgrounds but share a generally leftist view of politics. Most members would agree that the problems of Korean and Latino workers derive from some underlying inequality that is perpetuated in both the ethnic and mainstream power structures, but their interest in workers' issues may have different roots—some from labor unions, others from coalitional work, and still others from leftist Korean student activism. Despite coming from diverse backgrounds, members rarely adopt an essentialist perspective on any one political issue and provide full-fledged support for others' causes as long as they emerge from a sincere desire to promote some form of social equality. In fact, the one member who seemed to cause the greatest political commotion internally during my time there antagonized other staff members with his nationalistic rhetoric and derogatory comments about other ethnic groups. He later left his position because of these and other political differences.

As described in the previous chapter, KIWA has built an organizational structure that balances democracy with strong leadership. As a result, interviewees have noted that one of the positive aspects of KIWA is its general openness to alternative viewpoints among its members. One twenty-three-year-old female organizer explains, "[KIWA's] strength is that openness and the openness enough to create a direction together and not have maybe three or four people sitting in a room deciding it. And it seems like even though there is a goal to work with workers, I mean it's flexible, and I feel free enough to really talk about objections I have and bring in new ideas." Compared to more hierarchically structured organizations, women, workers, and youth generally have more opportunity to express their political views, or give their input in decision-making processes, although not without occasional problems. Within this spirit of inclusiveness, KIWA can draw strength from the dynamic and innovative ideas of its diverse membership and minimize the risk of directly or indirectly excluding the insights of marginalized groups within the organization.

Politics is central to the organization's mission, because it is viewed as the most effective way to break the bonds of eth-class exploitation, to share publicly the personal trials and experiences of marginalized groups, and to combat all manners of social injustice. Unlike KYCC, KIWA has demonstrated a greater willingness to step up to the immigrant elite leadership when it is unwilling to concede to the larger issue of social justice. Indeed, it is generally believed among the staff that the unquestioned power of hegemonic groups lies in their ability to enforce silence, ignorance, and accommodation and their failure to question their own position of privilege within the multiple hierarchies of race, class, and gender.

As a result, members regularly engage in open political discussions from the workspaces of the general office to the social spaces of the kitchen. These congregations offer staff members the opportunity to recap and strategize over problems they had negotiating with business owners that day, exchange information on new labor laws and political goings-on within the community, connect with interns and workers on a more personal level, and share memories of political protests and activities of the past. The abridged excerpt below is one example of our typical "kitchen conversations."

Sarah asked me if I had gotten involved with any of the students protests while I was in Korea. I said that I had not heard of any type of student protests while I was there, and Sarah speculated that the government had cracked down hard and kept them to a minimum. Sarah said when she was there (near the time of the Kwangju Rebellions in 1984–85), she joined in a lot of the protests. She said she would be riding on a bus and, spotting a protest, would hop off the bus and join the protesters. She said one time when President Ro Tae Woo got caught with some cash box in his house, students started protesting and the police came out with tear gas. She said that she was caught running away from the tear gas and thought she would die from the toxic gas. Jacob followed up with a story about how he had been followed by the police the summer of the Kwangju Rebellions. [Jacob tells his story]. Both Jacob and Sarah then traded stories about a program they had partook in Korea where they worked on a farm for eight days and helped to organize farmworkers.

In this sense, "airing the dirty laundry" of a community is seen as central to achieving its goal of empowerment and liberation. As the above passage shows, these conversations also help to cultivate feelings of solidarity and comfort between staff members and workers to counter the day-to-day anxieties and confrontations associated with community work.

Nor is any one group immune from such inquisitions. The organization nurtures an environment in which affiliates are pushed to question and challenge the privileged position of all Korean Americans, including themselves. During my time with KIWA, the members of the organization seemed to display a relative frankness to educating and informing incoming members about the organization and its history, including its past mistakes. The following passage is an example of how one female staff member took the time to update me on different political conversations and events. I walked in on a heated conversation that was taking place between two male staff members over some politicking that was going on over the M. S. Lee suicide case with the leader of one elite 1.5/second generation organization.

I wasn't clear about what Peter meant by "this," but unprompted, Sarah came up to me after he had retreated to the inner office and explained to me what happened over the weekend. [Sarah explains the incident to me in detail]. I inquired about KIWA's own involvement in the case, and Sarah informed me that KIWA had assisted the man a couple of years ago by setting him up with a lawyer, among other things. She told me that now they were helping out with things like funeral arrangements. She suggested that I read up on the case in the newspapers.

Sometimes, members would encourage me to bring the politics home to my own life.

The previous week, Peter approached me and asked me how the change in affirmative action policies had affected my graduate department. Then, he informed me that someone from the law school was preparing a demonstration against these antiaffirmative action policies and suggested that I try organizing my department to join them. (I later called her and left a message, but she never returned my call.) He joked how I would probably end up doing what he said and get kicked out of the department.

The staff encouraged me to sit in on case management sessions where prospective clients would relay their grievances and ask for assistance. I was also invited or permitted to attend most staff meetings, conferences, lunches, and negotiation discussions with business owners that took place at KIWA, where bilingual staff members would explain to me what was being said by Korean and Spanish speakers without my asking. Needless to say, my Korean and basic Spanish abilities improved tenfold and I gained tremendous insight on the lives and experiences of staff members and workers.

The driving force of KIWA's political work comes from the strong political bent of its members. The fact that the small membership is committed to similar ideologies of social justice helps the organization to be politically active without violating the letter of the law. As one organizational official points out, there is a fine line between an organization officially advocating for a specific candidate or issue and the numerical majority of individual members personally supporting one on their own time. KIWA has been able to participate in a variety of political actions, because the dominant majority of members support one another on these issues and sustain a commitment strong enough that they are willing to work overtime without pay. Because the type of activities in which members engage does not require significant financial resources, KIWA is able to provide support to social movements in a manner that does not undermine their status as a nonprofit organization.

Considering their position of marginality within local power structures and their lack of financial resources, how is KIWA able to fulfill its political agenda of empowering workers against business owners who have on their side blacklisting tactics, organizational support, and financial resources? The organization has pursued two relatively effective strategies for dealing with unrelenting business owners when all attempts at negotiation fail. One is focused on addressing grievances through conventional mechanisms, such as pursuing claims through the legal system, and the other involves the more aggressive tactics of direct action reminiscent of grassroots movements in the

It's always been you know more mainstream issue or like kind of a White-centered movement so they're really interested in the fact that we're talking about this in this setting. *So how does mobilizing on these type of issues fit within the goals and strategies of KIWA?* Yeah, you know our mission is not only to empower low-wage immigrant workers, but also to create a progressive constituency within the Korean community. I mean I think our organizing base is among low-wage workers but we also want to be a progressive voice in the Korean community that brings the community's attention to broader issues in American society and to promote civil rights for minorities and also you know issues that involve marginalized groups whether that be people of color or women or other groups that are marginalized and are not respected equally in society. [Interviewer's questions in *italics*]

In this sense, KIWA could provide an "in" for outside LGBT organizations while also garnering support from outside to promote issues of social justice from within.

Although they regard electoral participation as an important way to enact social change, KIWA has generally operated on the premises that mainstream institutions and government representation are not always the most effective means of addressing the needs and problems of oppressed groups. As one 1.5 generation member points out:

> A lot of progressive groups spend time trying to hold political offices and government bureaucrats accountable. I've always been a believer that immigrant workers are somewhat less impacted by government, especially undocumented workers. The government is supposed to enforce the law so the employer treats the worker well. [But] unless employers themselves change their attitude, government never has enough resources to enforce all the laws. I know that holding government accountable is relatively easier, because they are susceptible to public opinion and votes and we can effectively organize and influence their outcome. But they are operating on much stricter restrictions in those cases. If you keep going to the government, we're gonna always lose out in the end.

From this perspective, small grassroots-based community organizations such as KIWA tap into an oft-neglected part of the enclave community that cannot overcome its problems through traditional political processes. Taken together, it is clear that KIWA has dedicated itself to creating a community-based political entity for disempowered and underrepresented groups within the ethnic enclave community.

Political Visions and Youth Leadership Programs

One of the more important ways that ethnic nonprofits have contributed to the political development of the Koreatown community is through the creation of different leadership programs dedicated to training, educating, and guiding future generations of Korean American leadership. Youth leadership programs are one powerful way nonprofit organizations can indirectly promote their political agenda without overtly engaging in politics. These types of programs proliferated in the wake of the 1992 civil unrest as a way to harness the political energy of young Korean Americans and lay the foundations for addressing, voicing, and mobilizing on the diverse social needs of the broader ethnic community. The movement to incorporate college-age Asian Americans into local organizational structures was greatly facilitated by the strong institutional linkages that had been cultivated between universities and CBOs over time.

In general, Asian American organizations in Los Angeles have carried on a long-standing tradition of collaborating with student organizations and academic departments within local university campuses. More so than other private universities and local community colleges, larger public universities such as the University of California Los Angeles (UCLA) and the University of Southern California (USC) have served as important feeders and breeding grounds for community activism, because of the higher class status of Asian Pacific American students, the substantial presence of 1.5/second generation students on campus, and the individual initiatives of departments and student organizations to establish these types of connections. Student organizations like Asian Pacific Student Outreach at USC and academics from the Asian American Studies Center and the Urban Planning Department of UCLA have worked to maintain this relationship through active involvement in community events and demonstrations, collaboration on related programs and conferences, and various types of intellectual exchanges.

An observational survey of the Korean American community alone is replete with examples of such mutually supportive partnerships. KIWA, KYCC, and the UCLA Asian American Studies Center cosponsored The National Korean American Studies Conference in April 1997 to commemorate the five-year anniversary of the Los Angeles civil unrest. During my time with these two organizations, I witnessed professors bringing their classes to KIWA and executive directors and organizers from these two organizations giving presentations to students at UCLA on a regular basis. Select Korean American professors and graduate students themselves have made it their obligation to volunteer for and work with both immigrant and 1.5/second generation organizations within the community as organizational researchers, board members, and active staff. Students from both universities were also an important source of warm bodies for protests and demonstrations organized by KIWA or community events and programs at KYCC.

Realizing the need to tap into rising enthusiasm among the younger generations, Korean American organizations, including KIWA, KYCC, KAC, and the Korean Exposure and Education Program (KEEP), have created a variety of leadership training programs as a way to shape the ethnic leadership of the future. Not surprisingly, each organization has found very different ways of developing the political consciousness of young future leaders in terms of the content of training, the type of networks they develop, and how strongly they link them to the grassroots ethnic community. KAC for instance focuses on placing students into elite institutions within the ethnic and mainstream communities, such as corporations and politicians' offices, with less emphasis on developing community-related projects. On the opposite end of the gamut, a unique summer program sponsored by KEEP provides participants from diverse backgrounds, including students, with the opportunity to learn about the culture and history of Korea through meetings with workers and student activists, organizational visits, and experience working alongside farmers in Korea.

Even prior to the emergence of leadership programs, the youth leadership base had always been an integral feature of KIWA's historical evolution. Glenn Omatsu (September 23, 1999 interview) explains how UCLA students disillusioned with the privileged viewpoints of upper-class males in the established Korean Student Association (KSA) had formed a new organization called Korean American United Students for Educational Services (KAUSES), which participated in community activities by providing riot victim relief and various social services. Students from this organization formed strong linkages with KIWA, which unlike most community organizations of the time, were eager to recruit and train students. Omatsu states:

> KIWA strategically worked with the students for that purpose, meaning that they saw students as an important force, not something that's peripheral to the community. They wanted to carve out a space within their organization to have students take an active role [and] also felt that the students could play a certain role on campuses in terms of bringing more conscious Korean American students.

Harnessing the energy of youth activists, KIWA incorporated student activists on a large-scale level in the Asian Immigrant Workers Advocates (AIWA) campaign against Jessica McClintock garment industries. To this day, many of KIWA's major restaurant campaigns continue to draw on the support of student activists at UCLA and USC.

In 1994, KIWA, in coalition with the Pilipino Workers Center (PWC), the National Coalition for Redress/Reparations, and Thai Community Development Center (Thai CDC), organized the first Student Activist Training (SAT) program, the goal of which is to "offer young Asian Pacific Islander Americans an opportunity to identify and examine various models of community organizing and direct-action organizing campaigns," according to the application brochure. The three-day program covers a variety of areas in political activism, including organizing skills, media relations, and a sophisticated analysis on power dynamics within the ethnic and mainstream communities. As Omatsu describes it, "the Student Activist Training is an extension of KIWA's attention to try to develop forums like incorporating younger activists and then trying to use their energies as a certain kind of conscious force for redefining community politics."

The driving ideology of course is not to simply strive for the upper echelons of mainstream politics or to work within the system as a representative of the ethnic community to bring about social change, as it is in KYCC. Rather, it is to use one's skills to protest social injustices and learn how to help marginalized ethnic groups empower themselves from the bottom up. Oftentimes, students from these workshops go on to work or volunteer at KIWA to get hands-on experience in grassroots community work. Even those students who do not participate in the workshops or work at KIWA are often exposed to community organizing through their involvement with the organization's different protest campaigns.

Observations on the day-to-day operations of KIWA today reveal the extent to which KIWA continues to actively promote the development of youth leadership. As opposed to being assigned to monotonous secretarial duties, student interns are constantly encouraged to partake in case management, negotiations, and protest demonstrations even in situations where language barriers and youth might be perceived as an obstacle in other more professional organizations. In addition, older staff members rarely treat youth interns as their subordinates and instead make constant efforts to be honest and informative about any new occurrences within the organization or the broader community. A twenty-nine-year-old Chinese American who had worked as a student intern in both KYCC and KIWA compared his experience as such:

> The level of engagement was very different because we were more engaged in what was going on with the Jessica McClintock campaign as students, whereas the KYCC voting thing was very much a technical assistance and you know collaborative project, but it was very professionally linked so it was work. The relationship between KIWA and students was fluid in that we were being utilized to organize and help them at the rallies to increase the numbers, but we also were utilizing them and their knowledge to do education on campus. So I think it really helped to spur a lot of labor activism among students.

Based on stories of other interns, it seems that KIWA taps into student organizations that spring from student discontent with the traditional Korean Student Associations on campus and growing interest in engaging with CBOs on a grassroots level.

In terms of leadership training, KYCC has established two different programs since the outbreak of the 1992 civil unrest under the leadership of Bong Hwan Kim and the support of the board members. One focuses on developing Korean American leadership, and the other links Korean American leadership to those in other racial and ethnic communities. The first program, the Korean American Leadership Program (KAYLP), allows select high school student interns to "develop leadership skills, explore their culture and history, experience hands-on community organizing, and develop a larger perspective of themselves in relation to their own community as well as the larger public arena." The second, the Multiethnic Youth Leadership Collaborative (MYLC), has formed partnerships with a Central American and an African American youth center to attend conferences and collaborate on specific community projects over a six-month period. Other programs such as the Youth Drug Abuse and Prevention Program (YDAPP) and Gang Awareness Program (GAP) have indirectly functioned in building leadership skills by building self-esteem and teaching youth how to both lead and democratically work with other coethnic and ethnic members.

Having evolved under the guidance of a progressive program coordinator and executive director, KYCC's leadership-based programs have tended to fall somewhere between the corporate model of KAC and the grassroots organizing model of KIWA by providing youth with ties to ethnic and mainstream elite networks as well as community organizing skills based on a broader understanding of power. Hence, these programs are ideologically similar with KIWA in terms of educating youth on the power structures that undergird society but find more traditional ways of bringing about social change such as education and electoral politics. Even those within KYCC who were resistant to the idea of politicizing the organization recognized the need for political leadership programs in the wake of the 1992 riots. One such thirty-seven-year-old, 1.5 generation leader states:

> I think KYCC responded to [the 1992 Riots]. We really felt that we should not necessarily be political, but we really lacked leadership and that's one thing that we realized in the community. And I think our community has made that as one of the priorities. If there had been more policy programs available in Korean community nonprofits, like us started developing leadership programs for high school and college kids [so that] they would understand what this community is about, they would understand what their identity is about, they also would understand how to mobilize community, how to use authority and power, more like you know with the tools so that they can be a better leader tomorrow is what we provide here.

Here, the emphasis is not so much on community service but on learning how to empower oneself and the community of which one is a part.

For instance, KAYLP has concentrated on three areas of youth leadership development, including education, skills development, and community projects. The education component involves teaching youth the dynamics of community organizing, power, politics, cultural diversity, and intraethnic issues, such as gender and generational issues. Skills development includes knowledge and training on how to organize, build coalitions, and acquire job-training skills. And the final and most significant part of the program uses community projects developed by the youth interns to apply what they have learned to empower the community. Among other things, the program has educated youth on issues such as the history of comfort women, media bias, the prevalence of liquor stores, and mainstream political issues such as affirmative action. In a similar light, the MYLC guided interns in researching, writing, and producing public service announcements for TV around issues of racism, police brutality, and injustices against juveniles.

The program directors for these programs have generally taken the approach of letting youth debate among themselves what project they would like to focus on, thus emphasizing the simultaneous importance of consensus-

coordinators. For instance, some of the more progressive or antiestablish-ment coordinators at KYCC run their programs in a relaxed and open man-ner so that youth have more flexibility to decide for themselves where their political vision lay and what type of community projects they want to pro-mote. Youth from this program have even participated in KIWA's political campaigns against specific businesses, although not officially as members of KYCC. Such activities still have to comply with the unsaid rules of the larger bureaucracy so that anything that goes against the general interest of the organization is likely to be contained by supervisors or through informal pressure. Staff members are so preoccupied with their own programs that collective consciousness on an organizational level has remained relatively underdeveloped.

In addition, the rigid, hierarchical structure of the agency focuses its mis-sion by enabling organizational superiors to exercise firmer control over the political actions of staff members—or at least the views they project to the public. Accountability to supervisors in such hierarchical structures reinforces this so-called "apolitical" image by allowing superiors to curb the political ac-tivities of individual staff. An example of this is when the youth interns of one leadership program at KYCC decided to protest the selling of a liquor license to a business in Koreatown. The business was specifically targeted because it was situated in a new building that would also offer different youth recre-ational activities and space for a daycare center. The interns of the program planned to rally community and mainstream support by collecting signatures to protest the liquor license, attending public hearings, and publicizing the issue to the media. However, the young leaders encountered internal criticism, because the business owner was well connected with the organization.

As one twenty-one-year-old second generation intern explains:

Our project was trying to prevent his business from getting their liquor license, because that was what the kids wanted to work on. It's on alcohol abuse. But it turns out that the owners of the business are connected with people and I'm starting to figure out who these people are. Even within KYCC, people were starting to backlash at me, saying, "Why are you targeting just this business? Why not other businesses?" And I was starting to see how people were connected with each other.

One of the staff members higher up in the organization discouraged them from going through with the project even before they had a chance to develop their plan, underlining the role of hierarchical authority in supporting such infrastructures.

Yet while KYCC has publicly detached itself from electoral activities and controversial political issues, it would be misleading to say that the organization is completely apolitical in terms of its orientation. Instead, they have found alternative ways of practicing politics. KYCC hones the political experience of youth and staff through regular exposure to elite networks, advocacy groups, and events within the community. The organization also nurtures the internal political culture of the organization through various public relations activities, such as press conferences and political fundraisers. KYCC is actively involved in different leadership and coalition-building projects with other racial and ethnic communities such as the Korean American Inter-Agency Council (KAIAC) and the Multiethnic Youth Leadership Collaborative (MYLC), a program that provides members with a sound introduction into the politics of crossracial networking. A former board member cited coalitions like these as "good forums where you can do a lot of political work," because they are not directly associated with one organization. In terms of general outreach efforts, newsletters, educational forums, and youth projects offer an important forum for political discourse for both the staff and the broader community.

The more explicit forms of electoral and community politicking occurs behind the scenes through board members and individuals higher up on the organizational hierarchy. Bureaucratically structured nonprofit organizations such as KYCC find other avenues through which to wield political influence as described in the following passage by one longtime 1.5 generation board member:

> I mean I'm not here to say that nonprofits are not very political. It's *very* political. But there are strategies and ways that you do political work. As a nonprofit, as a social service, you cannot completely stay away from politics. But there's a way to do political work and you don't always have to be in the forefront. You could work with the local politicians and you could work *through* a network or coalition that forms many times from leaders of the organization. But you still have to keep a distance or you have to distinguish the organization and its services with the political coalitions and political campaigns that you get yourself involved with. The way you approach political work is through your board members, through having other supporters of the organization to make contribution to your local politician, by volunteering in a campaign as an

oftentimes included requirements on serving racially diverse clientele. For instance, one after-school educational program experienced a decline in Black and Latino student enrollment when it lost city funding and had to charge a small fee for families interested in the program. At another program meeting, counselors expressed concern over what would happen to their non-Korean clientele once they instituted a new sliding scale based on changes in their mental health government contract. They claimed that most of their non-Korean clients approached KYCC over other centers only because they did not charge a fee. Generally, insufficient funding for specific programs may often result in either the elimination of the program or the establishment of fees, which causes greater homogeneity not only in terms of the socioeconomic background of clientele but also its ethnic composition. This factor highlights the significance of governmental support in facilitating multiethnic efforts in ethnic nonprofits like KYCC.

Aside from improving relations with other racial and ethnic groups, the coalitional approach benefits organizations like KYCC by allowing them to interchange information, expertise, resources, and clients that they could not otherwise obtain from their usual ethnic partnerships. Because they are still learning the tricks of the trade, newly emerging 1.5/second generation Korean organizations have much to gain from networking outside of their community. These interethnic partnerships have also made them privy to new political opportunities while allowing them to expand their clientele base and staff membership. The executive director of KYCC states:

> We're currently building a lot of collaborations with other nonprofit agencies who are not Korean American. So we work with many different Latino as well as other community-based organizations. Program development, program implementation, program design, outreach efforts—that's basically what we do with them. I think the time's changing a little bit in this area for nonprofits. We're doing more organization development work with other agencies, sharing our personnel, policies, and procedures, sharing administrative practices, what works and what doesn't work for organizational development, you know how do you deal with leadership and management issues so we could really practice what's best for the agency.

The root of KYCC's success lies in its ability to sustain its position within ethnic power structures while remaining open to new opportunities in mainstream society.

By expanding their concept of community to include other racial and ethnic groups, the organization can also gain more support from funders. A second generation manager at KYCC noted that government agencies often have a restrictive notion of "community" that causes problems in terms of applying for funding. He states:

> One proposal I just wrote funded through the Department of Children and Family Services is formatted so that the County Board of Supervisors select high-need areas, and we weren't included in that high-need area. And I think when we're talking about most agencies that are multicultural, it's focused geographically. Where we being a Korean American organization, we focus on a target population. So in this particular proposal, it's very difficult to define where our geographic area is, because it is so spread out countywide. So we would target the San Fernando Valley, the South Bay, the Cerritos area, the Diamond Bar area, you know things like that.

The incorporation of Latino clientele helps to resolve some of these difficulties by giving the organization an opportunity to sell itself as an advocate of the Koreatown community rather than on a narrowly defined ethnic community.

The following passage comes from my observations of a counselors' meeting at KYCC. The encounter below captures the ways in which the organization must balance the needs of servicing the Korean American community, while fulfilling their governmental contracts by servicing the broader Koreatown population.

> Julie told us how she had run into someone from one of the Korean newspapers, who suggested that KYCC should publish more articles in their newspaper, but they never did. As they knew from experience, such publicity brought in a lot of clients for their program, so for example, the day after they had appeared on TV, they had gotten a whole load of clients. Bryan agreed, but said that they should advocate not only through the media, but also other agencies and coalitions. He said that as much as the Korean media was important, they should try to reach out to non-Korean clientele as well. Julie suddenly asked Bryan why he was emphasizing non-Korean clients more this year and he responded that for practical reasons, they could make full use of their Medi-Cal contracts and second, the reality was Koreatown is 60 percent Latino. Other agencies that catered to Latino clients had long waiting lists, so KYCC needed

to fill in this gap and provide services to this underserviced population. He said, as an agency, we have an obligation to the entire Koreatown community, but as KYCC, we must focus on Korean American families and youths, so he wanted to balance both these obligations.

While governmental contracts are a concern, KYCC must balance between funding and program quality in making such decisions. The organization is relatively unwilling to relinquish their support base among Korean immigrants in order to promote their goal of interethnic cooperation.

KIWA, on the other hand, mainly views these alliances as a means to find greater empowerment for oppressed communities and more importantly marginalized groups within those communities. From a practical perspective, the incorporation of Latino immigrant workers and alliances with Latino organizations allows them to overcome some of the disadvantages they face in trying to challenge the stronghold of dominant groups within the Korean American community. Only by cultivating interethnic partnerships among workers can the organization hope to serve the needs of Korean immigrant workers. To a lesser degree, KIWA like KYCC does depend on funding from private foundations that support crosscultural organizing. Yet these types of alliances are not simply a means to end, but also a complement to the general ideological base of the organization, which recognizes the need to promote class solidarity across racial and ethnic boundaries as a matter of social justice.

KIWA engages in various coalitions with local and national progressive Latino-based organizations, such as the Coalition for Human Immigrant Rights L.A. (CHIRLA), CARECEN, the Mexican American Legal Defense and Educational Fund (MALDEF), and international labor organizations like Enlace. They have also supported and collaborated with other racial/ethnic organizations and leftist grassroots organizations, such as the Association of Community Organizations for Reform Now (ACORN), the Bus Riders Union, the Garment Workers Center, the Asian Pacific American Legal Center (APALC), and the PWC. Like the leaders of KYCC, KIWA leaders believe that they must first integrate Latinos into the organization and assume a mentorship/supervisorial role by providing them with the knowledge, skills, and experience to go out on their own. Yet whereas KIWA provides this training on a grassroots worker level, KYCC views itself as cultivating elite leadership within the Latino community. In other words, KIWA takes a bottom-up approach to collective empowerment, whereas KYCC takes the top-down approach.

The official languages of KIWA are Korean, Spanish, and English. Most organizational media distributed by KIWA are written primarily in Korean/Spanish or Korean/Spanish/English, and as stated, the organization itself is staffed by members proficient in these three languages. KIWA publicizes its events and demonstrations to both Korean and Spanish media and occasionally to American news when they are interested. Furthermore, meetings that have any Spanish-only or Korean-only speakers are translated by one of the many bilingual and trilingual staff in the organization. A presentation at one of the fund-raising dinners I attended in the spring of 2000 was translated into Korean, Spanish, and English for each segment of the given speech. Although the meals eaten at KIWA are primarily Korean, the staff also enjoys Mexican food at times.

This type of cultural infusion and social bonding is best captured in a striking dialogue I observed at one consultation meeting I attended with KIWA workers and organizers. During the meeting, a middle-aged Korean waitress explained through a translator how she had been physically assaulted after confronting her employer about unpaid wages and how she had been sexually harassed as well during her employment. After she related to us her touching story, she said in Korean in a small voice "Ji-gum do-wah-jwo-yo (Please help me now.)" A Latino member of KIWA responded in Spanish to a Latino-English translator, who translated his remarks to a Korean-English translator, who in turn communicated his words to the waitress in Korean. The Latino worker communicated to her that she should not be afraid and that they could move forward through KIWA, who always confronted those who treated workers like slaves. He said that Korean and Latino workers were working together as part of the Restaurant Workers' Association of Koreatown (RWAK) to make things better. The conversation was most fascinating because of the way these strong words of support had been communicated across three languages, although the two workers barely looked at one another during the entire conversation.

Having established a name within both the Spanish media and the Latino workers network over the years, KIWA has primarily relied on the networks of their clientele and employees and only secondarily on referrals from other labor or Latino organizations. Workers are less likely to be involved in organizations in general, because they are caught up in the day-to-day struggle to survive and are also unaware of the services available to them. Furthermore, there are virtually no Latino workers' organizations like KIWA other than

CHIRLA, which mostly caters to day laborers who seek employment on the streets, not in a regulated workplace environment. In the absence of local organizations, this method is an effective way for workers affiliated with KIWA to learn the practice of organizing fellow workers and to also use their own personal relations and knowledge to make workers feel more comfortable seeking assistance. Thus, the individual social networks of workers are the main conduit for clientele recruitment.

Driven by the philosophy that the ultimate goal should be to provide workers with the tools to organize themselves, KIWA has taken several steps toward helping workers reach that state of independence and self-empowerment. Below is an excerpt from a thirty-eight-year-old Mexican restaurant worker who initially approached KIWA about workplace concerns and eventually became involved with the organization:

> *In relation with the association, what did you learn and what are you still going to learn?* I am learning to express myself in giving my opinion. When I first came to the organization, I learned to give opinions, talk with the co-workers about work, everything, everything. Some people that are not with the organization, they criticize that KIWA doesn't work. They tell us, "Ah, KIWA doesn't work. It closes the door." But those of us who are in the organization are seeing we are getting support for everything. Well we see that it is good. I myself think that here, it doesn't matter who you are or where you come from. The thing is to unite once we are here. If it's just us Latinos, if it's only Latinos, we cannot translate or do things with other people. If we separate Koreans, Latinos, and others, well, no, it's not going to work. [Interview translated from Spanish, Interviewer's questions in *italics*]

Not surprisingly, the worker focuses on the confidence and skills he was given to empower himself against exploitation.

After a couple of years of learning the ropes of organizing, the members of the restaurant workers' committee officially launched their own workers' organization, RWAK, in the summer of 2000 as an off-shoot of KIWA. Back then, it was envisioned that the organization would take over case management responsibilities and educational seminars, among other things. Because it is in the fledgling stage of development, KIWA believes it is important for RWAK to maintain a separate identity so that employers and employees do not associate the workers' association with the negative image and aggressive reputation of its parent organization. However, Latino restaurant workers have worked closely with staff organizers on all levels of collaboration.

KIWA also has greater flexibility in terms of the alliances it creates because of the extent to which the organization is willing to challenge the views of conservative-minded immigrants and mainstream Americans in order to form these interethnic partnerships. Although mostly centered on the issue of worker empowerment, KIWA has been a strong supporter of the general movement for racial and ethnic equality on issues such as Proposition 209 and police brutality. In such collective movements, KIWA's general strategy has been to vocalize its political views and to steer public opinion away from racialized interpretations of such issues. Former executive director, Roy Hong, explains:

> Through KIWA—an organization representing Latino workers—the race factor is taken out. And today's politics, especially racial politics, that's critical, so much so that after 1992, my contention is that every group that wants to do anything should think about what race implication it has before they do it. We hope to organize Latinos and give as much power and voice for their concerns in our community so that it's dealt with in a proper manner and not just continuing bullshit dialogue about how we need to do better with the Hispanics; you know the situation's getting worse, all this yakety-yak about race relations, and yet they have no idea what to do with it. What they need to do is really look at where do we come in contact with these community members on a day-to-day situation. It's the workplace, and if our community does not treat people fairly and respectfully, they're gonna have race problems.

As suggested in the passage, KIWA members generally find the dialogue-oriented, humanitarian approach of Koreans in the aftermath of the riots to be largely ineffective in addressing the real structural issues that underlie interethnic tensions.

Despite their focus on both first generation Korean workers and Latino workers, KIWA has had to fight the image that it has been assisting Latinos at the expense of the Korean immigrant community. Most of this misperception has to do with KIWA's stance against the most visible constituency of the ethnic community, the Korean immigrant entrepreneurs, who feel most threatened by KIWA's aggressive actions. But the motivation for KIWA members has been to avoid projecting a false image of ethnic unity and to follow the political movements that best reflect the core mission of their organization.

Although the general public has largely ignored conflicts between Korean employers and Latino workers, the exploitative practices of Korean employers became more visible as a result of KIWA organizers who spoke out against these injustices. As stated, Light, Chvi, and Kan (1994) could not find any articles on Korean-Latino conflicts in issues of *La Opinion* prior to the 1992 riots, but in the following years, KIWA protests against Latino worker exploitation have made the pages of the Spanish-language newspaper *La Opinion* several times (for example, Treviño 1998). At the same time, their participation in such protests has helped to prevent observers from interpreting these conflicts as the outcome of racial tensions.

In the decades following the Los Angeles civil unrest, nonprofit organizations have made it their responsibility to cultivate greater political representation, leadership, and empowerment within the Korean American community. To this end, 1.5/second generation ethnic organizations have adopted a variety of approaches in terms of creating an ethnic political culture among the membership, depending on the internal structure of the organization and their relations with immigrant power holders. In downplaying the inherently political nature of community work, ideologies of mainstream liberalism help KYCC to consolidate a diverse membership base and maintain strong networks with the ethnic elite, corporations and governmental agencies. As a result, the organization promotes political activities in more subtle and indirect ways, including activism within individual programs, behind-the-scenes activities of board members, and conversations in informal social spaces. In contrast, the politicization of members and clientele is central to the work of organizations like KIWA. Political tactics offer organizations on the peripheries of ethnic power structures with an economical and effective strategy to contest the powerful resources of immigrant powerholders and achieve organizational goals. KIWA has utilized its outside networks to gain invaluable political experience, politicized its membership to promote advocacy on a personal and interpersonal level, and employed militant, direct action strategies and coalitions with diverse organizations to fight the exploitative practices of coethnics.

The case studies clearly demonstrate the inherently political nature of nonprofit organizational work and the enormous impact that changes in federal legislation may have on the internal power dynamics of ethnic organizational structures. Because of their dependency on the surrounding enclave, bridging geoethnic organizations must adapt their political agenda to new conceptualizations of community, even if their interests remain rooted in the coethnic population. Bridging organizations that reach out to other racial and ethnic groups have access to wider resources and greater legitimacy within Los Angeles politics. In the end, the chapter has shown how these organizations must constantly navigate their political agenda within the constraints of ethnic and mainstream power structures—the outcome of which will determine the role they play within the broader community. However, how these abstract political visions begin to address the personal ethnic-centered struggles of the 1.5/second generation staff membership and clientele is another story that involves the visions and efforts of female "bridge-builders" within the organization.

9 Organizational Carework and the Women of KYCC and KIWA

STAFF MEMBERS OF ETHNIC COMMUNITY-BASED organizations (CBOs) struggle with a range of internal pressures that get buried under the day-to-day realities of leadership, money, bureaucracy, and politics. Among other things, they must juggle the physical and emotional burdens of working long hours for little pay, dealing with daily conflicts with co-workers, clientele, and community leadership, balancing their home life with their work life, and negotiating their personal practices with their public persona and political beliefs—all in the name of "giving back to the community." The rapid expansion and diversification of Korean American organizations in the past few decades have only served to aggravate these tensions by increasing bureaucratic responsibilities in the workplace, heightening political and ideological conflicts among various constituencies, isolating staff members within their respective programs, and concentrating power in the hands of a few. It is only in nurturing the humanistic ideals, the personal drive, and the spiritual development that brought them to the organization in the first place that members are able to last long in the nonprofit sector.

In this sense, Korean and Korean American women in these organizations have taken on a variety of functions that help organizations to manage the microlevel aspects of organizational growth and political leadership. In general, women help to bridge the growing disjuncture between the abstract, political, and aggressive aspects of community work and the concrete, personal, and humanitarian realities that inspire them. The women of organizations such as the Korean Immigrant Workers Advocates (KIWA) and the Korean Youth and Community Center (KYCC) assume certain caretaker roles and responsibilities, cultivate and personalize intimate relationships, humanize the political goals of nonprofit organizations, and develop innovative programs that connect the abstract politics with the lived experiences of clientele. In so doing, they create crucial linkages between the staff and the clientele, between leadership and community, between work and home, and between the personal and the political. At the same time, these contributions often become shrouded in the political agenda of newly empowered organizations and take shape within the confines of traditional ethnic and mainstream hierarchies.

This chapter explores the ways in which women contribute to the cohesiveness and basic functioning of bridging organizations by essentially "grounding" the politicization of the membership through renegotiated gender roles and responsibilities. Korean American women have only a few venues for articulating their political concerns and cultivating formal spaces to pursue their interests within the male immigrant-dominated institutional structures of Koreatown. Within this context, the chapter considers how female community workers foster the more personal, empathetic, and humanistic aspects of community work through existing ethnic organizations, even as they are constrained by their individual and collective subordination within them. Mindful of their relations with the immigrant elite and the population they serve, Korean American women must strategically navigate traditional hierarchies and find a way to strike a balance between cultural respect and individual empowerment through organizational carework. In particular, KIWA and KYCC's respective frameworks of ethnic political solidarity help to mold women's right to political expression and responses to gender inequality.

En-"gendering" Political Spaces

Major transformations in the structural and ideological foundations of Koreatown organizations have opened up the doors of opportunity for Korean and Korean American women in the post-civil-unrest era. Although the dominance of the male-led ethnic elite had precluded women from key leadership positions in the past, newly emerging organizations among the 1.5/second generation have nurtured the leadership potential of men and women alike. These organizations have provided women with jobs, invaluable skills and experience, a political space, and a means to challenge racism and sexism outside the organization. Bridging organizations have also contributed to the changing ideological climate of Korean American politics, with new ideas about gender equality, equal opportunity, and democratic rule. Particularly for those who are excluded from the traditional institutions of power in both

the immigrant community and mainstream society, 1.5/second generation ethnic organizations provide an important setting within which women can cultivate their political awareness and exert greater control over their personal identities and lives.

The growing involvement of women reflects not only the personal initiatives of female leadership and the more democratic atmosphere of contemporary ethnic organizations but also the practical need for warm bodies within the growing ranks of social service and advocacy organizations in Koreatown. As stated earlier, the expansion and diversification of ethnic organizational structures have created new leadership positions and political spaces where women can gain influence within the community. Greater access to government and institutional resources have created new organizations and job positions for aspiring social workers, teachers, activists, and other types of community caregivers. As ethnic organizational structures slowly expand, they must reach out to any Korean American able and willing to devote time to nonprofit work, regardless of gender.

Particularly in a culture where male breadwinners are supposed to take on more lucrative, "masculine" enterprises like law or business, it is the feminized imagery of humanitarian work within both Korean and mainstream American culture that has contributed to the growing presence of women in male-dominated organizations. As one twenty-seven-year-old female Korean American board member explains it:

> I had this long talk with my friend, because we just could not find any guys who were willing to work for nonprofits. I think first is that, especially if you're a Korean male, your parents force you to think you have to bring in the money and if you go work for a nonprofit, you're not going to do that. And you know, having a career that makes a lot of money, you know, is like an ego thing or is something that's necessary for Korean men to have. For Korean women, number one priority for women or their parents for their daughters is to get married [snort].

Similarly, one male social worker related to me an anecdote that represented to him Korean people's attitude toward his career in nonprofit. When his girlfriend's dad asked him what he was doing for a living, he told him he was working at a Korean American organization, to which her dad promptly responded, "No, that's volunteer work. What are you *really* doing for your career?"

While women have made some progress in terms of penetrating the ranks of organizational staff and leadership, these few instances do not necessarily indicate that women have achieved complete parity with men within Korean American politics. For one, organizations serving the specific social and political needs of Korean American women beyond familial issues have yet to garner significant support or attention within the community. In terms of formal institutional representation, a few organizations like the Korean American Family Service Center (KAFSC), the Womens Organization Reaching Koreans WORK), and the Korean Business and Professional Women's Association have provided leadership positions and political spaces for active women in the Korean American community.

However, the membership and activities of these organizations fluctuate depending on the initiative of select individuals. With the exception of KAFSC, which broadly services Korean families, they have still not attracted the kind of support or reached the level of political prominence seen among other ethnic organizations in the community. Few organizations have built working relationships with them on a regular, sustained basis. Programs that specifically cater to women's and children's issues are instead subsumed and marginalized within preexisting male-dominated organizations in Koreatown.

Surprisingly, a general survey of organizational activities among women in the community indicates that Korean immigrant women are more likely to establish their own womens' groups and organizations, whereas 1.5/second generation Korean American women are more likely to be incorporated into existing ethnic-based organizations. At first glance, this trend seems to contradict the common belief that American-born women have a stronger awareness of women's issues and are thus more likely to establish their own organizations than immigrant women, because of their supposed socialization into a more "gender-conscious" American culture.

There are a few ways to explain this apparent contradiction. First, Korean immigrant women generally have a more difficult time penetrating the more visible and prestigious positions in male-led immigrant organizations, beyond their role as administrative assistants, event planners, and invisible members. Immigrant women are particularly disadvantaged in political and business associations—a situation that has motivated some to form their own women's organizations. Nor is working in mainstream organizations an option, considering their language disadvantages, cultural barriers, and social marginality. In contrast, Korean American women have plenty of opportunities to take an active and visible role at most levels of 1.5/second generation organizations and, if necessary, American organizations. Because of their dual exclusion, Korean immigrant women have created their own subcultural spaces for socializing with other like-minded women and also achieving social status as organizational leaders, in the manner of their male immigrant counterparts.

Second, both their lack of acculturation into American society and the stronger domestic orientation of Korean immigrant women can in fact work to their advantage when it comes to bonding with their female counterparts. In other words, Korean immigrant women are bound to one another by common interests arising from home, neighborhood, and place. My observation of various social and organizational spaces, including organizational meetings, kye groups, church meetings, community events, and even day spas reveal how well these women can connect with complete strangers by starting up a conversation about their families. How this type of sociopsychological connection can potentially translate into political consciousness has been relatively understudied, but it is apparent that domesticity can lay the foundations for shared political interests among immigrant women.

Nevertheless, Korean American female leaders overall are caught at the crossroads of racial and gender marginality in an organizational structure that draws heavily on both ethnic immigrant and mainstream powerholders for manpower, legitimacy, influence, and resources. Because power in Koreatown continues to be definitively concentrated in the hands of the male-dominated ethnic elite, women confront a number of cultural and structural barriers in trying to facilitate greater awareness of gender issues and lack the type of networks, status, and money necessary to establish their own organization within the Korean American community. For example, political "powwows" and networking sessions can take the form of informal male rituals, like drinking at a bar with other male community leaders. Women are thus indirectly excluded from informal spaces that provide an entryway into ethnic power structures.

Gender inequality and sexism become even more deeply engrained in ethnically enclosed political structures, because conservative discourse on women and family is less likely to be contested and traditional avenues of empowerment closed off to segments of the population. For this reason, a couple of the women in the study would often wistfully refer to San Francisco as offering a much more open, supportive, and progressive space for Asian American women. This difference may be partly attributed to the socially insular and institutionally complete nature of L.A.'s Koreatown power structures, whose male immigrant-centered leadership easily monopolizes the discourse of the ethnic community. Women do not have as many non–Korean Asian American outlets through which to express their grievances.

My attendance at one fledgling women's association meeting exemplifies the way women's associations are treated by established institutions within the community.

> Before the meeting began, a middle-aged female reporter from *Korea Central Daily* briefly stops by but hurriedly informs Mina that she cannot stay because of another organizational meeting she has to attend. As she rises to leave, Mina grabs her hand and asks her to stay a little longer until the meeting starts, but the reporter insists she has to leave. As she begins to rush out the door, Mina calls out to her not to treat this association lightly and to write a good article in the paper. Later, Rosa the organizer comments in a distasteful tone that she refuses to read the newspaper, because the current editor is very conservative and rarely takes notice of women's issues.

As suggested, Korean American women lack the kind of political legitimacy, social status, and support networks they need to command attention from the media and infiltrate the power structures of the ethnic community.

Without access to such networks, they also miss out on opportunities to interact with mainstream institutions that most often work with leaders who can claim a solid constituency within the ethnic community. More importantly, it is their marginal treatment as Asian American women by mainstream institutions that impedes their ability to achieve progress within the Korean American community and makes it that much more difficult for them to "rat on their own."[1] Lack of political presence and visibility outside the Korean American community thus prevents these women from pursuing alternative venues for political empowerment. Until recently, Asian women were both legally and informally discouraged from becoming active participants in mainstream politics, as a result of American laws and attitudes that regarded them as noncitizens and the patriarchal influence of immigrant homeland cultures that relegated them to the domestic sphere (Espiritu 1997; Glenn 2002). The mainstream women's movement was more interested in advocating for middle-class White women's issues and did little to address the needs and concerns of minority and immigrant women. Despite the enormous strides Asian American women have made in the socioeconomic arena, the relative absence and invisibility of Asian American women in both electoral and community politics underscores the extent to which this historical legacy persists to this day.

Although some activists have nevertheless drifted toward community work in leftist American associations, the type of female community leaders who were active in Korean American politics felt that these organizations were not equipped to represent the specificity of their experience as Korean American women and occasionally noted struggles dealing with racial and gender exclusion in American settings. Other community workers envisioned their time with the organization as a stepping stone for better or diverse opportunities outside the ethnic community in the future. For example, a number of women who were at KIWA moved on to work for other American labor unions and minority women's organizations, while some women in KYCC decided to work for other social service agencies outside the Korean American community. Not only were there an abundance of entry-level positions available for women in this ever-expanding organizational structure, but community work allowed them to pick up language skills and networks that would prove to be invaluable should they choose to work in organizations that catered to more diverse populations in Los Angeles.

The absence of female leadership and women's organizations in Koreatown is also inextricably intertwined with what goes on in the personal and familial lives of Korean American women. Cultivating and maintaining the type of networks that lead to leadership opportunities requires enough people who are able to commit a significant amount of time and resources to community work. In some ways, women are in the position to take on the more time-consuming tasks involved in maintaining organizations, which is partly why they have become such key players in Korean American organizations today. However, when it comes to building and managing their own organizations, women face a host of burdens and responsibilities that extend beyond the normal trials of community work—from the daily anxieties of managing the gendered expectations and sexist treatment of their ethnic and nonethnic counterparts to the struggles of balancing their responsibilities in the home and workplace.

When asked why Korean American women do not start up their own organization in Koreatown, a 1.5 generation female board member of one prominent Korean American organization responded, "You know, it's so difficult when you're a board member and you have a full-time job and you're married and have kids. Just getting involved with an agency is half the battle, so initiating something different may be difficult. If it does happen, it will probably happen from like people like me, who are not married yet and who are just starting out with our career." The interviewee notes the difficulties of separating the personal from the political since women's roles are partly defined by their familial obligations.

One single immigrant community organizer in her fifties explains how it was futile to expect Korean American women to begin a woman's organization until they learned to confront the bonds of patriarchy in the home first. She recalls:

> People [said], "Mina, let's together and organize something." So, I said, "Well, unless you guys do something, I am not gonna do anything." But, they said, "You do it, and we'll help." And then, within that same month, they say, "Oh, no, my husband, no way, you know, he doesn't want me to involve in the Korean organization." So after that experience, I was so disappointed. I will be single and I am single. So I will never have any man behind me, in front of me, telling me what to do and what not to do, ordering me go ahead, or stop. Anyway, I was so disappointed after that experience, you know. When I organize something and when I do something, when some married women promise something, I always say you go ahead and discuss with your husband and if your husband says it's OK, then I will take what you say seriously.

The interviewee reminds us how, unlike their male counterparts, Korean American women must deal with all kinds of pressures from the homefront when it comes to organizational involvement. Because of the deep conservatism of the Korean immigrant culture, gender roles, sexism, and other inequities in the domestic sphere become key factors in determining the fate of women's organizations.

For this reason, community leaders explain that women's groups will succeed only if they function as a space for connecting with and educating like-minded women. Anything beyond that would fail to attract the kind of broad active membership that launches fledgling organizations like these. At the planning meeting for Korean American Women United (KAWU), the four female immigrant professional leaders in attendance agreed that they had little desire to start a formal nonprofit, because they wanted to avoid the impersonal businesslike atmosphere of such organizations and the personal politics involved in dealing with other organizational leaders (for example, whom to invite to organizational affairs). Instead, they wanted to build a place where women can feel free to come and socialize at their own will. One leader suggested that they work through existing organizations by encouraging and helping them to sponsor programs focused on Korean American women, such as an exhibit on Korean American women at the Korean American Museum. Otherwise, the organization would consume too much of their time and money.

Because of the heavy burdens placed on Korean American women in their day-to-day lives, women's groups tend to be more successful when they can help their members to deal with personal affairs, including the burdens of building relationships, confronting overbearing parents, managing work and family, and coping with racial and gender discrimination. In the passage below, a twenty-six-year-old, second generation graduate student active with WORK, a 1.5/second Korean American women's organization, explains how the organization adapted to the personal needs of their membership.

> Two years ago, when all the former board members decided that they weren't 'gonna continue, we actually had a debate on whether or not to dissolve WORK, and it was really an interesting conversation. Because on maybe a practical level, a lot of women weren't willing to commit another year of their time, but at the same time everyone got really upset at the notion that WORK would be dissolved. I think that's when we realized even though we're not a huge, strong active voice in the community, a lot of people know we exist and that's just comforting for people to know that there is this space for Korean American women. And so then we decided to be maybe a little more informal than we've been. So that's how it continued.

The organizational meetings I attended primarily revolved around discussions on career pressures, the difficulties of balancing home and work life, the desire for Korean American female role models, dating and divorce, breaking racial and gendered stereotypes about Korean American men and women, and the burdens of being a woman in a Korean immigrant family. WORK itself had no formal budget, no office space, and no regular meeting time. It was mostly driven by the active involvement of a few core members and their networks with other middle-class and professional women.

"The More Things Change . . ."

In the face of impediments to self-organization, female staff members have alternatively carved out their own political niches within existing male-dominated ethnic organizational structures.[2] However, this also means that they must work within the gendered constraints of ethnic power structures. In a community that is still heavily influenced by the traditional male elite, female staff members must find ways to deal with the gendered expectations and condescension of immigrant leaders, clientele, and some co-workers, who are not accustomed to treating women and the work they do on an equal level, regardless of their age, position, skills, or experience. In this sense, women and workers have fewer options when it comes to navigating the hegemonic context of immigrant-dominated, capital-rich communities. Even those 1.5/second generation organizations whose ideals about gender relations may be more progressive must learn the tricks of working and engaging with male immigrant leaders and clientele in a political structure where the fates of different generations and different organizations are inextricably tied to one another.

Gender roles set the context for structural inequities even within 1.5/second generation organizations, because the criteria for securing the position of executive director is based on male-dominated notions of "leadership" or other areas where men are more likely to be advantaged and masculine interpretations of community work prioritized. Political status, opportunity, and voice are meted out according to the dictates of a political culture—both Korean and American—that defines political leadership and community work in distinctly gendered terms. Community leaders and organizations earn their political legitimacy and respect through power, money, and visibility, as well as strong networks with others with power, money, and visibility.

The board member of a prominent Korean American organization related to me how she had been passed over as president, because she couldn't bring in the kind of money that the current male president brought in through his networks. Instead, she was asked to take a less prestigious and more demanding position within the board, which irritated her even further.

> So I could understand, but then, they asked me to be a membership coordinator or whatever it was. And as a membership board member, you do a lot of work. Like every month, you're organizing events. You know, you have to find like a speaker every month and you gotta get everyone to RSVP. You know like they kept calling all the female board members, asking them to be the membership director, and that's a hard job. I didn't really like the fact that just because they couldn't find anyone, they were trying to give this board membership to someone who was a woman. And they weren't going with a guy cause they didn't think a guy could do that kind of job or should do that kind of job, but yeah, for some reason, they kept asking all the females. And I didn't think that was right at all. Eventually a guy took it, cause everyone kept saying no.

Thus, aside from being given more tedious, unrewarding positions on the board, the interviewee shows how women were being pigeonholed into positions that reflect gendered assumptions about their organizational and administrative skills.

To be a leader, you must also have a practical goal to pursue and find the most efficient means to achieve that goal, even if it involves employing a more aggressive approach in dealing with those who oppose you. From the perspective of many female staff members who were interviewed, ethnic organizations often underemphasize nurturing, people-oriented projects in favor of such aggressive, status-oriented programs. The following twenty-eight-year-old second generation female organizer claims, "With campaigns and stuff, if you're in a fight with someone, it's like—I don't know if it's a male thing—but it's sort of like a posturing thing. Like if they do something, then we have to respond in a certain way. I don't really have a feel for it, because I don't really like to fight with men generally. That part is very difficult for me." Organizations are less likely to experiment with alternative modes and frameworks of empowerment when they're otherwise preoccupied with the struggle to survive.

Yet even women who manage to penetrate the upper ranks of organization leadership based on their aggressive, goal-oriented approach to community work were ironically criticized for possessing these very same qualities. Below is an excerpt from the same second generation woman who had been passed up for the presidency.

Are there any other instances where you encountered discrimination? Um, I've heard a lot of criticisms of the female board members who you know were presidents of [name of organization omitted], but I haven't heard negative stuff about the male presidents, which is odd, 'cause you know, I'm sure they've done things wrong too, but that's not really discussed. *Like what kind of criticisms?* You know, how they're too detail oriented, like they nitpick on every little thing, um they don't give enough leeway to the staff to do their job, they're always like overwhelming. Not only the staff but like the other board members as well. [Interviewer's questions in *italics*]

Thus, even when they are seen as meeting the standards of leadership, they are likely to be criticized as being overly aggressive and domineering as leaders.

The gendered nature of organizational carework can be particularly con-
straining for women when it is marginalized within the male-oriented framework of organizational politics. I experienced this myself when I was volunteering at one community event.

> I couldn't figure out how to fold the tissue paper for the gift bags we were
> making, so in a teasing manner, one of the male staff members made comments
> like "girls are supposed to be able to do things like that" and "you have delicate
> fingers so you can do this." After hearing this a couple of times, I couldn't
> help myself and snapped back in the same teasing manner, "I can probably
> beat you up with these delicate fingers" to which he blushed but laughed
> good-naturedly.

When asked if she faces any type of differential treatment because of her
sex, another second generation Korean American lawyer responds, "Not so
much when I talk to community members, but sometimes clients come in
and they're like, 'Do you have a male lawyer [laughs]?' You know they want to
talk to the man or something. Or if they don't know I'm a lawyer, they talk to
me like they think I'm the secretary or something." As suggested, this type of
dismissiveness or disrespect that female community workers encounter stems
from certain preconceived notions that immigrants hold about the "proper"
role and status of women within the community.

Furthermore, the type of work that women do behind the scenes or in day-
to-day routines is oftentimes regarded as inconsequential or not central to the
"real work" of the organization. As an example of this, I attended one organizational meeting where a woman's attempt to upkeep the physical spaces of
the organization was dismissed as a petty form of "nagging."

> One female program manager announced to the group, "I don't want to nag
> and make 'jan-so-ri [nagging],' but people need to clean up after themselves
> in the kitchen and bathrooms." She said it was embarrassing to bring visitors
> to the back part of the office. At this point, the male executive director
> interrupted her, dismissively joked that she was indeed nagging, and then
> asked her in a more serious tone if she was going to talk about the insurance
> changes instead.

In this scenario, the director trivialized her effort to make the area attrac-
tive to visitors and recentered the discussion on more "important" organizational matters related to bureaucratic issues.

Keenly aware of the predominance of immigrants in the surrounding Koreatown community and sensitive to the norms and values of Korean immigrant culture, 1.5/second generation female staff workers continuously struggle with ways to ignore or overcome these cultural barriers without alienating their constituency. Consider for instance the following quote by a thirty-year-old second generation program manager.

> Me being a woman and being young, I tend to not get a lot of respect from the business owners. I think they don't take me very seriously. They don't take my advice very seriously. Sometimes it makes me lose respect for them, you know. I was born here so I guess that technically makes me second generation. I try as hard as I can to understand where they're coming from. And I'm trying to do it with as much humility as I can.

The interviewee underlines the struggles that Korean American women face in trying to be empathetic to the norms of immigrant cultures while still being accepted and treated as equals.

Although the pervasiveness of immigrant traditions has somewhat weakened in Koreatown politics, cultural values about women and family can also trickle over into the next generation of leadership in more subtle and informal ways. As a thirty-nine-year-old 1.5 generation male staff member admits, men have a tendency to take their male privilege for granted, unless they actively work to stay aware of this privilege.

> We're living in a male-dominant society so as a male, there's a constant struggle, not just ideally sexism is wrong, but reality is unless you check yourself every day you get up, you fall into the routine, which is that men are dominant in society, you're not treated differently. As a man, sexism is something that I need to put myself on guard about every day I wake up so I try to work on it.

The temptation to exercise gender privilege in a society that otherwise marginalizes Asian American men provides a compelling incentive to maintain the male-centered status quo within the ethnic community.

The pervasiveness of sexism in Korean American politics discourages some women from getting too deeply involved. For example, one former female executive director describes the context within which she decided to apply for this high-level position only with the encouragement of a fellow Japanese American male colleague.

And so he was asking you know why don't you apply, and I said I don't think I should be applying, because the Korean community still has this concept of executive director being a man's job, something more masculine than a woman. At the time, if you look at all the organizations like han-in-hoi [the Korean-American Federation], all the presidents were headed by men and whenever I went to community meetings, I think I was the only woman there. And usually they ask me to become a secretary, you know, so that I can take notes and that's what they thought a woman's role would be. In other Asian communities, it wasn't as big a deal as our community was, but it certainly was a challenge being a woman, single, and young.

Even those women who are able to reach the top echelons of ethnic organizations must often deal with the gender norms of the traditional Korean American leadership. The interviewee refers to the way she was relegated to traditional, "domesticated" roles even as a designated leader within the community. Interestingly, she was motivated to break tradition only with the encouragement of an Asian American male colleague outside the community.

Certainly, not all male staff members directly exhibit such blatantly sexist attitudes and may be sensitive to the plight of women in the community. In many instances, I observed male co-workers insist on helping out with menial tasks assigned to female staff members, complain about the way women are treated in these organizations, or show respect for the views and contributions of women in the organization. At a going-away party for one male staff member at one organization for example, a first generation female administrative assistant remarked on how unlike other men in the organization he did not just take things without asking and would always treat her respectfully.

However, some second generation female organizers argue that the general complicity and failure of leaders to deal with sexist behaviors has helped to passively legitimate and perpetuate such attitudes and behaviors on an institutional level. Women who complain about subtle gender discrimination are labeled as being overly emotional, and fighting sexism is perceived as divisive to the organization's work or the community at large. The "divisiveness" of gender struggles may be couched in terms of class solidarity and/or ethnic solidarity. For instance, one female community worker related to me that one man's response to her complaints about sexism in the organization was "that I had become a bourgeois middle-class White feminist, and if I was truly Korean, I would've been able to understand the situation. So obviously I'm not Korean anymore [sarcastic tone]."

Female community workers argue that men not only need to treat women as equals in the workplace but need to recognize the way this is intertwined with what they do in the privacy of their homes. Oftentimes, sexist attitudes are not so much directed at co-workers, but at spouses and girlfriends—the attitudes and effects of which carry over into the workplace environment. A thiry-two-year-old second generation Korean American female organizer explains:

> I think what really, really disturbed me was this attitude, kind of women got in the way of organizing, because women suddenly if they have children, they want more money, they want you know healthcare. They wanted things that they didn't want before. And you know I heard it from several staff members, like before I married and you know, when I was dating, she seemed like the revolutionary woman, you know willing to sacrifice everything, and then after I married, she becomes this middle-class housewife kind of thing. It was really critical. I was like, excuse me, you guys are talking about women in front of me.

In the preceding excerpt, we see how women's issues are viewed as personal, individualistic, and trivial and thus antithetical to the larger organizational goals of ethnic political solidarity. What's more interesting is the way in which men supposedly feel free to make these statements in front of their female co-workers, because they're seen not so much as "women" as "sexless political organizers."

During some of my informal conversations, female members expressed frustration with even the hypocrisy of so-called "progressive" leaders, who preach equality for all and then look for a domesticated housewife to take care of them. Such observations are based on what they perceive as men's inability or unwillingness to incorporate their political beliefs into their personal lives. Others have expressed incredulity that men often make sexist kind of remarks about their wives right in front of their female co-workers, as if their co-workers were "androgynous" or "invisible." One woman told me that one male co-worker even said, "Why can't other women be like you?"

The organizational culture can in fact serve to legitimize and institutionalize gender relations in the home. The following is an interaction I observed between a husband and his wife at one Korean American organizational meeting.

At one point, both Michael and Susan wanted to say something at the same time and they briefly bickered over who would go first. Michael finally overruled her in a stern tone with "No, I'll go first." He added, "Men should always go first." One of the female immigrant staff members at the meeting then pointed to him laughing and said, "See? He's a Korean male." People laughed and one of the female staff members pointed out that he was second generation though. Someone else commented on how Michael had regressed in his attitudes toward women since he started working with this organization. I'm not sure if he had been joking about going first, but he proceeded to speak before his wife anyway.

One woman complained to her co-workers that working in a particular Korean American organization had made her husband more traditional in his views on his wife and family. Such observations make us wonder to what extent general attitudes and behaviors like this legitimize and perpetuate unequal gender relations among staff members, especially when they go unchallenged.

From the Personal to the Political

Although not completely unreasonable criteria in themselves, women have pointed out to me that ethnic organizations can oftentimes lose sight of those conceivably "feminine" aspects of leadership that stress empathy, negotiation, and compromise. They argue that leaders should consider placing as much importance on the process of nurturing the emotional self, building relationships, and promoting the personal well-being of the membership as achieving organizational objectives. Korean American women are able to relate to the humanistic aspects of community work, having felt for themselves the contradictions and tensions of trying to negotiate their personal obligations with their political lives. Some women's very involvement in community work may be attributed to inequities or struggles they personally experienced or witnessed as daughters, mothers, sisters, partners, and friends of other women in the community. Drawing on these experiences, they are able to reappropriate traditional roles and responsibilities and employ gendered frameworks of understanding that enable them to become active contributors within the organization.

Women's ability to see beyond the abstractions of organizational goals partly originates from their embeddedness in "place." Numerous studies (Hondagneu-Sotelo 1994; Robnett 1997) have shown that women are in the position to mobilize localized networks of friends, neighbors, and community institutions through their multiple roles as mothers, neighbors, domestic workers. and active participants in local CBOs and institutions. While men

may opt for more visible, prestigious positions that offer them status and privilege within ethnic politics, women are more likely to be responsible for the
detailed, menial, but critical "grunt work" that enables organizations to function (Horton 1995). As Hondagneu-Sotelo (1994) puts it, "If men are the community pioneers, it is women who are the community builders" (174).

Korean American women have achieved more political visibility as community leaders in recent decades, but they generally tend to predominate in
critical lower-level positions within organizations as staff, interns, and caregivers of organizational leaders. In addition to fulfilling the formal requirements of their given job positions, many female staff members take on more
informal duties that reflect "gendered" roles, such as secretarial and household
functions like cooking. In KYCC, for instance, women predominate among
the clinical social work staff and teaching positions of after-school programs,
with the exception of those dealing with leadership programs and juvenile delinquents. In KIWA, Korean immigrant women have usually been in charge of
overseeing the Korean workers branch of the Restaurant Workers Association
of Koreatown (RWAK), primarily because an overwhelming majority of Korean clients in this industry are first generation women. These gender-defined
positions are less likely to garner status and respect within the organization,
but those in the lower strata of organizational hierarchies are more involved
with the daily operation of organizations and are thus in tune with the needs
and well-being of clients and co-workers within the community.

Because of their care and attention to the humanistic aspects of personal
relationships, careworkers in crossracial organizations like KIWA and KYCC
can more easily traverse the social boundaries of race/ethnicity, class, and
gender. In this light, the following passage describes one first generation Korean woman's relationship with a fellow Latino co-worker in RWAK.

> During my last conversation with Myung-Hee, she had mentioned how Jose
> was currently living with about ten other people in a one-bedroom apartment.
> Because of living costs, she said, they could not afford things like medicine
> when they got sick. When she said this, I recalled a similar incident a few
> months ago when Jose had gotten sick and Myung-Hee had kept on urging
> him to go to the doctor, but he had politely declined. So she argued that the
> micro-loan program that they were starting with Latino workers could be
> used for those kinds of basic necessities.

Carework is an often overlooked way to equalize hierarchical relations
within the organization and help clients learn the skills to empower them-

selves. Although Myung-Hee was ultimately unsuccessful in convincing Jose to see a doctor, the kind of work that she does and the care that she displays help to bridge the personal lives of fellow co-workers in a way that humanizes their relationship beyond the formality of work relations. In so doing, she creates relationships with others that transcend the organizational hierarchies of race, class, and gender.

Spouses are also one of the oft-forgotten caretakers of leaders and staff members of organizations like these. One way they indirectly contribute to organizational carework is by ensuring that men do not risk their personal health and well-being, which as the following second generation female interviewee states, can have serious ramifications on their politics as well. The interviewee claims that labor-intensive organizations can sometimes lose sight of the humanistic aspects of people's lives and remarks that wives can play that role even for community leaders. Within this context, she makes the following observation on the wife of one executive director.:

> She was more the voice of reason. Meaning that he's kind of a workaholic, you know and he's really into this martyrdom. And I just felt like she sometimes reminded him that he's got family, he's got another life you know beyond his work. And I felt like that was the healthier way of looking it than to be so absorbed by the work.

Although most of this kind of carework occurs behind the scenes (namely, at home), I've observed numerous occasions where wives, and only rarely husbands, of staff members also help cook and set up at various organizational functions.

Several male and female interviewees have suggested that women who are influential in the private lives of male leaders also play an integral part in transforming their political consciousnesses in the workplace by enforcing equal gender relations at home. In the following quote, a 1.5 generation male staff member explains how knowing about the experiences of his female co-workers in dealing with sexism is very different from actually living through it.

> You know, at home, we talk about [how] we have to do the same house chores. It should be divvyed up evenly, but I do last dishwashing. Knowing about it and having to do it is different 'cause it's much easier not to do it. And thanks to my wife, she consults me and I realize every time that having to have such consciousness, it has nothing to do with really doing it.

He goes on to say, personal education by his wife at home helped him to recognize his privileged position with respect to gender politics in the workplace.

Based on these gendered roles and responsibilities, many female community workers have worked to nurture a more personalized organizational culture that they find lacking in male-dominated organizations. Undoubtedly, male staff members are quite knowledgeable on the abstract dynamics of ethnic, class, nativity, and gender status and may help others to articulate their political concerns, but female community workers can be particularly sensitive to the conflicts, burdens, and struggles of clientele as they relate to the political visions of the larger organization. One female interviewee noticed that as people became overworked and neglectful of their own personal lives and well-being, they became less sensitive to women's problems and more likely to make what she perceives as sexist comments and adopt disparaging attitudes toward both staff and workers. Thus, the concept of nurturing is not so much an innate quality of women, but also a political statement that links the personal lives of the membership with the politics of their work.

Referring to specific problems within her organization, the following second generation female community worker pushes us to consider other ways of approaching community activism from this vantage point.

It was just a little too crazy so that a lot of times, we just use the people. Meaning like okay, we're gonna have a press conference, let's call as many workers as possible and let's have them read this, and we will write the script for them, this is what you say in front of the media. So I just felt like we didn't really develop them as leaders. And even when we called for a strike and the workers didn't want to strike, you know basically we know what's best for them. So I didn't necessarily agree with that kind of attitude. Like you have to nurture those relationships, and you have to get to a point where people not only trust you, but also believe that this is a position that they can make and feel good about. And it was like rush, rush, rush, rush, and I really never felt like we brought the workers with us. It was more they were behind us, driving them along and not always in agreement. Sometimes in agreement and not always in agreement. When you're in a campaign, you're kind of always in crisis mode.

The interviewee reminds us how easy it is to forget the true purpose of nonprofits when facing the day-to-day constraints and pressures of achieving organizational goals with limited time and resources. To make that link between the personal and the political, female organizers like this feel that it is necessary to analyze critically one's own organizational culture.

She goes on to advocate for more programs that cater to the personal well-being of staff members.

> I said, you know I really think we should have healthcare as an organization. Why is it that we want to like live on nothing, you know barely get paid enough to pay our bills and not have healthcare and not have any benefits. That's exactly what we're fighting for the workers, saying that they should have these wages, they should have decent work hours. We [the staff] didn't have any decent work hours; you know we should have decent healthcare benefits. And basically, he said to me, you know what, if you can't sacrifice yourself for the cause, then you shouldn't even work here. And it was really a harsh blow to me. I truly don't believe that you can take care of other people's needs if you can't take care of your own. The reason I also said that was because at that time, there were only four of us. And two of the employees, two of the staff members had children, and one of them was having lots of problems with his child with him all the time. You know and I felt like healthcare was so important in those kinds of situations.

The interviewee argues that organizational introspection, internal development, and concern for staff members within the organization should be valued just as highly as the services they provide to the outer community. Only then can the organization not only preach empathy for those exploited within the community but also act as a model for other institutions.

In addition to more formalized programs, female careworkers create informal social spaces, where staff members can bond with their co-workers on a more personal level. In most cases, these social spaces do not take place in physical settings separate from the rest of the working environment. For example, I have conversed with KYCC women in the office kitchen, where in the midst of envelope-stuffing for upcoming events, they chat about raising children and about their husbands, exchange grievances they may have at work, remark on the organizational managerial staff and leadership, and share the stress of juggling dual responsibilities in the workplace and at home.

> When I came back, Bryan gave me some corporate packet stuffing. Esther and Julie were sent over to help me in the kitchen. While we did this, we chatted. Esther was pregnant, so we talked a lot about babies, nursing, husbands, household chores, and other things. Esther and Julie joked around a lot like

close friends. Julie, who was enrolled in the rigorous MSW program at UC in addition to her KYCC job and household/childcare chores, talked about how she felt bad that she could not spend enough time with her child. Esther said that she was a true working mother, balancing job and childcare. Later, Bryan stopped by and sat around talking with us. They launched into a heated discussion about how the organization had a way of making male staff members even more traditional and conservative about their wives at home and named various managers and executive directors who claimed to be progressive but made comments like "needing a woman to cook and take care of them."[3] Esther and Julie joked how they preferred doing this type of boring envelope-stuffing task rather than the bureaucratic paperwork they would be doing instead.

This particular conversation shows how personal and familial experiences are in many ways inseparable from the politics of community work. Thus, even seemingly "apolitical" topics like home and family can transition into lively discourse about the politics of organizational leaders within the community. Interestingly, the women also find that these group projects, along with the social bonding that goes with them, help to overcome the tedium of "bureaucratic paperwork."

This passage suggests that social spaces can become important breeding grounds for the politicization of staff members and clientele. An excellent example of this comes from the activities of women in the Korean part of the RWAK, which is dominated by female immigrant waitresses. Female bonding sessions are one compelling strategy that these women have employed to recruit and politicize other immigrant women in the community. For example, one of the first generation Korean female organizers explains: "We constantly encourage Korean female restaurant workers to get involved with the association by offering such legal services and supports to fight against the abuse of the owners. They are aware of such programs, but we still struggle from lack of participation from the workers. [However,] if we make the problems personal then changes can be made" [Interview translated from Korean]. Such social spaces create a space for women to work out the daily anxieties and burdens they experience in the home and workplace. Although oftentimes these meetings take place in the office setting, RWAK representatives have also arranged social gatherings at local restaurants or created a "tea-time" environment at KIWA for women who do not have time to eat and rest before rushing home or to the workplace.

From the perspective of immigrant organizers in KIWA, social gatherings are not just a means to attract members to the organization, but also a strategy to politicize women by sharing their grievances as a group and articulating their concerns in broader political terms. Recognizing that case management provides only temporary relief for workers, RWAK organizers have attempted to come up with more long-term projects, which can attract members by gradually linking the personal experiences of workers to this broader sense of political consciousness about their day-to-day struggles as women and as workers. Because the Korean branch of RWAK is spearheaded by female immigrant workers, these women have been better able to incorporate these types of "personal-to-political" philosophies into their formal programs through workers' meetings and projects to recruit members.

The leaders of RWAK argue that these social spaces can engender future political action by sparking interest among mothers to change the environment around them for their children and eventually give back to the community.

> We talk about our kids and how it is to live in America, like our struggles through conversations. Talking amongst workers motivates them to want to give back to the community, even though they might be busy working all the time. At least they have the desire to get involved within the Korean community. We like the Korean restaurant workers or any minimum-waged workers to get interested and involved in such activities as parenting, getting information about American customs, language schools for those who want to learn more about English and even literacy clubs to promote more reading, labor laws, immigration laws. [Interview translated from Korean]

Thus, social spaces provide an opening for women to make the transition from recognizing their problems to dealing with them. Such discussions help to enhance their desire to become involved with the ethnic community, which in turn is expected to increase their political awareness under the guidance of KIWA organizers.

Two programs RWAK women had been trying to establish at the time of the study demonstrate the creatively gendered ways these leaders aim to nurture social awareness among other female restaurant workers: namely, organizing monthly "kye" groups among Korean immigrant women and establishing a nonprofit daycare center for working mothers, who cannot afford to put their children in one of the many private daycare businesses in Koreatown. Kye groups are a form of an ethnic credit-rotating financial system through which Koreans pool their money so they can raise funds when other financial sources are absent, difficult to access, or undesirable for other reasons. As Yoon (1997) notes, kye groups have become a common practice among immigrant Korean women seeking to "vent stress accumulated from daily household chores" (144). In particular, kye meetings offer low-income immigrant women who must struggle with domestic and economic responsibilities with the only means to get together with friends and relatives. Because it requires a great deal of trust among the participants, kye groups also promote ethnic and gender solidarity, as well as political awareness.

The daycare center meetings seemed to attract more attention from female workers than the kye groups, underlining the importance of personal responsibilities many Korean immigrant women feel as mothers and wives over mere financial and social interests. Mothers involved with KIWA often complain about their inability to raise their family properly because of workplace stresses; generational conflicts with their children; or the growing negative influences of karaoke, cafes, and nightclubs in Koreatown. An RWAK organizer in her forties who had first approached KIWA as a clientele explains that the thinking behind this strategy is to attract working-class women, who are more interested in getting together at social events like these, as opposed to attending political meetings about workers' rights.

> Korean workers are all aware of KIWA in case of victimization. However, they change their phone numbers if their case has been settled. They have to continue attending meetings and seminars, but they just stop at that point. This is why we do these coffee-tea time meetings. This is how we gather our members at a more personal level. They enjoy this personal contact. I keep this list of restaurant workers where I meet them as friends. Nevertheless, as soon as I bring up the issue of labor laws and KIWA, they change their attitude to me. It is harder to gather people for meetings to discuss labor laws and so on. It is also harder to approach the newcomers to KIWA even though we might have met before working. They get this impression of me being the leftist or communist. This is the reason why we are motivated for the mutual financial association where we can simply meet in a social setting. [Interview translated from Korean]

The organizers attribute this reluctance to attend political meetings to their relative vulnerability as Korean immigrant female workers. They feel that, culturally, most women are used to working in anonymous and passive roles and have not yet built their confidence to confront business owners through political actions.

She goes on to explain how difficult it is to force these women to break the bonds of traditional gender roles, to balance hardships in the home and hardships in the workplace, and to risk getting arrested or deported for labor activities, not only as a woman but as a mother and a wife. Because of the way community work intrudes on the personal lives of women, the organizer argues that it is best to begin by helping such women to deal with their day-to-day struggles with home and family first and only gradually develop stronger relationships and a more developed political repertoire over time. At one meeting, for instance, the Korean female organizers of the RWAK encouraged the potential members at the meeting to stop by during lunch breaks, to find out what work people here were doing, and to see if people got any sleep the previous night. One member urged the attendees not to see the organization as a "bu-dam," or burden, and expressed her hope that they would become "eon-ni" and "dong-saeng" (big sisters and little sisters) to one other.

Community work can also take the form of traditionally female-dominated roles and responsibilities. Cooking has become one particularly interesting way in which first generation and 1.5 generation women have made their mark on organization-building processes, particularly in an ethnic culture where food is central to bringing together members for social, political, religious, and cultural occasions. My observations and interviews with various organizations and churches have revealed the centrality of food preparation in all occasions that involve social networking and political discussions. Although confining in their own way, gender-proscribed roles and responsibilities at home and in the workplace offer a natural platform from which to help fellow members to overcome their daily anxieties, to strengthen interpersonal relationships across social boundaries, and to push forth an introspective approach to organizational development.

On this point, the former first generation president of the Korean Business and Professional Women's Association explains:

When we introduce our country's culture at the museum on Wilshire, we join with other women's organizations. We cook food to make people aware of Korean culture. After the 1992 civil unrest, the organization got very famous. I thought we could not stand still since many people were affected, so I took five members and we went to all the people that we knew to ask for donations.

And we went to Radio Korea and had a bazaar with the food that we prepared to raise a lot of money. With the money we raised, we gave it to the people that were affected by the 1992 civil unrest. [Interview translated from Korean]

From her perspective, cooking becomes a way of educating and connecting with American society—a need that became particularly compelling in the aftermath of the 1992 civil unrest.

Women who are hindered by language barriers and do not have the skills for other job positions within 1.5/second generation organizations find that their ability to give something special to the organization in the form of cooking as personally empowering. KIWA offers a particularly interesting example where staff and volunteers gather together over meals prepared by female members of the staff. A middle-aged female immigrant who prepares meals at KIWA explains:

I do it because I want to do it especially for our KIWA family. Especially in my case, I can't eat in Koreatown, because there are so many restaurant owners who recognize my face so if I go there, they keep looking at me. Our KIWA family cannot really go out and eat and some owners had complaints against us. There are people who don't accept our money after we eat. Even if we go out and eat, there are many phone calls here and if we can't answer the phones, we can't really listen to as many of the workers' stories so it is inconvenient. It is more comfortable to eat at KIWA and it is more comfortable since we save money. I just make it at home and bring it here since I always make kimchi. [Interview translated from Korean]

The above statement captures several ways female workers have played key roles in groups like KIWA that must struggle against the ethnic elite. Because of their oppositional stance against restaurant owners, KIWA staff members feel that they must find alternative ways of finding food. This also helps them to avoid uncomfortable situations where employers try to foster goodwill with staff members by refusing to accept payment for their meals.

In addition, their busy schedules, small staff size, and lack of a formal hierarchical structure that prevent them from doling out secretarial duties and designating set breaks do not always allow them the leisure to take time off for meals. Lack of money is thus an issue for organizations and members with low budgets. In this context, the interviewee pictures KIWA as a "family," and the work that she does indirectly helps them to better serve the needs of other workers like her. Although feeling conflicted by her cooking responsibilities, another younger first generation woman relayed to me similar sentiments during one of our informal conversations.

> When Jee-Hyun went over to the computer next to me, I told her I felt bad because she was cooking all the time. She said that she was cooking for everyone anyway so I should go eat. I said she shouldn't have to do that all the time, and she said that she was arranging for Kwan-Soo, Jacob, and the others to cook. She said she had just "ya-dan cheot-sseo" (scolded them) today about that. I asked if they were good at cooking, and she laughed saying they were great cooks (eol-mah-na jal ha-neun-deh! You don't know how good they are!). I said that once in a while, we should go out and eat instead, but she replied that she would only end up paying for the meals. She said that before she used to go out to eat, but her personality was such that she couldn't go out and eat alone. So she would ask people what they wanted her to pick up, but most of the time no one had enough money to pay so she had to pay herself. I said, "What, as if you're rich or something?" And she said that she was broke too, but no one else had money so what could she do? She said to me, "It's not like I could ask them to give me money! None of us have any money, so I have to pay." She said that a while back, she had thought to herself what can I do here to be most helpful? And she thought that this was the best way she can give "jeh-il keun do-um" (most help). I told her I always thought that cooking was much more difficult than washing dishes, and she said it was a little difficult, but she found out it was so much better when people were working together like this. If instead they took turns cooking, people would eventually get tired of it, and it wouldn't work.

The fieldnotes interestingly show how class inequality and budget constraints can reinforce gender hierarchies within the organization. Jee-Hyun comments that such responsibilities and expectations can become tedious at times, but she is willing to do something valuable for the organization. Thus, women who take on these kinds of roles help to equalize class differences within the organization as well.

During my attendance at various organizational functions, I noticed how food played a key role in personalizing the environment and encouraging people to put aside time to share their experiences and develop feelings of intimacy among the members. This is particularly true for smaller organizations that have little space or opportunities for social gatherings or lunch

positions, which includes a good mix of women in managerial positions and a few on the board. Thus, greater management control and adherence to regulations helps to temper more overt expressions of sexism in politically liberal and formally structured organizations like this.

Stronger emphasis on training, supervision, and leadership development within KYCC provides women with the opportunity to secure top-ranking positions. The mere fact that KYCC has more than one upper-level position, mainly in the form of managerial jobs, also leaves more room for women to take on leadership roles. The governing board currently includes a few women, although it is still dominated by men. Throughout its long history, KYCC has had at least one female executive director, but it should be noted that this was facilitated by the intervention of Asian American officials from Youth Drug Abuse and Prevention Program (YDAPP). Another minor factor is that the type of business and organizational skills that are most important in top managerial and leadership positions at KYCC are more attainable for incoming female staff members; in contrast, the top position at KIWA requires strong labor and community leadership background and extensive organizational networks. This is harder to come by for Korean American women who are often excluded from positions that would allow them to acquire these skills before joining KIWA.

Organizational structure is also reinforced by liberal American norms about equal opportunity and diversity. Within this type of culture, KYCC is less likely to encounter problems with more blatant forms of sexism and gender hierarchies associated with the immigrant culture. A Korean American KYCC program manager in her forties explains:

> I think that we are a multiethnic diverse agency and so there is a level at which we need to be respectful of everyone's differences in background and account for not only culture but also gender. So we have a certain organizational cultural norm where I think that respect is all around something we need to have for each other, but you know I still hear folks saying some stuff. Like I had a lunchroom discussion the other day where you know a guy was saying "well the women are so whining" and I'm like "what're you talking about?" But I can engage him without feeling like, "oh am I saying something that's completely out of the cultural norm here?" So I know he's gonna be respectful of my view as much as I am gonna challenge him in a way in a public setting that is okay within the culture of the agency. I think in a lot of places, it's not even okay to challenge it.

On the other hand, sexism still pervades the organization in more discrete and informal ways. An example of this is when leaders and staff members use ideologies of multiculturalism and democracy to dismiss allegations of inequality or hold onto the belief that sexism is individual, cultural, and violent in order to conceal other forms of gender inequality. In general, KYCC downplays the kind of self-politicization that pervades the internal culture of KIWA and does little to provide a broader framework for understanding social disparities. For example, many members tend to conceptualize sexism as an individual act or an extreme form of discrimination that is more likely to occur among people outside the organization rather than within themselves. When asked if they felt disadvantaged by their gender status, the few who responded yes most often referred to their interactions with clients or immigrant leaders.

Problems can arise because supervisors are generally perceived as being responsible for controlling the behaviors of individual employees, and members are less likely to take it upon themselves to reprimand the attitudes and behaviors of their co-workers. Furthermore, only more extreme forms of sexism are likely to be reported to managers, while more subtle forms of sexism tend to be dismissed or ignored. The structured nature of dealing with internal discrimination and the tendency to avoid confrontation seems to account for the relative lack of internal strife that is more common in other types of organizations. The subtle nature of internal sexist practices and the conservatism of KYCC's supporters also help to prevent outside activists from pressuring for changes within the organization.

Female interviewees seemed to feel that sometimes they are subjected to differential treatment or exclusion within the organization but are reluctant to label such experiences as signs of "sexism." Those men and women who do acknowledge gender inequality within the organization are often unable to cite specific incidents of sexist views or behavior, but rather, refer to it as some vague entity that prevents women from partaking equally in decision-making processes or taking leadership within the organization. Of course, there are many exceptions to this general pattern, especially in an organization as large as KYCC, but my interviews and observations show that this type of mentality is more indicative of the general culture of KYCC.

More importantly, I have seen very few staff members actively challenge sexist comments, beliefs, and behaviors of other co-workers and supervisors when they do arise. Take for instance the following anecdote of a conflict that occurred within one of the youth programs and the male program manager's response to the incident.

We once had a gender session, and there were tensions between girls and guys right there. One of the guys had a very conservative outlook on gender roles. He was saying that bottom line, guys need to do this, girls need to do that. And the girls are like, that's not right. And so that was one of the things I didn't expect. I didn't intervene by saying, oh I think so-and-so is right or I think the girls are right. Because I think part of being a leader is you gotta look through the eyes of the other person, try to understand where they're coming from.

In contrast to the political confrontations seen within KIWA, this response—that leaders must understand the viewpoints of both sides—is more commonly practiced within the organization. Although a few members consider themselves "feminists," I have not encountered many women who have made any visible effort to challenge gender inequity within the organization, as compared with the women of KIWA.

KIWA is based on a more informal, highly driven, and politicized organizational culture that considers the open politicization of its staff an integral part of its broader mission, at least in theory. In comparison to KYCC, staff members are more likely to be encouraged to bring internal issues such as race, class, or gender inequities to the forefront of organizational discourse. Formal bureaucratic control over interpersonal relations and the content of public discussions is less rigid in KIWA, in the interests of promoting greater democracy. However, the relative absence of an established decision-making structure, ambiguous bureaucratic procedures, and undeveloped staff-oriented programs also make it difficult for the organization to ensure equal gender relations and to deal with gender-based conflicts among the staff.

The general ethnic organizational culture of KIWA may be characterized as closer to a 1.5 generation culture in that it combines different elements of first generation and second generation cultures in its ideologies and organizational practices. Staff members converse with each other in both Korean and English, partly out of necessity, but also because of personal styles. Congregating for Korean "hot-pot" meals is one example of how Korean culture permeates the organization. Of course problems arise when gendered aspects of immigrant culture occasionally seep into the ideological views and practices of the organization, as in the case of female kitchen workers. Furthermore, the small size of the staff and KIWA's marginal status within ethnic power structures have fostered a strong sense of solidarity among its members in the face of external opposition so that the tendency has been to overlook individual transgressions. As a result, it has been reported that accusations of sexism regarding one of its male staff members were initially met with disbelief and reluctance to sever ties with the accused. Although individuals made attempts to keep the group united without alienating anyone, the failure to confront such behavior in an aggressive manner ironically led to deeper divisions within the organization.

In terms of ideological standpoint, it has been noted in previous chapters that KIWA's general stance has been to acknowledge the multiple intersectional systems of stratification that shape individual and collective experiences. The politicization of its membership and its attraction to progressives from different backgrounds inject an element of dynamism, broader political awareness, and ideological balance that is lacking in other organizations such as KYCC. In addition, the organization's roots in progressive networks that include many feminist supporters help to apply pressure on leadership to deal with internal sexism. Strong orientation toward equality and social justice minimizes the likelihood of internal marginalization along lines of race, class, gender, religion, and sexual orientation, as compared with other organizations. Because KIWA lacks the rigid hierarchical structure of organizations like KYCC, staff members are more likely to treat each other equally in their informal social interactions. As compared with KYCC, the female members in the organization today reported that they generally do not feel that they are treated differently than male members.

Regardless of intention and guiding philosophy, incidents do happen and because of the complexity of this type of intersectional thinking, ideology does not always carry over easily into everyday attitudes and behaviors of staff members. KIWA is certainly not the only organization to experience incidents of sexism internally, but it is one of the few that has openly acknowledged these problems (partly due to the insistence of female staff) and has made active efforts to address them, even though these efforts have not been seen as successful by many of its critics. One 1.5 generation male interviewee feels that they are held up to higher standards so that when they fail, people feel greater disappointment than they would with other organizations. He argues that KIWA does not have an ideal Korean America model to follow in order to remedy such problems and is given all kinds of contradictory advice from outside groups on how to deal with internal sexism. Amid such ideological diversity, KIWA is more likely to have to deal with internal conflicts than other organizations. Yet rather than viewing these types of conflicts as inherently problematic, we might view them as the type of soul-searching and growing pains necessary for greater equality.

On the one hand, one of the main advantages of a flexible and informal internal structure is the relative ease with which it can incorporate some of the changes necessary to deal with internal issues. In response to allegations of sexism in the past, KIWA has in recent years set up a new decision-making body that deals with complaints of sexual harassment and discrimination through outside mediators. In addition, incoming interns and staff are honestly informed about KIWA's past problems with sexism and educated on their rights should they encounter such discrimination in the future. Although changing the mindset of individuals may be more difficult, KIWA at the very least continues to grapple with these issues.

On the other hand, the internal structure of the organization is a key element both in reinforcing gender hierarchies and affecting the organization's capacity to respond to such problems. To explain, most of the older ethnic organizations in Koreatown began from the efforts of male leadership mainly because of the pervasiveness of traditional patterns, which privileged men in both the ethnic community and mainstream society. Among other things, general sexism prevented Korean American women from gaining the adequate skills, mentorship, experience, and status necessary to garner the social and financial capital to start up an organization. However, in more recent years, 1.5/second generation organizations have been able to elevate women into top executive positions, because these organizations have the capacity to mentor and cultivate leadership skills among women. KIWA on the other hand cannot offer this type of guidance, because it is constantly in battle against outsiders and lacks the rigid hierarchy to formally train and supervise its staff. Because of the intensive nature of its work, the organization finds it difficult to gain the introspective insights necessary to find alternative remedies.

As a result, interviewees have related to me that this structural weakness has helped to reinforce the dominance of men in leadership positions. A former twenty-nine-year-old second generation female staff member argues that ethnic-based organizations like KIWA need to devote more of their time toward creating programs that focus on personal growth, staff education, training, and workplace benefits in order to prevent what she feels are "incidental" gender inequities.

There are certain issues of low personal growth here, personal opportunities to grow as individual staff like staff training, staff development, and with that kind of thing, feeling powerless. I think with nonprofits if you can't afford to pay the staff well, the one way you can really help them is by helping them to really grow professionally in their field. I mean we're all here because we believe in certain issues and causes and believe in the organization. And we're here for a very low wage, you know; at least we can get paid by helping us as a staff professionally. And um, if you're not trained, I think there's a feeling of frustration that your self-confidence goes down, and then you also feel powerless in the organization. I think it just has a lot to do with people that have been here, not really knowing how to pass their knowledge on to new people. And it just turns out that the people that know most of it that have been here are male but in the newer staff, they're female, you know, and I think that gender's more by accident.

Not all former members would agree that these structural inequities are not deliberately gendered in some manner, but the interviewee does point out that the absence of internal development can at least indirectly reinforce gender differences within the organization. Notably, KIWA's peripheral status within ethnic power structures also undermines its capacity to address such imbalances internally, because it lacks the time and resources to put people through training and implement a systematic procedure for dealing with grievances. In this sense, gender inequities can also be attributed to larger hierarchies within Koreatown politics.

In a previous chapter, it was discussed how the executive director of KIWA has taken on the primary role of accountability and visionary for the organization for all practical purposes. Although this allows the organization to retain focus within the complex ideologies of intersectionality, this type of structure is problematic when the organization has had only one leadership for most of its history and the leadership is male. When unsatisfied with the actions of a director, women have no one to turn to internally to address their grievances. In addition, staff members have pointed out that the informal nature of decision-making processes is structured so that stronger personalities and politically experienced staff are more likely to dominate discussion in the absence of formal rules and procedures. So although the organization has tried to battle gender hierarchies within, the secondary consequence of its internal structure has ironically been the perpetuation of such hierarchies.

Korean American women play a type of brokering role between the abstract, instrumental mission of the organization with the lived experiences of staff members and clientele. It is their empathy for and engagement with the personal and emotional aspects of people's lives that allows them to stay in tune with their membership and the communities they serve without seriously undermining the status quo. Immigrant and American-born women in the community have been active in cultivating the subjective, nurturing, and inclusive dimensions of community work by taking on diverse gendered responsibilities, fostering interpersonal relations among staff and community members, and pushing for new people-oriented programs and perspectives. Women have also created their own spaces within these organizations where they can share their hardships and create a nurturing environment that is often lacking in most male-dominated organizations.

At the same time, the rigidity of these gender roles and responsibilities have also curbed other opportunities for empowerment and laid the groundwork for their further marginalization within ethnic power structures. Indeed, their very rootedness within the political structures of the immigrant enclave may enable them to connect with the surrounding community, but it also subjects them to the gendered norms and values of the male-dominated ethnic leadership. While it is relatively easy to challenge exploitation and oppression when it comes from the outside, organizations have found it more difficult to confront their own internal organizational problems depending on their status within ethnic power structures. This chapter has demonstrated how gender relations and responses to sexism are mediated by the different organizational cultures and internal structures of these 1.5/second generation organizations as they are shaped by their position within traditional ethnic hierarchies. For women, working within these enclosed power structures requires negotiating the cultural terrains of working in an immigrant-dominated community and finding other avenues for individual empowerment.

10 United We Stand, Divided We Speak

AS WE ENTER A NEW PHASE in the evolution of racial and ethnic communities in America, we are faced with the formidable task of cultivating alliances that enable us to break the chains of social inequality. Clearly, this task has been complicated by increasing class polarization within minority communities, the growing diversity of incoming immigrant groups, and the divisive effects of globalization in recent decades that have made lines of commonality with political allies as unclear as the adversaries we must confront in order to address our social ills. It is with this in mind that this book considers an alternative approach to ethnic political solidarity—one that finds as much potential value in welcoming new political actors and their diverse perspectives as coming together as a single, homogeneous constituency.

As this research suggests, political dissonance does not necessarily detract from the healthy functioning and internal cohesiveness of ethnic communities undergoing generational transitions in leadership, but instead enriches political discourse through the incorporation of diverse coethnic constituencies. Among other things, challenging the status quo is one way of introducing new methods for addressing old problems, giving voice to those without a voice, uncovering new bases of empowerment for communities with limited resources, and most importantly, building bridges with groups where there once were none.

Be that as it may, the main challenge is to determine whether or not there is a basis for collective unity and empowerment when class differences, residential dispersal, intergenerational conflicts, and gender inequality seem to be pulling ethnic communities apart. In traditional assimilation models, it was

Notes

1. See Herman 2004 for a more detailed discussion on the different names of sa-i-gu.

Chapter 1

1. "Coethnic" refers to those who are members of the same ethnic community. Hence, "non-coethnic" refers to anyone who is not (e.g., non–Korean Americans.)

2. See the special issue on immigrant organizations in vol. 31, no. 5 of *Journal of Ethnic and Migration Studies* for more on this topic.

3. The potential for greater political empowerment within the Korean American community has noticeably increased as the population of American-born children of Korean immigrants begins to grow and more Korean Americans overall begin to pursue citizenship status. Recent 2000 census data collected by the Center for Korean-American and Korean Studies at California State University, Los Angeles (CSULA), indicate that today about 22 percent of Korean Americans are citizens by birth, and 45 percent have become naturalized citizens as compared with 34 percent who remain noncitizens (Korean American Coalition and Center for Korean-American and Korean Studies 2003).

4. Although scholars concede that some groups (namely, Black Americans) may be impeded by racial barriers, most of the earlier scholars generally considered assimilation as an inevitably irreversible and monolithic process by which most groups would be incorporated into the institutions of mainstream society.

5. The study draws on multiple methodological techniques with particular emphasis on personal interviews and participant observation methods. As its primary methodology, I conducted in-depth, semistructured interviews with twenty-four affiliates from KYCC, seventeen affiliates from KIWA, seventeen affiliates from other

Korean and Latino organizations, and twelve active community members (business owners, workers, church leaders, academicians, and so forth). Of those interviewed, sixteen were first generation Korean immigrants, eighteen were 1.5 generation Korean Americans, twenty-two were second generation Korean Americans, and fourteen were non–Korean Americans (usually Latino or non–Korean Asian American). In addition, I devoted a total of 15–25 hours of volunteer work per week at KIWA and KYCC from October 1999 to November 2000. I also incorporated four years of field observation with various groups and organizations, including protest demonstrations, annual fundraisers, interorganizational meetings, political study groups, social events, canvassing, and conferences. The above data were supplemented with other available material, including (1) media sources, such as ethnic and mainstream media, documentaries, and organizational newsletters; (2) preexisting surveys of Korean American organizations; (3) statistical data from the U.S. Census and GIS Mapinfo program; and (4) official records and documents.

Chapter 2

1. "Vertical integration" refers to a situation where a given ethnic group dominates all levels of production within the enclave economy, including not only the businesses but also the suppliers, financiers, and manufacturers higher up on the economic chain.

2. Because of their relatively higher socioeconomic and educational background, Korean immigrants have access to more *class resources* than some other ethnic groups. These include financial resources, as well as specific cultural class-related values, knowledge, and skills that predispose them to enterprise and help them to succeed (Light and Bonacich 1988). In particular, Korean immigrants draw on a variety of sources, including personal savings and family loans, in order to start up their businesses. In addition, *family resources*, or "private goods that are exchanged and kept within a closed circle of family and kin," are important for obtaining business advice, financial information, and sources of unpaid labor (Yoon 1997, 45). Scholars have found that Korean immigrant entrepreneurs also receive invaluable assistance and resources from strong networks of ethnic solidarity. These *ethnic resources* include business information, organizational representation, financial aid, coethnic customers and suppliers, and job training experiences (ibid., 45). This sense of solidarity is best exemplified by the group's effective use of kye groups that allow members to acquire financial capital to establish and maintain their businesses. In addition, some scholars argue that certain values deriving from the group's ethnic heritage, such as Confucian values on hard work and meritocracy, may also aid in entrepreneurial success.

3. The intense religiosity of Korean immigrants can be attributed to three factors: the predominance of urban, middle-class Koreans among immigrants to the United States; the high proportion of North Korean immigrants fleeing religious persecution;

and the greater tendency of Christian Koreans to immigrate as a result of Western and modern influences (Min 2000).

4. The zip codes for Koreatown are 90004, 90005, 90006, 90010, 90019, and 90020. Note that parts of this zip code region may extend outside of Koreatown (especially 90019). However, the concentration of Korean-owned businesses is not as visible in these outlying areas so that the figures are expected to be roughly accurate.

5. My count of "established" organizations includes those well-known CBOs that I have encountered through my field research or read about in the Korean newspapers. These organizations have more than ten members, have regular organizational agendas or meetings, actively participate in Korean American events, or are well-recognized within the Koreatown organizational community.

Chapter 3

1. One exception to this is the Cholla province, which is marginalized within the Korean nation-state as the breeding ground for radical, dissident politics based on its long history of class struggles. Notably, the Kwangju Rebellions broke out in the Cholla province. See Yea (2005) for more information on Cholla's historical status within Korea.

Chapter 4

1. I would like to give special acknowledgment to Minjeong Kim for her assistance in researching and writing portions of this section on reunification.

2. Aside from Mitchell's death, the involvement of Reverend Boyd was also linked to a long-standing conflict with the nearby market, which sold liquor on Sundays and sold drug-related items (Freer 1994).

3. Among other things, the coalition was unable to deal with both internal divisions and outside pressures from the media and the community because of lack of funding; inability to move beyond dialogue and education to deeper economic issues; the divisive loyalties of different representatives to their ethnic constituencies; and lack of involvement from those community members actually involved in the conflicts—namely, Korean immigrant merchants and Black residents and activists (Chang 1992).

4. Among other problems, only 35 percent of Korean Americans were insured during the civil unrest, and of those insured, many policies turned out to be meager in sum or offered no riot coverage.

5. This is partly attributed to California state laws, which impose few restrictions on store locations. Underlining the race-class dynamics of the general market economy, the liquor store trade builds on the profitability of serving alcohol to low-income, minority residents who generally lack the political influence to resist the influx of liquor stores. These market dynamics set the stages for the entrance of Korean immi-

grant entrepreneurs, who have little sense of the history of substance abuse in racial minority communities and seek the most profitable business with which to overcome their disadvantaged status in American society.

Chapter 5

1. "Comfort women" are women from Korea, China, Philippines, and other Japanese-occupied Asian countries who were used as sex slaves for Japanese soldiers during World War II. A coalition of Asian American organizations have filed lawsuits and sought both symbolic and financial reparations from the Japanese government in recent decades.

2. Edward Park (1998) provides a good discussion on how 1.5/second generation organizations have been divided by differences in political partisanship.

Chapter 7

1. Portions of this chapter were taken from Chung, Angie. 2004. "Giving Back to the Community." *Amerasia Journal* (30)1: 107–124; and Chung, Angie Y. Forthcoming. "Re-assessing Ethnic Political Solidarity: A Case Study on Bridging Organization in Koreatown." *Negotiating Space: New Asian American Communities*, ed. Huping Ling. Monograph under review.

2. KCTU represents workers in the manufacturing heavy industries (e.g., auto, steel, and shipbuilding) and white-collar workers in banking, media, and other economic sectors.

Chapter 8

1. A different version of this chapter was published in Angie Y. Chung. 2005. "'Politics without the Politics': The Evolving Political Cultures of Ethnic Non-Profits in Koreatown, Los Angeles." *Journal of Ethnic and Migration Studies* 31(5): 911–29. (See http://www.tandf.co.uk)

2. The controversy focused on a series of proposed initiatives directed against homosexuals on the November 2000 and March 2001 ballots. The first piece of legislation, the California Defense of Sexual Responsibility Act of 2000, prohibited "public entities from endorsing, educating, recognizing or promoting homosexuality as acceptable, moral behavior, and prohibits public entities from using the phrase 'sexual orientation.'" Proposition 22, written by Republican Senator William Peter Knight, defined marriage as being between a man and a woman. Although the second initiative may seem innocuous in its simple wording, opponents of the legislation have pointed out that the statement implies something deeper about the social acceptability and legitimacy of homosexual partnerships and denies gay and lesbian couples certain rights and privileges, including tax benefits given to married couples.

The controversial issue of gay marriage is particularly telling in the way it clarified political fault lines that had arisen within the existing Korean American power structure as well as the type of relations that 1.5/second generation leaders had fostered and sought to maintain with the traditional immigrant leadership. Interestingly, the movement against gay marriages was the first large-scale effort by Korean American church leaders to participate in American politics through coalitions with outside groups. Among other things, Korean American church leaders set up several meetings to rally support among religious leaders, published ads in local Korean newspapers, made regular announcements to their congregations, and helped to gather signatures for a petition in support of the Sexual Responsibility Act and Proposition 22. Members of the ethnic elite including representatives from the Korean-American Federation (KAF) and conservative leaders of 1.5/second generation organizations like KAC and the Korean American Republican Association (KARA) are said to have offered more tacit, individual support for the initiative, although they state that their names, along with their affiliated organizations, were included on the petition without their permission (Ma 2000).

In response, the Los Angeles-based KACR, an ad hoc coalition of LGBT organizations and various progressive groups throughout California, planned an organized response to these initiatives, beginning with a series of press conferences, community meetings, and protests that would lead up to a purchased ad in the two leading Korean-language newspapers. The ad framed the debate as one of ensuring "fair and equal treatment . . . for all members of society" and not granting "privileges" to homosexuals as supporters for the legislation would like to claim. Out of the twenty-seven organizations that signed the ad, at least eight organizations were Korean/Korean American.

Chapter 9

1. See Espiritu (1997) for a more detailed discussion on the dilemmas Asian American women face in trying to deal with both sexism within their own community as well as racial-gender marginalization in American society.

2. This is not to claim that Korean American women, particularly more gender-conscious 1.5/second generation leaders, have been completely stripped of their ability to articulate their political concerns to others within and outside the community. As a result of continuing exclusion from and discrimination in formal political spheres, women have carved out their own informal "politicized" spaces either within non-gender-focused institutions within the community (e.g., churches) or in the form of arts and culture, study groups, educational seminars, and the Internet that cross not only local and state but also national boundaries. I've attended a number of political language study groups and spoken word performances where women have vocalized their concerns on topics ranging from family to career to community.

One second generation leader informed me about Korea-based bulletin boards like lesbian websites that enable Korean Americans to link up with Koreans abroad on specific political issues.

> It's virtual but it's definitely an actual space in L.A. [where] they utilize resources from Korea to link up with other Korean lesbians. So actually the group of Korean lesbians I know who mostly work in Koreatown are more in touch with what's going on in Korea rather than white mainstream gay and lesbians scene here so like they wouldn't necessarily go to like a pride march but they would visit Korean language websites for lesbians, you know that sort of thing. And the websites I think are interesting too because some people really just meet and gather and organize specifically with this virtual space, but I think the more interesting phenomenon has to do when this overlaps with actual physical organizing so there's people who actually hook up with people they meet in chat rooms and that sort of thing.

The interviewee notes that Korean Americans can find like-minded "coethnics" through websites that transcend physical space. Of course, 1.5/second generation women are also active in physical spaces like the kitchens, classrooms, and bible study groups of local churches, but such virtual spaces can help Korean Americans from diverse backgrounds to overcome some of the difficulties of finding a fitting political forum within the confines of geographically defined communities. Indeed, such alternative spaces open up the range of political expression and activity among women in the community, yet it should be noted that they tend to be isolated niches that have been unable to challenge the patriarchal underpinnings of Koreatown politics.

3. Details of this part of the conversation omitted to protect privacy and confidentiality.

Works Cited

Abelmann, Nancy and John Lie. 1995. *Blue Dreams: Korean Americans and the Los Angeles Riots*. Cambridge, MA: Harvard University Press.

Agocs, Carol. 1981. "Ethnic Settlement in a Metropolitan Area: A Typology of Communities." *Ethnicity* 8: 127–48.

Alba, Richard and Victor Nee. 2003. *Remaking the American Mainstream: Assimilation and the New Immigration*. Cambridge, MA: Harvard University Press.

Alba, Richard D., John R. Logan, Brian Stults, Gilbert Marzan, and Wenquan Zhang. 1999. "Immigrant Groups and Suburbs: A Reexamination of Suburbanization and Spatial Assimilation." *American Sociological Review* 64: 446–60.

Bonacich, Edna. 1973. "A Theory of Middleman Minorities." *American Sociological Review* 38: 583–94.

Bonacich, Edna, Mokerrom Hossain, and Jae-hong Park. 1987. "Korean Immigrant Working Women in the Early 1980s." In *Korean Women in Transition: At Home and Abroad*, eds. Eui-Young Yu and Earl H. Phillips, 219–47. Los Angeles: Center for Korean-American and Korean Studies, California State University, Los Angeles.

Breton, Raymond. 1964. "Institutional Completeness of Ethnic Communities and the Personal Relations of Immigrants." *American Journal of Sociology* 70(2): 193–205.

Burgess, Ernest W. 1925. "The Growth of the City: An Introduction to a Research Project." In *The City*, ed. Park, Robert E., Ernest W. Burgess, and Roderick D. McKenzie, 47–62. Chicago, IL: University of Chicago Press.

Cha, Marn J. 1994. "Korean Americans Seeking Elective Office." In *Community in Crisis: The Korean American Community After the Los Angeles Civil Unrest of April 1992*, ed. George O. Totten and H. Eric Schockman, 275–80. Los Angeles: Center for Multiethnic and Transnational Studies, University of Southern California.

Chang, Edward T. 1988. "Korean Community Politics in Los Angeles: The Impact of the Kwangju Uprising." *Amerasia Journal* 14(1): 51–67.

———. 1991. "New Urban Crisis: Intra-Third World Conflict." In *Asian Americans: Comparative and Global Perspectives*, ed. Shirley Hune, Hyung-Chan Kim, Stephen S. Fujita, and Amy Ling, 169–78. Pullman: Washington State University Press.

———. 1992. "Building Minority Coalitions: A Case Study of Koreans and African Americans." *Korea Journal of Population and Development* 21: 37–56.

———. 1995. "The Impact of the Civil Unrest on Community-Based Organizational Coalitions." In *Multiethnic Coalition Building in Los Angeles*, ed. Eui-Young Yu and Edward T. Chang, 117–33. Los Angeles: Institute for Asian American and Pacific American Studies.

———. 1999. "The Post-Los Angeles Riot Korean American Community: Challenges and Prospects." *Korean and Korean American Studies Bulletin* 10(1–2): 6–26.

Chang, Edward T. and Jeannette Diaz-Veizades. 1999. *Ethnic Peace in the American City: Building Community in Los Angeles and Beyond*. New York: New York University Press.

Chaves, Mark, Laura Stephens, and Joseph Galaskiewicz. 2004. "Does Government Funding Suppress Nonprofits' Political Activity?" *American Sociological Review* 69(2): 292–316.

Cheng, Lucie and Yen Espiritu. 1989. "Korean Businesses in Black and Hispanic Neighborhoods: A Study on Intergroup Relations." *Sociological Perspectives* 32(4): 521–534.

Cho, Namju. 1992. "Check Out, Not In: Koreana Wilshire/Hyatt Take-Over and the Los Angeles Korean Community." *Amerasia* 18(1): 131–39.

Cho, Sumi K. 1993. "Korean Americans vs. African Americans: Conflict and Construction." In *Reading Rodney King, Reading Urban Uprising*, ed. Robert G. Williams, 196–211. New York: Routledge.

Choy, Bong-youn. 1979. *Koreans in America*. Chicago, IL: Nelson-Hall.

Chung, Angie Y. 2001. "The Powers That Bind: A Case Study of the Collective Bases of Coalition-Building in Post-Civil Unrest Los Angeles." *Urban Affairs Review* 37(2): 205–26.

Cota-Robles, Eugene. 2000. "Latino Students in the Academic Pipeline." Paper presented at UC Accord: Education and Equity: Research, Policy, and Practice, in San Jose, CA.

Espiritu, Yen L. 1992. *Asian American Panethnicity: Bridging Institutions and Identities*. Philadelphia, PA: Temple University Press.

———. 1997. *Asian American Women and Men: Labor, Laws and Love*. Thousand Oaks, CA: Sage Publications.

Fernandez-Kelly, M. Patricia. 1995. "Social and Cultural Capital in the Urban Ghetto: Implications for the Economic Sociology of Immigration." In *The Economic Sociology of Immigration: Essays on Networks, Ethnicity, and Entrepreneurship*, ed. Alejandro Portes, 213–47. New York: Russell Sage Foundation.

Freer, Regina. 1994. "Black-Korean Conflict." In *The Los Angeles Riots: Lessons for the Urban Future*, ed. Mark Baldassare, 175–203. Boulder, CO: Westview Press.

Glenn, Evelyn N. 2002. *Unequal Freedom: How Race and Gender Shaped American Citizenship and Labor*. Cambridge, MA: Harvard University Press.

Gordon, Milton. 1964. *Assimilation in American Life: The Role of Race, Religion, and National Origins*. New York: Oxford University Press.

Hahn, Harlan. 1996. "Los Angeles and the Future: Uprisings, Identity, and New Institutions." In *Rethinking Los Angeles*, ed. Michael J. Dear, H. Eric Schockman, and Greg Hise, 77–95. Thousand Oaks, CA: Sage Publications.

Herman, Max. 2004. "Ten Years After: A Critical Review of Scholarship on the 1992 Los Angeles Riot." *Race, Gender & Class* 11(1): 116.

Hondagneu-Sotelo, Pierrette. 1994. *Gendered Transitions: Mexican Experiences of Immigration*. Berkeley: University of California Press.

Horton, John. 1995. *The Politics of Diversity: Immigration, Resistance, and Change in Monterey Park, California*. Philadelphia, PA: Temple University Press.

Hum, Tarry. 2002. "Asian and Latino Immigration and the Revitalization of Sunset Park, Brooklyn." In *Contemporary Asian American Communities*, ed. Linda T. Vo and Rick Bonus, 27–44. Philadelphia, PA: Temple University Press.

Hurh, Won M. and Kwang C. Kim. 1984. *Korean Immigrants in America*. Cranbury, NJ: Associated University Presses, Inc.

Johnson, James H. Jr. and Melvin L. Oliver. 1994. "Interethnic Minority Conflict in Urban America: The Effects of Economic and Social Dislocations." In *Race and Ethnic Conflict: Contending Views on Prejudice, Discrimination and Ethnoviolence*, ed. Fred L. Pincus and Howard J. Ehrlich, 194–205. Boulder, CO: Westview Press.

Kim, Elaine H. 1993. "Home Is Where the *Han* Is: A Korean American Perspective on the Los Angeles Upheavals." In *Reading Rodney King, Reading Urban Uprising*, ed. Robert G. Williams, 215–35. New York: Routledge.

Kim, Ilsoo. 1981. *New Urban Immigrants: The Korean Community in New York*. Princeton, NJ: Princeton University Press.

Kim, Rebecca. 2004. "Made in the U.S.A.: Second-Generation Korean American Campus Evangelicals." In *Asian American Youth: Culture, Identity, and Ethnicity*, ed. Jennifer Lee and Min Zhou, 235–50. New York: Routledge.

KIWA. 2000. *"Workers Empowered": A Survey on Working Conditions in the Koreatown Restaurant Industry*. Los Angeles: Korean Immigrant Workers Advocates.

Korean American Coalition. 2003. *Sample Survey of Korean Churches in Southern California, 2003*. Los Angeles: Center for Korean-American and Korean Studies, California State University, Los Angeles.

Korean American Coalition and Center for Korean American and Korean Studies, CSU-LA. 2003. "Census Tables: Korean Population in the U.S." http://www.calstatela.edu/centers/ckaks/census_tables.html (accessed May 30, 2004).

Kwong, Peter. 1993. "The Los Angeles Riots: Lessons for the Urban Future." In *Inside the Los Angeles Riots: What Really Happened and Why It Will Happen Again*, ed. Don Hazen, 88–93. New York: Institute for Alternative Journalism.

Lee, Dong O. 1995. "Koreatown and Korean Small Firms in Los Angeles: Locating in the Ethnic Neighborhoods." *Professional Geographer* 47(2): 184–95.

Lee, Kyung. 1969. "Settlement Patterns of Los Angeles Koreans." Master's thesis, Department of Geography, UCLA, Los Angeles, CA.

Lewis, Helen G. 1974. *The Korean Community in Los Angeles County*. San Francisco: R and E Research Associates.

Li, Wei. 1998. "Anatomy of a New Ethnic Settlement: The Chinese Ethnoburb in Los Angeles." *Urban Studies* 35(3): 479–501.

Li, Wei, Gary Dymski, Carolyn Aldana, Maria Chee, Hyeon Hyo Ahn, Jang-Pyo Hong, and Yu Zhou. In press. "How Minority-Owned Banks Matter: Banking and Community/Economic Development." In *Landscapes of the Ethnic Economy*, ed. David Kaplan and Wei Li. Lanham, MD: Rowman and Littlefield.

Lien, Pei-Te. 2001. *The Making of Asian America Through Political Participation*. Philadelphia, PA: Temple University Press.

Light, Ivan and Edna Bonacich. 1988. *Immigrant Entrepreneurs: Koreans in Los Angeles, 1965-1982*. Berkeley: University of California Press.

Light, Ivan, Hadas Har-Chvi, and Kenneth Kan. 1994. "Black/Korean Conflict in Los Angeles." In *Managing Divided Cities*, ed. Seamus Dunn, 72–87. London: Keele University Press.

Lin, Jan. 1998. *Reconstructing Chinatown: Ethnic Enclave, Global Change*. Minneapolis: University of Minnesota Press.

Ling, Huping. 2004. *Chinese St. Louis: From Enclave to Cultural Community*. Philadelphia, PA: Temple University Press.

Massey, Douglas. 1985. "Ethnic Residential Segregation: A Theoretical Synthesis and Empirical Review." *Sociology and Social Research* 69: 315–50.

Massey, Douglas, Rafael Alarcon, Jorge Durand, and Humberto Gonzalez. 1987. *Return to Aztlan: The Social Process of Migration From Western Mexico*. Berkeley: University of California Press.

Min, Pyong G. 1989-1990. "Korean Immigrants in Los Angeles." Paper presented at the Conference on California's Immigrants in World Perspectives, in Los Angeles, CA.

———. 1990. "Problems of Korean Immigrant Entrepreneurs." *International Migration Review* 24(3): 436–55.

———. 1996. *Caught in the Middle: Korean Communities in New York and Los Angeles*. Berkeley: University of California Press.

———. 2000. "The Structure and Social Functions of Korean Immigrant Churches in the United States." In *Contemporary Asian America: A Multidisciplinary Reader*, ed. Min Zhou and James V. Gatewood, 372–91. New York: New York University Press.

_____. 2005. "Intergenerational Transmission of Religion and Ethnicity: Indian Hindus and Korean Protestants." Paper presented at the CUNY Asian American/Asian Research Institute Lecture Series, in New York, NY.

Morris, Aldon D. 1984. *The Origins of the Civil Rights Movement: Black Communities Organizing for Change*. New York: The Free Press.

Morrison, Peter A. and Ira S. Lowry. 1994. "A Riot of Color: The Demographic Setting." In *The Los Angeles Riots: Lessons for the Urban Future*, ed. Mark Baldassare, 1–46. Boulder, CO: Westview Press.

Navarro, Armando. 1993. "The South Central Los Angeles Eruption: A Latino Perspective." *Amerasia Journal* 19(2): 69–85.

Oliver, Melvin L. and David M. Grant. 1995. "Making Space for Multiethnic Coalitions: The Prospects for Coalition Politics in Los Angeles." In *Multiethnic Coalition Building in Los Angeles: A Two-Day Symposium*, Eui-Young Yu and Edward T. Chang, 1–34. Los Angeles: Regina Books.

Omatsu, Glenn. 1995. "Labor Organizing in Los Angeles: Confronting the Boundaries of Race and Ethnicity." In *Multiethnic Coalition Building in Los Angeles*, ed. Eui-Young Yu and Edward T. Chang, 81–116. Los Angeles: Institute for Asian American and Pacific American Studies.

Ong, Paul and Suzanne Hee. 1993. *Losses in the Los Angeles Civil Unrest*. Los Angeles: UCLA Center for Pacific Rim Studies.

_____. 1994. "Economic Diversity: An Overview." In *The State of Asian Pacific America: Economic Diversity, Issues and Policies*, ed. Paul Ong, 113–37. Los Angeles: Asian Pacific American Public Policy Institute, LEAP. Ong, Paul, Doug Miller and Doug Houston. 2002. "Economic Needs of Asian Americans and Pacific Islanders in Distressed Areas: Establishing Baseline Information." http://lewis.sppsr.ucla.edu/research/publications/projreports.cfm (accessed May 30, 2004).

Park, Edward J. W. 1998. "Competing Visions: Political Formation of Korean Americans in Los Angeles, 1992–1997." *Amerasia Journal* 24(1): 41–57.

_____. 1999. "Friends or Enemies?: Generational Politics in the Korean American Community in Los Angeles." *Qualitative Sociology* 22(2): 161–75.

_____. 2001. "The Impact of Mainstream Political Mobilization on Asian American Communities: The Case of Korean Americans in Los Angeles, 1992–1998." In *Asian American Politics: Perspectives, Experiences, Prospects*, ed. Gordon Chang, 285–307. Stanford, CA: Stanford University Press.

Park, Kyeyoung. 1997. *The Korean American Dream: Immigrants and Small Business in New York City*. Ithaca, NY: Cornell University Press.

Park, Robert E. 1950. *Race and Culture*. Glencoe, IL: The Free Press.

Pfeifer, Mark E. 1999. "'Community,' Adaptation and the Vietnamese in Toronto." Ph.D. dissertation, Department of Geography, University of Toronto, Canada.

Portes, Alejandro and Ruben G. Rumbaut. 1996. *Immigrant America: A Portrait*. Berkeley: University of California Press.

Portes, Alejandro and Alex Stepick. 1993. *City on the Edge: The Transformation of Miami*. Berkeley: University of California Press.

Reid, Elizabeth J. 1999. "Nonprofit Advocacy and Political Participation." In *Nonprofits and Government: Collaboration and Conflict*, ed. Elizabeth T. Boris and C. Eugene Steuerle, 291–325. Washington, DC: The Urban Institute Press.

Robnett, Belinda. 1997. *How Long? How Long?: African American Women in the Struggle for Civil Rights*. New York: Oxford University Press.

Rodriguez-Fraticelli, Carlos, Carlos Sanabria, and Amilcar Tirado. 1991. "Puerto Rican Nonprofit Organizations in New York City." In *Hispanics and the Nonprofit Sector*, ed. Herman E. Gallegos and Michael O'Neill, 33–48. New York: Foundation Center.

Saito, Leland. 1998. *Race and Politics: Asian Americans, Latinos, and Whites in a Los Angeles Suburb*. Urbana: University of Illinois Press.

Saito, Leland T. and Edward J. W. Park. 2000. "Multiracial Collaborations and Coalitions." In *Transforming Race Relations: A Public Policy Report*, ed. Paul Ong, 435–74. Los Angeles: LEAP Asian Pacific American Public Policy Institute and UCLA Asian American Studies Center.

Sassen, Saskia. 1988. *The Mobility of Labor and Capital: A Study in International Investment and Labor Flow*. New York: Cambridge University Press.

Shin, Gi-Wook and Kyung M. Hwang, eds. 2003. *Contentious Kwangju: The May 18 Uprising in Korea's Past and Present*. Lanham, MD: Rowman & Littlefield Publishers.

Smith, Michael P. 2001. *Transnational Globalism: Locating Globalization*. Oxford: Blackwell Publishers.

Suttles, Gerald D. 1972. *The Social Construction of Communities*. Chicago, IL: University of Chicago Press.

Tierney, Kathleen J. 1994. "Property Damage and Violence: A Collective Behavior Analysis." In *The Los Angeles Riots: Lessons for the Urban Future*, Mark Baldassare, 149–73. Boulder, CO: Westview Press.

Valdez, Zulema. Forthcoming. *Economic Strategy of Survival or Mobility? Ethnic Entrepreneurship in the United States*. Monograph in progress.

Vo, Linda. 2004. *Mobilizing an Asian American Community*. Philadelphia, PA: Temple University Press.

Vo, Linda T. and Rick Bonus. 2002. *Contemporary Asian American Communities: Intersections and Divergences*. Philadelphia, PA: Temple University Press.

Vo, Linda and Mary Y. Danico. 2005. "Transforming the American Suburb: The Renaissance of Little Saigon and Koreatown." Paper presented at the Annual Association for Asian American Studies, in Los Angeles, CA.

Waldinger, Roger and Mehdi Bozorgmehr, ed. 1996. *Ethnic Los Angeles*. New York: Russell Sage Foundation.

Ward, David. 1989. *Poverty, Ethnicity, and the American City, 1840–1925: Changing Conceptions of the Slum and Ghetto*. Cambridge, MA: Cambridge University Press.

Gang Awareness Program (GAP)Korean American Leadership Program (KAYLP)

Multiethnic Youth Leadership Collaborative (MYLC)

Student Activist Training (SAT)Youth Drug Abuse and Prevention Program (YDAPP)

Asian Immigrant Workers Advocates (AIWA)

Asian Pacific American Dispute Resolution Center

Asian Pacific American Legal Center (APALC)

Asian Pacific Americans for a New Los Angeles (APANLA)

Asian and Pacific Islanders for Community Empowerment

Asian Pacific Planning Council (APPCON)

Asian Pacific Student Outreach

Brotherhood Crusade

Bus Riders Union

California Black Commission on Alcoholism

Central American Resource Center (CARECEN)

Coalition for Human Immigrant Rights L.A. (CHIRLA)

Coalition L.A.

Coalition of Asian Pacific Americans for Fair Redistricting (CAPAFR)

Community Coalition for Substance Abuse Prevention and Treatment

El Centro Del Pueblo

El Rescate

Enlace

Garment Workers Center

Hotel Employees and Restaurant Employees Local 11 (HERE Local 11)

Korean Confederation of Trade Unions (KCTU)

Liberty Hill FoundationLittle Tokyo Service Center

Los Angeles County Human Relations Commission (LACHRC)

Martin Luther King Jr. Dispute Resolution Center

Mexican American Legal Defense and Educational Fund (MALDEF)

Multicultural Collaborative (MCC)

National Asian-Pacific American Women's Forum

National Association for the Advancement of Colored People (NAACP)

National Coalition for Redress/ Reparations

Organization of Mutual Neighborhood Interest (OMNI)

Pilipino Workers Center (PWC)

Rebuild Los Angeles (RLA)

Search to Involve Pilipino Americans (SIPA)

Southern Christian Leadership Conference (SCLC)

Sweatshop Watch

Thai Community Development Center (Thai CDC)

United Way

Urban League

Youth Empowerment Project

Wilson, Kenneth L. and W. A. Martin. 1982. "Ethnic Enclaves: A Comparison of the Cuban and Black Economies in Miami." *American Journal of Sociology* 88(1): 135–60.

Wilson, Kenneth L. and Alejandro Portes. 1980. "Immigrant Enclaves: An Analysis of the Labor Market Experiences of Cubans in Miami." *American Journal of Sociology* 86(2): 295–315.

Yea, Sallie. 2005. "Maps of Resistance and Geographies of Dissent in Cholla Region." Paper presented at the Korean Society and Culture, Auckland, New Zealand.

Yoon, In J. 1997. *On My Own: Korean Businesses and Race Relations in America*. Chicago, IL: University of Chicago Press.

Yu, Eui-Young. 1987. *Juvenile Delinquency in the Korean Community of Los Angeles*. Los Angeles: The Korea Times.

Yu, Eui-Young, Earl H. Phillips, and Eun S. Yang, eds. 1982. *Koreans in Los Angeles: Prospects and Promises*. Los Angeles: Center for Korean-American and Korean Studies.

Zelinsky, Wilbur. 2001. *The Enigma of Ethnicity: Another American Dilemma*. Iowa City: University of Iowa Press.

Zelinsky, Wilbur and Barrett A. Lee. 1998. "Heterolocalism: An Alternative Model of the Sociospatial Behaviour of Immigrant Ethnic Communities." *International Journal of Population Geography* 4(4): 281–98.

Zhou, Min. 1992. *Chinatown: The Socioeconomic Potential of an Urban Enclave*. Philadelphia, PA: Temple University Press.

Zhou, Min and Rebecca Kim. 2001. "Formation, Consolidation, and Diversification of the Ethnic Elite: The Case of the Chinese Immigrant Community in the United States." *Journal of International Migration and Integration* 2(2): 227–47.

Zhou, Min and Xijuan Li. 2003. "Ethnic Language Schools and the Development of Supplementary Education in the Immigrant Chinese Community in United States." In *New Directions for Youth Development: Understanding the Social Worlds of Immigrant Youth*, ed. Carola Suarez-Orozco and Irina L. G. Todorova, 57–73. Hoboken, NJ: Jossey-Bass .

Newspaper and Magazine Articles

Ahn, Sangho. 1992a. "Problems of the Korean American Community: Irresponsible Operation of Organizations." *Korea Times,* April 8.

———. 1992b. "Problems of the Korean American Community: Mismanagement of Donations." *Korea Times,* April 9.

Carvajal, Doreen. 1994. "Koreatown Seeing Quiet, Steady Exodus." *Los Angeles Times,* January 9.

Chua, Linus. 1994. "Opening Up for Business Koreatown Looks to Other Ethnicities for Post- Riot Patrons." *Los Angeles Times,* April 25.

Dunn, Ashley. 1992. "Looters, Merchants Put Koreatown Under the Gun." *Los Angeles Times,* May 2.

Hall, Carla. 1997. "A Dialogue, Five Years Later." *Los Angeles Times,* April 28.

Kang, K. Connie. 1992. "Understanding the Riots—Six Months Later." *Los Angeles Times,* November 16.

_____. 1994. "A Cause for Korean American Celebration—and Controversy." *Los Angeles Times,* May 13.

_____. 1994. "Store Owners to Fight Restrictions on Reopening." *Los Angeles Times,* July 21.

———. 1996. "Riots' Effects Are Still Smoldering in Koreatown." *Los Angeles Times,* April 29.

_____. 1998. "41 Restaurants Violated Labor Laws." *Los Angeles Times,* August 22.

Katz, Jesse and Frank Clifford. 1992. "Many Find Verdict Fair, but There Is Still Outrage." *Los Angeles Times,* October 12.

Korea Central Daily. 1992. "Korean American Seniors Association Donated $2190 to Judge Joyce Karlin," April 16.

Korea Times. 1997a. "Korean Restaurant Owners Association Should Set an Example in Resolving Labor Disputes," September 19.

_____. 1997b. "Consulting With the Labor Administration On Protecting Workers," October 24.

Lee, Kapson Yim. 1994. "Koreans Want an Equal Treatment From the Mainstream Media." *Korea Times,* May 4.

———. 1997a. "Sa-Ee-Gu (April 29) Was a Riot, Not 'Civil Unrest.'" *Korea Times,* March 26-April 29.

_____. 1997b. "Postmortem." *Korea Times,* June 24.

Lee, Seung Gwan. 1996. "KIWA and KROA in a Lawsuit." *Korea Times,* August 29.

Lope, Robert J., Lucille Renwick, and Diane Seo. 1993. "Charting a New Course." *Los Angeles Times,* May 28.

Los Angeles Sentinel. 1992. "Slanted Media Coverage of Uprising Is Disgraceful," June 25.

_____. 1993. "King Case Just One Example," April 8.

Ma, Jason. 2000. "Straight From the Church: How Korean American churches in California rallied against gay rights." *Asianweek,* January 20.

Marquez, Jeremiah. 2004. "Los Angeles: N. Korean Diplomats' Visit Exposes Rift." *Min-Jok Tong-Shin,* http://www.minjok.com/english/index.php3?code=23865 (accessed December 10, 2006).

Min, Byong-Won. 1994. "Time to Reconsider Korean American General Political Activities." *Korea Central Daily,* September 3.

Mitchell, Marsha. 1992. "Activists Win Small Victory, But Karlin Fight Not Over." *Los Angeles Sentinel,* February 5.

Park, Bong-Hyun. 1993. "Korean Ethnic Organizations Are Undergoing a Generational Transition." *Korea Central Daily,* August 21.

Smith, Matthew. 1997. "Why Rebuild L.A. Didn't Work." *L.A. Weekly,* April 25–May 1.

zations like KIWA and KYCC, we saw how the inclusion of Latino clientele and staff members allowed them to legitimize the work they are doing in the community to funders, politicians, and other mainstream constituencies. Interethnic partnerships may become an even more invaluable tool for Asian American organizations as their community becomes increasingly dispersed into suburbs and their numbers remain small in proportion to the rest of the American population. Despite making tremendous strides in education and income, Asian Americans have not yet achieved parity with other native-born Whites, especially in the arena of social relations, media, culture, and politics. Particularly in a mainstream society that continues to classify heterogeneous ethnic groups under one racial label, Korean Americans may become increasingly aware of the uses of "pan-Asianism" as a political rallying point and as a means to draw funding as they gain greater experience within the political processes of mainstream America.

Ironically, cultivating strong bases of ethnic political solidarity can also open the doors to more powerful alliances that transcend the boundaries of race and ethnicity. As coalitional studies have shown (Chung 2001; Espiritu 1992; Saito 1998), racial groups that engage in coalitional work must have a means to enforce equal representation and access within the organization. Part of this balance is achieved through the cultivation of *collective organizational bases*, or a group's ability to organize itself and coherently express its needs on a collective level through organizational solidarity, effective leadership, and preestablished support networks (Morris 1984). Organizing as an ethnic constituency, mobilizing ethnic-based resources, and establishing an ethnic presence enables groups to better articulate their interests to coalitional partners, promote their ethnic-specific needs, and develop the resources they need to appeal to other racial and ethnic participants. Studies on interethnic alliances show how the interests of participating groups that have little to bring to the table get drowned out amid competing interests and political agendas (Espiritu 1992). For this reason, bridge-building leaders and organizations like KIWA and KYCC continue to mediate the diversity and shifting context of the ethnic enclave and create new lines of communication with other racial and ethnic communities. Progressive Korean American organizations like KIWA, for instance, have been active participants in movements to protest legislation targeting undocumented Latino immigrants, including the "A Day Without Immigrants" marches in May 2006 that nearly shut down local economies nationwide.

causes in a power structure that is controlled by large-scale, bureaucratic entities—namely, big government and multinational corporations. As Suttles
(1972) notes, the growth of these institutional bodies has heightened the need
for "bigger" alliances and more so, with the growing scale of political issues
themselves in the current global era. As an example of this, we've seen how
KIWA's circle of allies include not only labor unions, pan-ethnic alliances,
and Latino organizations in Los Angeles, but also international groups like
Enlace and transnational organizations such as the Korean Confederation of
Trade Unions (KCTU) that are better able to tackle the issue of labor exploitation within the context of the global economy.

Of course, this has not rendered the work of more traditional, localized CBOs
obsolete. Both KIWA and KYCC are living testaments to the importance of
addressing territorially based concerns through the medium of neighborhood-
based organizations. At the same time, the two case studies also reveal how
pan-ethnic organizations play an important role in jump-starting marginal
organizations within the ethnic community by giving support to newly emerging organizations excluded from the immigrant networks of the ethnic community (KYCC) and creating a progressive model for activism among marginalized organizations in conservative, immigrant-dominated communities
(KIWA). Once established, Korean American organizations like KIWA and
KYCC have continued to recognize the political potential of forging coalitions
with other Asian American organizations, even as they maintain their roots
within their own ethnic communities. Large-scale organizations can speak to
a wider range of issues that affect the broader racial community through their
diverse membership and high-status leadership (Suttles 1972). Depending on
the flow of immigration in coming years, pan-ethnic organizations will have
a greater impact on issues of national interest, both because they offer the
advantages of size as well as visibility to a political structure that categorizes
groups into socially constructed categories of race. On a more grassroots level,
the racialized nature of day-to-day experiences will serve to reaffirm symbolic
affinities among socially conscious Asian Americans, allowing the membership of organizations like these to expand.

Furthermore, strengthening political linkages within and across ethnic
boundaries becomes increasingly crucial for Asian American communities
whose socioeconomic achievements have scattered them across geographical boundaries, but whose sociopolitical interests have yet to be adequately
represented in mainstream society. In the case of enclave-centered organi-

Redefining "Community" for Asian Americans

In traditional assimilationist literature, immigrants are said to be socially bounded by similar life chances stemming from their common status as poor ethnic immigrants within a spatially isolated neighborhood. While the primacy of such ties may best describe the experiences of low-skilled European immigrants at the turn of the century, they are by themselves insufficient frameworks within which to understand the diverse experiences of post-1965 immigrants. What is astounding has been the rapid pace of mobility that has occurred within post-1965 immigrant communities even within the span of one generation. Unlike their European predecessors, select immigrant groups that enter the United States with premigration educational training, job skills, and financial capital are able to forego initial seclusion within low-income enclaves and move straight to White-dominated or even ethnic suburbs. Similar patterns can be observed within the Korean American population of Los Angeles, yet such trends have taken place even as the enclave economy continues to grow in size and influence. The sociospatial profile of Koreatown reflects some of the unique trends that have occurred among ethnic enclave communities in recent decades.

For this reason, ethnic solidarity may no longer be based on residential propinquity or day-to-day interactions among coethnics within a spatially isolated enclave setting. Unlike White immigrants before them, ethnic-based ties may still remain strong, even for the upwardly mobile. Assuming of course that globalization processes, immigration flow, and residential mobility stay at their current pace, ethnic political solidarity in select populations will stay rooted in the social networks and institutional structures of the broader ethnic community. Among other things, the case of Koreatown, Los Angeles, suggests that some ethnic enclaves may even be moving beyond their roles as temporary sanctuaries for incoming immigrants under conditions that did not exist for the first waves of White European immigration. In the early stages of development, the immigrant enclave provides a physical context for cultivating territorially based "communities of interest," where neighbors are bound by their shared daily routines, eth-class interests, and local issues. However, communities that have access to diverse resources both within and beyond the local ethnic neighborhood may evolve to include activities that transcend the traditional entrepreneurial, cultural, and mutual aid focus of their immigrant predecessors.

assumed that new generations of political leadership would find little value in the legacy created by their immigrant predecessors. The reliance of 1.5/second generation organizations on outside allies and the consequent segmentation of ethnic power structures might have been interpreted as a sign of the dissolution of ethnic politics. Perhaps some can argue that this was true to some degree when American society had little tolerance for racial diversity, lines of stratification were much less complicated, and globalization had yet to make the fate of nations intertwined with one another. However, the conditions that engender ethnic political solidarity have changed significantly for ethnic communities in the post–civil rights era.

The case of Koreatown politics demonstrates how ethnic organizational structures can create new ways of adapting to the internal fragmentation of post-1965 immigrant communities when there are both compelling reasons and substantial resources to mobilize on shared ethnic-based interests. The purpose of this book was to address how 1.5/second generation organizations construct a sense of ethnic political solidarity despite the residential dispersal, class polarization, and intergenerational division of the Korean American community. This study shows that the status of Koreatown as the institutional powerhouse of a spatially dispersed community provided ethnic organizations with the general resource base and infrastructure within which to pursue their political goals. In this sense, the rise of vibrant ethnic enclave economies in an era of globalization has created new incentives for political actors to engage with one another despite increasing dissonance over the terms of this partnership.

Because immigrant elite control enclave resources, the next generation of leadership has not simply detached from the immigrant leadership but has rather worked to negotiate their political agenda within traditional ethnic hierarchies. In the end, I find that 1.5/second generation ethnic organizations have not so much disengaged from ethnic politics because of these internal differences as some might argue, but rather, they have reoriented their organizations around more diverse and specialized frameworks of ethnic political solidarity based on unequal relationships with the ethnic elite, thus assuming a "bridging role" within the politically fragmented community. The diversification and specialization of ethnic organizations allows organizational leadership to better connect with an increasingly heterogeneous ethnic population and thus to enhance a sense of community and political unity across multiple lines of stratification.

rean men, who are themselves marginalized within the hierarchies of White American society. As a result, any type of reform that is to be made would have to also come from within.

Again, how women and the organizations they work for respond to sexism depends largely on the way the organization is shaped by its relations with outside constituencies. In particular, there are two features that determine how much room there is for gendered political expression within 1.5/second generation organizations: namely, the political culture of the organization that emerges from the fusion of ethnic and mainstream cultural influences and the extent to which the organizational structure is equipped to deal with internal grievances and inequalities.

In general, KYCC is based on a formalized bureaucratic organizational structure that on the surface promotes a "gender-neutralized" approach to interpersonal relations within the workplace setting. What this means is that the organization does what it can to ensure that gender inequities do not manifest themselves in any clearly visible or formal way. In theory, gender or race-based differences should not matter in an organization where decisions on hiring and promotion are based solely on merit, as the upper management has reminded me several times. Of course, what this does not control for are more subtle and informal inequalities that surface in everyday interactions among the leadership and staff. Furthermore, gender issues are implicitly considered to be private, personal matters left to the discretion of the individual, unless of course they interfere with the proper functioning of the organization overall.

In terms of its outward appearances, KYCC comes across more as a second generation style ethnic organization with a formal, corporate structure more reminiscent of American social service agencies or businesses than Korean ones. The staff has a stronger representation of second generation members than first generation or even 1.5 generation ones. As a result, meetings are primarily conducted in English, and the few times I have seen members converse in Korean are when they are in a social setting with one of the few first generation staff in the organization. However, even those members have a sufficient grasp of English comprehension and occasionally speak in broken English. Of course, this is not to say that the organization is not "ethnic" in any sense, but rather that the organization is bureaucratically structured to prevent offensive behavior.

The rigid hierarchical arrangement of the organization provides a system of checks and balances against those who may make blatantly prejudicial comments or act in inappropriate ways. Decisions are made along this hierarchy of respect and dignity. It is an expression of power, not of affection. Keeping incidents of sexual harassment within organizations hidden is unprincipled and objectionable. Whether or not organizations themselves take a stance against the incidents, by saying nothing openly, they allow for the actions to occur again. For the rest of us who hear about incidents but do nothing and say nothing, we also perpetuate the tolerance of sexism. We allow for sexist behavior and sexist attitudes to be continued. We cannot fight sexism if we cannot openly acknowledge its existence amongst ourselves. We should use our knowledge of incidents in the movement as a force for generating more discussions and solutions, not secrecy and denial. Sexual harassment is not something that should be whispered about after meetings. These incidents should be dealt with in an open and timely manner. . . . The movement for social change is not about winning a one-time, short-term victory against one person or organization. It is about building a community based on human rights and dignity. We cannot continue to ignore the interconnectedness of the oppressions we are fighting against.

The letter clearly shows how important Asian American alliances can be in not only confronting the individuals who commit sexist offenses, but also in breaking the coethnic bonds of silence that help to perpetuate such heinous attitudes and behaviors.

However, it is still unclear to what extent outside intervention alone will help to penetrate the powerful political structure that has institutionalized gender inequality within the Korean American community. The problem in part stems from the relatively isolated and hegemonic nature of Koreatown politics, which generally hinders women's ability to solicit intervention on matters arising from within the community. Ethnic political structures are much more secluded and elite groups much more protective of the status quo when they are built on a self-sufficient, thriving enclave economy. Although blatant cases of sexism do arise, gender-based hierarchies are enforced by more informal, indirect, and subtle means of exclusion that make them that much harder to defeat. Unlike larger subgroups that can employ outside pressure to achieve some of their goals, Korean American women have relatively weaker access to powerful institutions in American society to which ethnic organizations may feel accountable. Even if mainstream support was more easily forthcoming, the politics of inequality are trickier to navigate in light of racial/ethnic dynamics that would arise from pitting outsiders against Ko-

Partly because of this, I did not note these types of gendered responsibilities at KYCC. The most obvious reason is that KYCC is not in the same type of situation where they may experience discomfort or a conflict of interests when eating at local Korean-owned restaurants. Conversely, in trying to avoid the class hierarchies associated with "eating out," KIWA members have had to rely on the gendered contributions of women within their organization. In addition, the general corporate office setting of KYCC is structured so that members are also more likely to buy from local fast-food joints or bring their own packed lunches from home (although possibly prepared by wives in the case of male staff members). I have seen large congregations of people eat together during lunch breaks, but the organization is of the size that staff and interns are not likely to eat at the same time. The only "get-togethers" would take place in the middle of staff meetings when someone brought in a birthday cake for one of the members or *after* work when people decided to hang out at the local bars or restaurants. Because of the bureaucratic structure of KYCC, intimate Korean-style gatherings seen at KIWA would not fit well with this business-like context.

Gender and the Politics of Expression

Although bridging organizations have opened the doors to opportunities unavailable to women elsewhere, this incorporation has taken place within the hegemonic framework of gender roles and organizational hierarchies that force women to seek alternative strategies and venues for social justice. On occasion, Korean American women have reached out to outside groups either for support or assistance on gender issues from within. More politically active Korean American women have been involved in organizations outside the Los Angeles community, such as the Asian Immigrant Workers Advocates (AIWA) in Oakland and the National Asian-Pacific American Women's Forum. Indeed, Asian American networks and organizations are one powerful venue through which to express grievances or rally support against sexism within the Korean community. Women seem to feel that other non–Korean Asian Americans can relate best to the competing loyalties they face in trying to fight sexism and gender inequality within their own ethnic community as well as racial and gender marginality in mainstream American society.

For example, one of the few female executive directors in Koreatown's earlier history described to me how she relied on support networks from non–Korean Asian Americans to get advice and release tensions arising from everyday sexism, gender hierarchies, and pressures within the workplace. She states:

> Within the Asian community, we had a woman management type of support group and we supported each other in that sense. We talked about the problems that we're having and we used to discuss certain situations, conflicts and how we can resolve it. For example, you're supposed to supervise male staff person and they make certain remarks about what you look like, some kind of comment, and how we can deal with it in a very wise manner, instead of challenging and confronting him, you know. And it was social as well as professional.

The passage highlights the significance of non–Korean Asian American support networks in helping women deal with the difficulties of being a female leader in a newly emerging, conservative Korean immigrant community. In this particular case, the interviewee did not seek to be confrontational but rather sought strategic ways to deal with such offensive behaviors.

Women also recognize the potential for Asian American organizations to act as a powerful counterforce against the sexist undercurrents of individuals and organizations within the Korean American community. It is this very same recognition that prompted individual second generation Korean American women to groups outside Koreatown during one incident when a male community activist working for a leftist organization was charged with sexually harassing an intern. After several failed attempts to address the grievances through the organization itself, individuals solicited support from Asian American organizations including several women's groups from Los Angeles, San Francisco, and other major cities across the nation. Asians and Pacific Islanders for Community Empowerment and a coalition of progressive Asian American organizations including WORK banded together and posted an open letter deploring the way sexism continues to permeate both progressive and conservative community organizations within the Asian American community (http://home.earthlink.net/~blacklava/ action/main.htm). In it they proclaim:

> It is a contradiction for us to ignore the existence of sexism in the movement, while we continue to work on "women's issues" in our organizations (e.g., Workers' rights are women's rights! Immigrant rights are women's rights!). . . . Sexual harassment is a violent act that denies women their freedom,

Song, Jeongho and Kim Seongju. 2000. "Construction of a High School in Destruction of the Hotel Ambassador." *Korea Central Daily*, November 2.

Tran, Tini. 1999. "Korean Community Spreading Out." *Los Angeles Times*, July 19.

Treviño, Joseph. 1998. "Trabajadores Protestan Contra Un Restaurante." *La Opinion*, July 25.

List of Organizations and Programs

1.5/second generation organizations and coalitions

California Korean Student Association for Democracy (CKSAD)

Korean American Bar Association (KABA)

Korean Americans for Civil Rights (KACR)

Korean American Coalition (KAC)

Korean American Democratic Committee (KADC)

Korean American Family Service Center (KAFSC)

Korean American Inter-Agency Council (KAIAC)

Korean American Museum (KAM)

Korean American Republican Association (KARA)

Korean American United Students for Educational Services (KAUSES)

Korean Cultural Center (KCC)

Korean Exposure and Education Program (KEEP)

Korean Health, Education, Information and Research Center (KHEIR)

Korean Immigrant Workers Advocates (KIWA) (more recently renamed the Koreatown
Immigrant Workers Alliance)

Korean Labor Association (KLA)

Korean Resource Center (KRC)

Korean Student Association (KSA)

Korean Youth and Community Center (KYCC) (formerly known as the Korean Youth
Center (KYC) and more recently renamed the Koreatown Youth and Community
Center (KYCC))

Korean Youth and Student Union (KYSU)

Koreatown Community Center

Koreatown Organizations Association (KOA)

Mindullae for Korean Community Empowerment

National Korean American Service and Education Consortium (NAKASEC)
Womens Organization Reaching Koreans (WORK)
Young Koreans United (YKU)

Advisory Council on Democratic and Peaceful Unification (or pyong-tong)

Council of Korean Churches
Council on Korean Community Affairs (CKCA)
Immigrant Workers Union
Korea National Association
Korean American Federation (KAF)/ Korean Association of Southern California (KASC)
Korean American Dry Cleaners Association (KADC)
Korean American Garment Industry Association (KAGIA)
Korean American Grocers Association (KAGRO)
Korean American Veterans Association
Korean American Women United (KAWU)
Korean Business and Professional Women's Association
Korean Chamber of Commerce
Korean Garment Wholesalers Association
Korean Restaurant Owners Association (KROA)
Korean Senior Citizens Association
Korean Town Development Association
Koreatown Association
Koreatown and West Adams Public Safety Association (KOWAPSA)
Los Angeles Korean Chamber of Commerce
One Korea LA Forum
Restaurant Workers Association of Koreatown (RWAK)
Southern California Korean American Coalition of Business Association

Black-Korean Alliance (BKA) (formerly known as the African American-Korean Community Relations Committee)

Chingusai of Los Angeles
Korean American Race Relations Emergency (KARE)
Korean Coalition for Lesbian, Bisexual, Gay, and Transgender Rights
Korean Riot Victims' Association (KRVA)

Association of Community Organizations for Reform Now (ACORN)

African American Korean American Christian Alliance (AAKACA)
Asian American Drug Abuse Program (AADAP)

ers as fitting well with their broader vision of integration, upward mobility, and multiculturalism. The organization helps both Korean and Latino immigrants and their children to overcome the barriers of language, cultural insularity, and prejudice that prevent them from achieving the ideal goal of eth-class mobility. One thirty-eight-year-old, U.S.-born Latino interviewee for example hopes to start his own business in the future with the knowledge and skills he has gained as a manager at KYCC.

> I was a teamsters' union truck driver; I was a supervisor before in the past for other companies; I know how to do sprinkler system; I'm a plumber. I mean it's not like I don't know how to do manual work. I know a lot of trades of work. But I like this one, and I learn about managing. One day I want to be my own boss, I want to have my own business. And I think that's why I'm still here. I learn how to manage people, how to take care of people, how to pay people, how to pay my taxes, how to do a lot of things, how to operate a business. And I think what I like about it, because I'm learning how one day I want to be my own boss. I think they're giving me the opportunity to give me that respect and you know to make my own decisions and to lead this operation.

Working with Latinos in turn gives Korean Americans the opportunity to learn how to interact with other groups. As one board member proclaims, "Korean Americans need to be able to learn to interface with those various groups, because that in fact is why by and large the immigrants have chosen to live in this milieu so they might as well have organizations that help to facilitate that integration."

With this in mind, KYCC has pursued interethnic programs and projects that cultivate leadership and self-empowerment skills within a multicultural framework of integration and eth-class mobility. KYCC has collaborated with established social service agencies and race/ethnic organizations such as the Asian American Drug Abuse Program (AADAP), the Little Tokyo Service Center, the Urban League, the United Way, the Central American Resource Center (CARECEN), El Centro del Pueblo, and El Rescate on numerous service work and leadership programs. The efforts of KYCC have been largely concentrated on servicing Latinos as clientele, incorporating them into lower-level staff positions, and establishing coalitions with other Latino organizations. KYCC devotes most of its energies on organizing service-oriented, humanitarian activities and leadership-based coalitions at the individual and coalitional level.

sion, especially considering how inattention to changing demographics, inter-ethnic tensions, and cultural insularity have caused problems for the Korean American community in the past. Both recognize that Koreatown will thrive only if they recognize and interact with the multiethnic communities around them on their own terms. The following two statements from the leadership of KIWA and KYCC, respectively, show some of these underlying parallels.

In order to be an effective organization or activist or a community service person, people have to do a little bit of soul-searching to find out who you are first, because we live in a multicultural, multiracial, multi-ideal society. If you're confused about who you are, then you're gonna be confused about how effectively you can serve the community. People need to come together as a coalition because there's mutual issue that impacts all of us, but it's my view that the danger is when you don't have a base, you don't have institutes, you don't represent anyone. Then you're just an individual activist acting based on your own perspectives, and often that could put you in a situation where you misrepresent issues.

Another large area that I've tried to encourage in the organization has been dealing with Koreatown as a geographic phenomenon as well as the Korean American population as an ethnic population. When I say Koreatown, I refer to sort of a geographic area, but that geographic area is something that is multiethnic, multicultural. You know, it's important to reach out and integrate inward, [but] we also recognize the importance of dealing with a lot of energy towards our own ethnic community. So we don't for a moment see the organization as simply serving a geographic area. We know our mission has to do with dealing with the Korean population.

Both interviewees acknowledge that coalitions must bring together leaders who are linked to a strong ethnic community base and who do not simply act on their own individual visions, no matter how noble. Thus, working with other racial and ethnic groups on an organizational level is feasible only after the leadership has carved out its own role within the ethnic community.

While their overall political visions may coincide, KIWA and KYCC are driven by different ideological motivations and pursue divergent strategies in order to achieve their goals. Not surprisingly, each organization conceptualizes its work with Latino staff, clients, and leaders within their respective framework of ethnic political solidarity. In particular, KYCC sees these merg-

"You do that? You're so weird!" And my friends have to stop me so even when they come over, I feel like I should be cutting fruit and making coffee. And I like it so I feel that way, and on the other hand, women's rights! [laughs]. I like that diversity in myself, so I've come to appreciate it better. It was kind of confusing for a while. You know I kind of went through that period like, "Is that what I should be thinking about various serious feminist issues and political issues?" So it took me a while to really find what I really think and my happy medium. You know not completely rebelling against our parents' generation, but being more like, oh you have to appreciate what they did kind of thing. I don't know, I'm still trying to find myself.

Her comment does not so much validate the gendered nature of organizational work but demonstrates the complexities and difficulties of identity formation among second generation staff members. Particularly in organizations where identification with ethnic heritage is strong, women are often ambivalent about respecting their parents' cultural traditions while resisting the kinds of inequality and sexism they perceive in the immigrant community.

Even immigrant female workers who willingly partake in cooking duties occasionally grumble at the way their work is taken for granted. In the following passage, I describe how immigrant women of KIWA who oversee cooking duties tried to enforce a dishwashing schedule for other staff members, although this did not always work out as planned.

Jee-Hyun and Myung-Hee continue to put together the meals. Several times during or after the meals, Jee-Hyun tries to make sure that someone is in charge of doing the dishes. Once, she tried to put together an informal arrangement for two different people to do the dishes per day for the week. Eun-Ji and Peter said that it wasn't necessary to have two people do the dishes, but Jee-Hyun argued futilely that when it came to be someone's turn, that person would often have to go to some meeting and couldn't do their part. Last week, she sighed and grumbled, telling us that cooking like this so often was no longer fun for her. However, as of yet, the Korean immigrant female staff members continue to make the meals.

We can see why larger bureaucratic organizations that have fixed work schedules and more resources might be better able to avoid this type of informalized cooking arrangement.

breaks. In the following passage, members of KIWA are sharing personal stories about their children over Korean food prepared by the female immigrant staff members.

During lunch, the various staff members and I sat and ate a meal of rice, soup, and various Korean side dishes prepared by the female immigrant organizers. Myung-Hee told us how when she immigrated to the U.S., both parents were so busy with their work that their relationship with their children had become distant. As a result, the kids were sometimes rebellious. Sometimes Myung-Hee would tell the children they could not eat as punishment for something they did; one of the children finally caught on and said to her, "Fine! I won't eat and I'll die!" as a way to get her to cave in. The staff laughed over this. Jee-Hyun similarly told us how one of Jacob's children was punished in the same way and the child told her mom later that she had been so hungry she had eaten paper. Jacob said it was funny, because instead of being strict and telling the child that he/she should not behave like that anymore, the mom had felt really guilty and starting apologizing, saying that it was her fault. They thought that it was just the kid's trick to make the mother feel guilty. Jacob said he stood there trying not to laugh over the situation.

Compare this type of bonding session to the occasional times I would catch staff members grabbing a box of ramen from the kitchen cabinet or picking up a burrito at the local Mexican food truck while eating on the run.

Of course, relegating women to the kitchen also indicates deeper gender inequalities, especially in a power structure where much fewer women are seen in leadership roles. As such, second generation women are more likely to express aversion to assuming such domestic responsibilities in the workplace. In reaction to her observation that women do most of the cooking for the organization, one female intern states simply, "I try not to take on those traditional roles myself." Another second generation woman, who partakes willingly in these types of domestic activities at work, explained her own struggles between recognizing the need to protest such gender roles yet trying to hold onto the cultural traditions that had been passed down from her mother. She says:

I feel a pride in what our mothers have done and even though it seems to other people like oh it's very oppressive, I feel pride that a lot of Korean households are built on their mother's back. And part of me that's really Korean is like when people come over, I run to the kitchen and peel fruit. Everyone goes,

United States. Both strategies allow the organization to publicize injustices to institutions outside the enclosed power structures of the Korean community and bring to bear the external pressure of negative publicity and legal force.

Legal claims can be both time consuming and financially draining, as several organizers have pointed out. Thus, direct action is a critical tool for organizations situated on the peripheries of ethnic power structures, because it is a strategy that requires few resources from either the individual worker or the organization. Since it does not have the kind of elite support available to other more established ethnic organizations, one of KIWA's greatest weapons is to expose such abuses through visible acts of protest. Moreover, learning the methods of organizing and protesting allows workers to empower themselves and gain both leadership skills and greater political knowledge in the American system. The organization practices politics by utilizing the mainstream media to publicize grievances and endowing workers with the knowledge and skills to advocate for their rights.

KIWA's political sensibilities also work well with its small and informal organizational structure. The organization is better able to adapt to whatever strategy is needed to best contest the marginalizing and silencing tactics of elite groups that respond to KIWA's political actions. When it is found that the organization is not sensitive to the needs of its constituency, it is also small and flexible enough to incorporate whatever changes are required to meet those needs, although this would depend on to what degree the director and members can come to a consensus on how to do so. The following is a statement from the current executive director.

Have you ever felt a conflict between your values and anything that happens here? Not necessarily. If there are, it's thought out and talked about. And I think KIWA is small enough and progressive enough so that if that value should be considered I think we could adapt to that. There are things like as an organizer, as a community activist, we feel KIWA is not being sensitive to the issues or are not sensitive enough to the things that are happening in community or back in Korea. So let's set up a study session where reading material is distributed to all staff, study it, read it, and come to the table and talk about it. Or we bring other experts from outside and you know, something like that it's thought out and we adapt our schedules to make that happen. [Interviewer's questions in *italics*]

In this sense, KIWA's emphasis on political education is integral to adapting to the needs of the membership and community.

On both an individual and organizational level, KIWA members have mo-bilized on key campaign-related issues, such as the statewide movement to eliminate affirmative action (Proposition 209) and efforts to deny social ser-vices to undocumented immigrants (Proposition 187). KIWA members have also been active participants in various political movements, such as cam-paigns for police accountability, North Korean Famine Relief, and gay/les-bian rights. The organization helped to raise political awareness through the development of a voters guide with Coalition L.A. However, KIWA members can also be selective in the issues with which they become actively involved in order to be able to maintain focus in its mission and rootedness in centralized bases of support.

In contrast to KYCC's reserved response, KIWA took the lead in orga-nizing a political response to the Sexual Responsibility Act and Proposi-tion 22. Leaders of progressive Korean American organizations like KIWA, the Korean Resource Center (KRC), and Chingusai of Los Angeles were ac-tively involved in the counteractive movement to protect and promote lesbian, gay, bisexual, and transgender (LGBT) rights through fundraising assistance, press conferences, ad endorsements, and organizing efforts behind the scenes. Of course, part of this has to do with the weaker link of KIWA members to Korean Christian churches, which tend to be conservative on many social is-sues. However, the politics of sexual orientation also goes hand in hand with KIWA's general mission to empower underrepresented and oppressed groups within the ethnic community. Although the initiatives were not directly re-lated to labor issues, organizers within KIWA conceptualized the issue of LGBT rights as one of social justice and inequality that if unprotected could lead to the prevalence of right-wing conservative attacks on a key civil rights issue and the ultimate downfall of minority rights.

As an organization, KIWA added its name to a public petition in a Korean newspaper denouncing the initiatives, but also unofficially supported indi-vidual staff members who became actively involved with KACR. One second generation female KIWA member who participated in this coalition explained to me that the organization's involvement was particularly crucial, not merely because of its relevance to issues of social equality, but also because the or-ganization could build a relationship with LGBT groups attempting to raise social consciousness within the Korean immigrant population.

We're getting like so much interest among mainstream LGBT groups um because no one is really doing stuff in first generation immigrant communities.

In the case of Korean Americans in Los Angeles, it is clear that Koreatown has served a variety of functions: as a residential space for the poor and the elderly, an economic outpost for larger global production processes, a venue for socioeconomic and political empowerment, and an institutional bridge for integrating with other racial and ethnic groups. Aided by both globalization processes and the influx of resources in the postriot era, the enclave has expanded beyond its traditional adaptation functions and reaffirmed its status as the institutional headquarters of the ethnic community. As Eui-Young Yu (May 2, 2000 interview) puts it, "You can define the community in different ways, like a territorial-based community—the Koreatown Korean community. But Koreans are pretty scattered all over so they form the community through organizational affiliations. [This] sense of identity is formed through the organization." In the process, Korean American communities of interest are being reconstructed to reflect both the residential needs of a multiethnic enclave community, but also, the political needs of a residentially dispersed ethnic community.

Nevertheless, the ability of community-based organizations (CBOs) to appeal to the political consciousness of their 1.5/second generation membership comes from something more than mere accessibility. In particular, the book has referred to the multiple ways race and ethnicity have had continuing relevance in the diverse lives of Korean Americans beyond the confines of place and space. As contemporary immigration scholars have noted, "growing up American" occurs in different residential contexts for children of immigrants in America, including White-dominated neighborhoods, multiracial neighborhoods, inner-city ghettos, or ethnic enclaves (Portes and Rumbaut 1996). The spatial dispersal of the ethnic community coupled with increasing dissent both within and across different generations of Korean Americans underline the fact that ethnic solidarity cannot be characterized as homogeneous or unifying as traditional theories might like to portray.

Yet it is my contention that such complexities indicate not so much the disappearance of race and ethnicity as a formative framework for understanding one's lived experiences, but rather the increasingly diverse ways race and ethnicity continue to shape people's lives. The 1.5/second generation Korean Americans in the study have brought to light the various tensions and struggles associated with "assimilating" into American society and the way CBOs have provided them with the political consciousness to make sense of these ethnic-centered experiences. Organizations have reconstructed the meaning of community to encompass a wide range of personal-political beliefs and interests that emerge from living in such distinctive neighborhood settings. Moreover, the growing diversification and specialization of ethnic organizations in institutionally developed enclaves like Koreatown enable them to relate to the peculiarities of different Korean American identities and experiences as they are shaped by these neighborhood experiences. Thus, staff members are able to feel like they are part of a "Korean American community," reconceptualized and practiced in their own individualistic way.

The Case for Ethnic Political Solidarity

As stated, the fragmentation of the Korean American political community is not so much indicative of the disintegration of ethnic solidarity or even the absence of good leadership, but rather the growing involvement of diverse ethnic organizations in the community's transition from a new immigrant community to an Americanized ethnic plurality. Thus, conflict in the postriot era is not so much about turning away from ethnic political solidarity than it is about accommodating ethnic-based political goals to the changing demographics of Koreatown and the metropolis of Los Angeles. It is not an effort to close bridges with other coethnic organizations but an effort to open access to new ones. It is not a means to close intergenerational lines of communication but instead a process of sharing the reigns of political leadership on more equitable terms.

This study addresses some of the complexities of nurturing ethnic political solidarity among post-1965 immigrant communities that are internally divided by multiple lines of stratification but whose life chances are conjoined by continuing racial exclusion and political disempowerment in the mainstream arena. The way it plays out for different immigrant communities varies. In the case of Korean Americans, social mobility has given individuals the opportunity to live in higher-quality neighborhoods, to send their children to better schools, and to maintain a higher standard of living overall. Social mobility, however, can diminish political influence on a group level when it is not accompanied by political representation either in the form of media representation, electoral influence, or politicians in office.

As a result, Korean Americans in Los Angeles have had to find ways to adapt to the constraints of small population size and the absence of a concentrated electoral bloc, even in its own ethnic enclave of Koreatown. One way they have achieved this is by using their socioeconomic resources and

At the time of the study, the majority of Latino employees of KYCC had their own separate program in the environmental unit, which relative to some of the other youth-oriented programs has had lower standing in the organization under the current director. Furthermore, only a few of the Latino workers from the environmental unit spent part of their time in the main office in a separate section near the front entrance. The vast majority of environmental workers, which also includes a small contingency of Asian, White, and Black employees, were located in a physically separate warehouse located miles away in neighboring Pico-Union. In more recent years, however, the organization has started to hire more Latino and non-Korean staff members to meet the diverse needs of youth and family clientele, the effects of which continue to unfold today.

The ethnic organizational culture of KYCC is not so much a fusion of Korean and Latino culture like KIWA, but rather a fusion of Korean and American culture overlaid by the organization's culturally neutral corporate atmosphere. Nevertheless, the official language of KYCC seems to be primarily English and then secondarily Korean, with attention to Spanish when it is necessary. Major organizational events target a mixed American audience, but the ambiance is affected by the occasional Korean cuisine, venues at local Koreatown restaurants, or the presence of Korean-language media. Most of the organizational media that is distributed is in English and Korean, while only a few brochures are translated into Spanish, depending on the program. Furthermore, the organization is less likely to publicize in the Spanish media than does KIWA. Of course, much has changed in KYCC's staff composition since the execution of the study, but patterns of Korean-Latino integration within the broader culture of the organization is still the same.

The general weakness of the Latino infrastructure in this area makes it difficult for Korean American organizations to recruit volunteers, staff members, and clientele through institutionalized community networks. KYCC primarily works through other governmental and social service agencies to recruit its non-Korean clientele, which fits well with the bureaucratic and regulated approach of the agency. Youth on probation from governmental agencies are required to attend the different juvenile delinquency or after-school programs offered by KYCC. Students from local school sites and clients from other social service agencies are referred to KYCC counselors. Latino and Black American youth leaders from CARECEN and the Youth Empowerment Project collaborate with Korean youth at KYCC through the MYLC. Social service agencies, such as CARECEN and El Rescate, offer important sources of Latino client referrals because of the need for more services than these organizations can provide. In that way, KYCC has more options for finding clients through Latino organizations than does KIWA. Thus, government and nonprofit organizational linkages provide the bureaucratic networks through which KYCC attracts its racially diverse clientele.

KYCC views service and collaboration as one of the keys to helping Latinos create their own political base within the community in the long run. Board members recognize that this type of crossethnic support allowed Korean Americans of KYCC to create their own independent organization as an offspring of AADAP. One 1.5 generation board member, who strongly advocated for this vision, presents this analogy in the following manner:

> I always believed in serving more than just Koreans. When we were growing up, there were no Korean organizations, and we were serviced by other ethnic organizations. KYCC started out through the work of Japanese Americans at AADAP. So I appreciate what they have done and I feel in turn that it is our obligation to work with other non-Korean populations, and particularly because of where we are geographically, Central Americans become the logical choice of ethnic that we should work with. I believe that we have a responsibility and obligation to assist Central Americans to develop an organization like what we have, just the way that AADAP has helped us out and helped us to form an independent service organization. I always thought that the best way to achieve that is by providing services for the population and be able to hire Latino workers who have the potential to become managers and have executive capacity, and to start building advisory members for that project to spin out and become a nonprofit board.

The above passage is especially telling not only because of KYCC's expressed commitment and felt obligation to play a more integral role in empowering Latinos, but also the specific approach it hopes to take in achieving this goal, in terms of bringing them in as staff members and then allowing them to work their way up the organizational ladder.

KYCC would not have been able to open its doors to non-Korean clientele without the funds to implement new programs and the broad support of groups both within and outside of the Korean American elite. Many of their programs that service other non-Korean constituencies came about in the aftermath of the 1992 riots and with the assistance of governmental funding that

ties with mainstream institutions to develop the overall capacity and diversity of ethnic organizations in Koreatown, while remaining politically centered on the spatially concentrated influence of the ethnic elite. Among other things, these organizations have recongregated 1.5/second generation Korean Americans from afar, organized a wide range of political activities and events, and cultivated coalitional partnerships with other racial and ethnic communities. Bridging organizations have been particularly critical in using these coalitions to work with groups that either have more experience dealing with mainstream politics (for example, labor unions and African American organizations) or have greater potential to influence the vote through numbers alone (for example, Latinos). In this way, the weakening effects of spatial dispersal have intertwined the political fate of Korean American organizations to the institutional power structures of Koreatown.

Future research studies should also explore how other newly arising ethnic communities compensate for their own disadvantages in mainstream politics in similarly strategic ways. For instance, larger, densely concentrated immigrant populations such as Mexicans in Los Angeles clearly have the demographic presence to demand greater electoral representation in the future but lack the same financial wherewithal to establish their own political base in the present. Other Asian American populations like the Chinese Americans are large enough to transform the neighborhoods they occupy through sheer numbers but occasionally struggle to find common political ground amid wide regional, linguistic, and cultural differences. Still others like the Vietnamese are densely concentrated enough in certain areas to elect fellow members to office but do not have the financial resources or the numbers to make their political presence felt beyond their local neighborhoods.

Working with immigrant elite groups may be seen not only as a way to compensate for internal weaknesses but also as a means to gain a competitive edge in politics. Despite intensifying competition and divergent political ideologies, more established CBOs have discovered the potential benefits of building on the resources of the immigrant population, because their enclave-based power complements their own invaluable ties with mainstream institutions. Simply put, the influence of the ethnic elite will persist as long as they have something valuable that the 1.5/second generation cannot as easily acquire—in this case, control over community resources within the institutionally developed center of Koreatown. Access to both ethnic and mainstream networks merely widens an organization's range of options, because it gives them more flexibility and resources to adapt to political exigencies, depending on specific needs and context. Therefore, bridging organizations cannot completely ignore immigrant powerholders but must engage with them even if it is in a conflictual manner.

My most recent visits to the Korean Immigrant Workers Advocates (KIWA) and the Korean Youth and Community Center (KYCC) testify to the continuing effects of both ethnic political solidarity and non-Korean partnerships and clientele on these bridging organizations. As of July 2004, KYCC had changed its name from the Korean Youth and Community Center to the Koreatown Youth and Community Center. According to Song, this transition was a planned one that required gradually changing the internal culture of the organization and the organizational image in the Korean media. The staff membership was more than half Korean, although many of them were still being trained in lower-level job positions. Nevertheless, when asked if the Korean part of KYCC's identity was still important, Song responded firmly that it was integral and that they were not trying to change their identity but rather balance the Korean identity with demographic shifts that had occurred in the community within the past few decades. In terms of its alliances with other Korean American community organizations, it should be noted that KYCC has also officially relocated its administrative staff to the Koreatown Organizations Association (KOA) building alongside the Korean American Coalition (KAC), the Korean American Museum (KAM), the Korean Health, Education, Information and Research Center (KHEIR), and the Korean American Grocers Association (KAGRO)—the goal of which is to strengthen ties among the established coethnic leadership and maximize interorganizational relations among the various Korean American organizations.

Like KYCC, KIWA decided to change its name to the "Koreatown Immigrant Workers Alliance" to reflect the changing demographics of the communities they serve. The last time I visited, the story of KIWA was a bit more difficult to read, however, because the staff membership was in a state of transition as a result of staff downsizing, budget constraints, and the departure of a few of its long-time core members, who moved on to other progressive organizations. In their stead, the organization has hired both non-Korean and Korean members, including the return of one younger Korean American staff member from graduate school. The internal culture still seems to be significantly influenced by the Korean immigrant politics of several of its remaining long-term members, but the final composition of its full-time staff

Korean Americans into the organization or even confronting the established ethnic leadership about its exclusion and exploitation of other racially marginalized groups.

However, not all organizations have been compelled to make the same type of groundbreaking changes that these two organizations have achieved. Multiculturalism may provide the ideological framework for interethnic cooperation, but 1.5/second generation organizations are primarily driven into action by a variety of pragmatic concerns—the most important of which may be the political niche they create for themselves within the ethnic and mainstream power structures. The degree to which organizations can become racially inclusive depends on the views of the organization in respect to its role within the community and its relations with the ethnic elite, practical needs arising from different areas of collective disempowerment, and the amount of funding and support that they are able to garner from mainstream institutions. Bridging organizations that can contextualize their work around innovative notions of community may come upon new and interesting political opportunities within the broader society. Under the guidance of a progressive-minded leadership, these organizations have the potential to work with the surrounding multiethnic communities and thoroughly transform the political consciousness of members in the process.

Organizations such as KIWA and KYCC have embarked on this journey by bringing in Latinos and other groups into the lower echelons of their organizational staff. In KYCC, Latinos have been at least minimally visible at all levels of affiliation, including clientele, staff member, program manager, and board member throughout its recent history, but are most dominant within certain programs such as the environmental unit and in the lower ranks of the organization. In KIWA, Latinos have been hired as organizers and also represent a significant portion of the organization's clientele base and support networks. The organizers of KIWA and the management team of KYCC have started to promote Latino members into higher-level positions, but it is still uncertain to what extent this will dramatically change the Korean-dominated decision-making structures of the two organizations.

Representatives from KIWA and KYCC feel that focus on Korean Americans allows them to maintain coherency in their general mission and stable support networks from which to pursue their political goals. At the same time, both groups argue that incorporating Latino residents and workers into their organization on some level is also integral to achieving their political mis-

making models and taking "ownership" of community projects, as one organizer describes it. While focusing on more traditional styles of leadership found in mainstream American society, the youth programs have found that the most effective means for realizing this vision is by connecting the ethnic community to powerful mainstream institutions—a relationship that is shaped by conventional forms of protest and cooperation. Through organizational experiences, youth may indirectly learn how to cultivate ties to powerful constituencies and avoid engaging in political activities that would substantially alienate them from these networks. The guiding philosophy is thus one focused on a combination of service, leadership, and socioeconomic mobility. Through such programs, youth interns learn to take on responsibility and develop invaluable networks and skills that are critical to the uplifting of the Korean American community they are taught to value.

Navigating Ethnic Boundaries

An analysis on the political potential of organizations like KIWA and KYCC would not be complete without an understanding of the relationships they've cultivated with other racial and ethnic groups both within and outside the Koreatown community. Drawing on lessons learned since 1992, Korean American organizations recognize the need to prepare a new generation of leadership willing and able to engage themselves within the multiethnic political scenes of Los Angeles and American society. While most organizations have focused their energies on building collaborative programs, events, and alliances, KIWA and KYCC both stand out in terms of their greater inclusion of non–Korean Americans at all levels of membership. This strategy has enabled them to strengthen their position within American politics while maintaining their roots in the Koreatown community.

Leadership and ideology can of course be a determining factor in the direction that an organization chooses to take in designing and implementing its political agenda. In the case of 1.5/second generation CBOs, this path was almost laid out for them when they were driven to speak out against the injustices played out during the Korean-Black conflicts and the 1992 civil unrest. Such political exigencies also led to the blossoming of alternative organizations like KIWA and the rise of new leaders who were daring enough to expand their organizational reaches into unchartered territory. Although still considered challenging in its own right, it was no longer inconceivable for organizations and leaders to explore more pervasive ways of integrating non–

has yet to be seen. KIWA is still actively working with both leftist Korean and Korean American organizations on workers' issues in both Koreatown and South Korea, as well as non-Korean supporters, who dominated the audience in a 2005 commemoration ceremony of the Los Angeles civil unrest. What was most striking about the audience though was first, the visible presence of Korean representatives from various politicians' offices in the front row and more importantly, the attendance of several religious leaders and Korean business owners, including a representative from the Korean American Business Association. As one former KIWA board member who spoke at the event noted, the notable presence of business owners and the location of the ceremony at the church clearly demonstrated how much things had changed since he had been a member way back. This shift may be a sign of improving relations with the Korean immigrant generation as well.

As KIWA organizers would be quick to point out, ethnic political solidarity also comes with its own set of disadvantages. Internal inequality is most apparent in capital-rich, institutionally developed, and relatively isolated political structures. In particular, the findings from this research emphasize the need to approach ethnic communities not as monolithic entities but as hierarchically organized systems that dole out opportunities, advantages, and resources according to the social status of the individual or group. Clearly, women, workers, and non–Korean Americans have been able to benefit from the expansion of organizations in Koreatown, but not to the same degree as their male, entrepreneurial, and coethnic counterparts. Furthermore, the power of ethnic political solidarity is often used either to ignore or contest the concerns and grievances of less politically empowered subgroups within the Korean American population. How ethnic organizations negotiate their political agenda within hierarchical ethnic and mainstream network structures will in turn determine the diverse benefits and constraints they derive from such associations.

Societal myths about the hard-work ethics, middle-class values, and assimilationist tendencies of Asian Americans emanate not from the ethnic community as a whole but rather from those ethnic elite groups that dictate the political discourse of the broader community. I use the term *projected ethnicity* to describe how such elitist interpretations of ethnic political solidarity conceal deeper inequities within the ethnic community. Centered on ideological notions of eth-class solidarity and conformity to mainstream values, the upper circuits of ethnic political structures have played a dominant role in shaping and representing community values to mainstream America. In contrast, the lower circuits have strategically utilized their outside support networks to contest the ideological dominion of the ethnic elite. While certain groups may project a particular image of what it means to be Korean American to the outside world, not all members of the ethnic community subscribe to such images, choosing instead to be "Korean American my way, not their way kind of thing," as the one organizer in Chapter 7 had stated.

This book's focus on ethnic stratification systems is not meant to diminish the significance of mainstream opportunity structures in determining the overall fate of ethnic politics. For one, organizations like KIWA, in challenging the authority of the ethnic elite, are in effect challenging the ways they support the same mainstream ideologies and institutions of power that confine them. Their political agenda focuses on how Korean American business owners, church leaders, and other elite groups not only legitimize the hegemonic practices and meritocratic ideologies of White male powerholders but also directly engage in the oppressive practices that bring about their own demise. By exploiting the labor of less fortunate Korean immigrants, entrepreneurs are using the potential force of ethnic political solidarity for unscrupulous purposes, while sacrificing their own families and personal well-being in the process. By looking down on other racial minority groups around them, Korean Americans are not only subscribing to the racial power of the (White) American Dream but also cutting off opportunities for long-term collective empowerment. Furthermore, those who avidly pursue their individual success and assimilation with little regard for issues of social justice merely reinforce popular stereotypes about their model minority status and hence alienate themselves from their true allies.

Second, I have suggested throughout this book that the ability of internally marginalized groups to contest ethnic hierarchies is contingent upon the support they receive from outside groups. As opposed to arguing that ethnic groups can lift themselves up by their own bootstraps, I show how CBOs rely on external bases of support to cater to the specialized needs of an internally diversifying population, including marginalized and noncoethnic groups neglected within traditional ethnic power structures. It is not only that more resources allow for more programs and clients, but it also gives peripheral organizations the opportunity to assert and promote the importance of their work to the ethnic community. In addition, the accompanying inclusion of such organizations contributes to a culture of democracy by broadening the range of political perspectives in public discourse.

As the culture, politics, and economy of American society become increasingly interconnected with those of other nations, both indigenous ties to ethnic-based structures and bridging networks to the host society may become valuable resources for post-1965 ethnic groups. Ethnic politics is not disappearing, nor is it retaining the same form that it did under the first generation of immigrants. Rather, this book suggests that because of the countervailing forces that arise from shifting political opportunity structures, ethnic political solidarity still matters for the second wave of ethnic leadership in resource-rich immigrant communities, but in more heterogeneous ways than described in traditional paradigms. In the end, this study underlines the need for scholars to reconceptualize ethnic political solidarity in a manner that recognizes the diverse and flexible ways post-1965 immigrant groups can adapt to their diversifying "ethnic" surroundings and make their voices heard in mainstream America.

Index